名/著/的/力/量

青闰 王艳玲 编译

世界经典名家名作赏析

★英汉对照★

传奇篇

大连理工大学出版社
DALIAN UNIVERSITY OF TECHNOLOGY PRESS

图书在版编目（CIP）数据

世界经典名家名作赏析．传奇篇：汉英对照／青闰，王艳玲编译．—大连：大连理工大学出版社，2014.7
（名著的力量）
ISBN 978-7-5611-9187-3

Ⅰ．①世…　Ⅱ．①青…②王…　Ⅲ．①英语－汉语－对照读物②世界文学－文学欣赏　Ⅳ．①H319.4：Ⅰ

中国版本图书馆CIP数据核字(2014)第112297号

大连理工大学出版社出版
地址：大连市软件园路80号　　邮政编码：116023
发行：0411-84708842　邮购：0411-84703636　传真：0411-84701466
E-mail:dutp@dutp.cn　　URL: http://www.dutp.cn
大连金华光彩色印刷有限公司印刷　　大连理工大学出版社发行

幅面尺寸：168mm×235mm　　印张：19　　字数：448千字
印数：1~5000
2014年7月第1版　　　　　　2014年7月第1次印刷

责任编辑：高　颖　　　　　　责任校对：杨晓慧
装帧设计：对岸书影

ISBN 978-7-5611-9187-3　　　　　　定价：29.80元

感受名著力量，点亮智慧心灯

——向文学大师致敬

谨以本套丛书献给那些深爱家人与朋友、有追求、有梦想、对生活有激情、对英语学习有热情的读者朋友们。

我们为什么阅读名家名作？因为艺术是生活的折射，阅读名家名作能够扩展我们的自我生活体验。艺术大师通过对现实生活富有想象力的艺术演绎，让我们从中得到某种意味深长的生活启迪。

我们为什么阅读名家名作？因为文学是语言的艺术，阅读名家名作能够给我们带来愉悦身心、陶冶性情、完善心智的艺术享受。艺术大师个个都是讲故事的高手，善于描绘充满悬念的场景，采用多种多样的叙事方式和叙事技巧，通过超凡脱俗的语言和奇特精巧的构思，将人物、情节、主题巧妙融入一个个或传奇、或谐趣、或唯美、或惊悚、或隽永的故事之中，制造险象环生的情景氛围和惊心动魄的情感冲击，既使作品意蕴深邃丰沛，又给读者带来回味无穷的阅读享受。

这是一套十分值得一看的英语学习与心灵成长读物。"名著的力量"系列丛书包括《世界经典名家名作赏析——唯美篇》、《世界经典名家名作赏析——谐趣篇》、《世界经典名家名作赏析——惊悚篇》、《世界经典名家名作赏析——隽永篇》和《世界经典名家名作赏析——传奇篇》五个分册。

《世界经典名家名作赏析——传奇篇》顾名思义就是以传奇为主线，遴选世界上最著名的小说家，如爱伦·坡、莫泊桑、霍桑、马克·吐温、奥斯卡·王尔德等名家的11篇经典力作，让读者充分领略到传奇文学的里里外外、方方面面。故事环环紧扣，悬念迭起，通过这些悬念紧紧抓住读者的心，刺激着读者的阅读欲望，推动着情节的发展。本集选文就是要引领读者在传奇的氛围中分享名家呈现的精彩故事，品味传奇人物的精彩人生。

可以说，所选作品无论是在主题思想、人物形象上还是在语言风格、故事结构上都各具千秋、精彩纷呈，同时写作手法所涉范围较广，这里提到的写作手法主要是小说的表现手法，主要有悬念、照应、抑扬结合、点面结合、动静结合、叙议结合、情景交融、首尾呼应、伏笔照应、承上启下、开门见山、烘托、渲染、虚实相生等等。不同的写作手法对小说故事的构成起到了重要的作用，产生了异乎寻常的艺术效果。

非常感谢大连理工大学出版社的编辑们对本书稿所提的修改意见及辛苦努力。在选材、翻译和点评过程中，也得到了宰倩、廉凤仙、宋娟、张连亮、张灵敏、刘君武等同志的热情支持和帮助，在此深表感谢。

尽管我们力求在翻译上做到信达雅，在点评上手到、眼到、心到，但仍不免会有遗珠之憾，恳请读者朋友们不吝赐教与雅正。

编者

2014年5月

目　录

Anton Chekhov

01 The Darling

宝贝儿

姓名	安东·契诃夫
出生日期	1860年1月29日
出生地	俄罗斯罗斯托夫省塔甘罗格市
性别	男

成就和特色

　　十九世纪末俄国伟大的批判现实主义作家、幽默讽刺大师、短篇小说的巨匠和著名剧作家。他一生创作了七八百篇短篇小说，还写了一些中篇小说和剧本。他的小说短小精悍，简练朴素，结构紧凑，情节生动，笔调幽默，语言明快，极富于音乐节奏感，寓意深刻。他的小说没有多余的东西，很少有抽象的议论。他善于用不多的文字表现深刻的主题。他的小说抒情气味浓郁，抒发了他对丑恶现实的不满以及对美好未来的向往，把褒扬和贬抑、欢悦和痛苦之情融化在作品之中，可见他生活的时代是一个多么阴暗的时代，而他就是这个阴暗时代的一根点燃的蜡烛。

写作背景

　　这篇小说讲的是可爱而可怜的奥莲卡一生的感情故事。她热爱生活，能从她所爱的人那里得到爱的源泉，关注自己的爱人，并因此关注生活，关心身边的人，也因此身边的人亲切地称她为宝贝。奥莲卡并不是没有自我，只是将自我依附在了爱上。

The Darling

Olenka, the daughter of the retired collegiate assessor, Plemyanniakov, was sitting in her back porch, lost in thought. It was hot, the flies were **persistent**[1] and teasing, and it was pleasant to reflect that it would soon be evening. Dark rainclouds were gathering from the east, and bringing from time to time a breath of moisture in the air.

Kukin, who was the manager of an open-air theatre called the Tivoli, and who lived in the lodge, was standing in the middle of the garden looking at the sky.

"Again!" he observed despairingly. "It's going to rain again! Rain every day, as though to **spite**[2] me. I **might as well**[3] hang myself! It's ruin! Fearful losses every day."

He flung up his hands, and went on, addressing Olenka: "There! that's the life we lead, Olga Semyonovna. It's enough to make one cry. One works and **does one's utmost**[4], one wears oneself out, getting no sleep at night, and **racks one's brain**[5] what to do for the best. And then what happens? To begin with, one's public is ignorant, **boorish**[6]. I give them the very best **operetta**[7], a dainty **masque**[8], first rate music-hall artists. But do you suppose that's what they want! They don't understand anything of that sort. They want a clown; what they ask for is **vulgarity**[9]. And then look at the weather! Almost every evening it rains. It started on the tenth of May, and it's kept it up all May and June. It's simply awful! The public doesn't come, but I've to pay the rent just the same, and pay the artists."

宝贝儿

退休的八品文官普列勉尼科夫的女儿奥莲卡坐在后门廊上，陷入了沉思。天很热，苍蝇飞来飞去，让她不胜其烦。一想到天马上就要黑，她又感到愉快。乌黑的雨云从东方聚集而来，空气中不时吹来潮湿的气息。

库金站在花园中央，望着天空。他是季沃里露天剧场的经理，暂住在这里的小屋里。

"又要下雨了！"他绝望地说，"天又要下雨了！天天下雨，好像是要拿我出气似的。我还不如上吊！要破产了！天天都要赔一大笔钱。"

他猛地举起双手，接着对奥莲卡说："好了！这就是我们过的日子，奥尔佳·谢敏诺芙娜。真够让人哭一场了。一个人工作，竭尽全力，筋疲力尽，夜不成寐，绞尽脑汁想做得最好。最后，结果是什么呢？首先，观众无知粗野。我为他们排最好的轻歌剧、雅致的假面剧，请一流的杂耍艺术家。可是，你认为这是他们想要看的吗？他们一窍不通。他们想要看的是小丑；他们想要的是粗俗。其次，看看这天气！差不多每天晚上都下雨。五月十号就开始下了，五月和六月都下个不停。简直太可怕了！看戏的不来，可我还得照样付租金，给演员们开工钱。"

奥莲卡为什么天一黑就会感到愉快呢？乌黑的雨云又预示着什么呢？作者为后文打下了伏笔。

10. scaffold
n. 绞刑台

11. tenor
n. 男高音

12. compassionate
adj. 富于同情心的；慈
悲的

13. rosy
adj. 玫瑰；红色的

14. mole
n. 黑痣

15. naive
adj. 天真的

16. refrain from
克制不住

17. gush
n. 倾泻；表现出过度
的热情与情感

18. entrenchment
n. 堡垒；阵地

19. foe
n. 反对者；敌人

The next evening the clouds would gather again, and Kukin would say with an hysterical laugh: "Well, rain away, then! Flood the garden, drown me! Damn my luck in this world and the next! Let the artists have me up! Send me to prison! —to Siberia! —the scaffold[10]! Ha, ha, ha!"

And next day the same thing.

Olenka listened to Kukin with silent gravity, and sometimes tears came into her eyes. In the end his misfortunes touched her; she grew to love him. He was a small thin man, with a yellow face, and curls combed forward on his forehead. He spoke in a thin tenor[11]; as he talked his mouth worked on one side, and there was always an expression of despair on his face; yet he aroused a deep and genuine affection in her. She was always fond of some one, and could not exist without loving. In earlier days she had loved her papa, who now sat in a darkened room, breathing with difficulty; she had loved her aunt who used to come every other year from Bryansk; and before that, when she was at school, she had loved her French master. She was a gentle, soft-hearted, compassionate[12] girl, with mild, tender eyes and very good health. At the sight of her full rosy[13] cheeks, her soft white neck with a little dark mole[14] on it, and the kind, naive[15] smile, which came into her face when she listened to anything pleasant, men thought, "Yes, not half bad," and smiled too, while lady visitors could not refrain from[16] seizing her hand in the middle of a conversation, exclaiming in a gush[17] of delight, "You darling!"

The house in which she had lived from her birth upwards, and which was left her in her father's will, was at the extreme end of the town, not far from the Tivoli. In the evenings and at night she could hear the band playing, and the crackling and banging of fireworks, and it seemed to her that it was Kukin struggling with his destiny, storming the entrenchments[18] of his chief foe[19], the indifferent public; there was a sweet thrill at

第二天傍晚，阴云又聚集起来，库金歇斯底里地笑道："好吧，那就继续下吧！淹没花园，把我淹死！我这辈子真倒霉，下辈子还是倒霉！让那些演员把我抓起来！送进牢房！送到西伯利亚去做苦工好了！送上断头台！哈哈哈！"

第三天还是这样。

奥莲卡默默地、认真地听库金说话，有时泪水涌进眼里。最后，他的不幸打动了她的心；她渐渐爱上了他。他又小又瘦，脸色发黄，鬈发向前梳向前额。他用尖细的男高音说话，说话时撇着嘴，脸上总是带着绝望的神情，但他还是在她心里唤起了一种真挚的深情。她总是得爱一个人，不爱就活不下去。早先，她爱她的爸爸，现在他呼吸困难，坐在一个昏暗的房间里；她还爱过她的姑妈，姑妈每隔一年总要从布良斯克来一次；此前，她上学时，爱过她的法语教师。她文静、好心、慈悲，目光温柔和善，身体非常健康。一看见她丰满红润的脸蛋，看见她带有一颗黑痣的柔白颈项，看见她一听到什么开心事脸上就露出的天真善良的微笑，男人们心里就想："是的，不错，"随后也露出微笑。女人们在谈话中间会情不自禁抓住她的手，喜不自胜地大声说道："你这宝贝儿！"

房子位于城郊的最尽头，离季沃里不远，她从生下来那天起就住在这座房子里，而且她的父亲在遗嘱里已把房子留给她。每天傍晚和夜里，她就可以听到乐队演奏，烟火噼啪作响；在她看来，这是库金在跟他的命运斗争，向主要敌人——冷漠的观众——的阵地猛冲；她

宝贝儿到底是一个什么样的人？她为什么见一个爱一个？

her heart, she had no desire to sleep, and when he returned home at day-break, she tapped softly at her bedroom window, and showing him only her face and one shoulder through the curtain, she gave him a friendly smile....

He proposed to her, and they were married. And when he had a closer view of her neck and her plump, fine shoulders, he threw up his hands, and said: "You darling!"

He was happy, but as it rained on the day and night of his wedding, his face still **retained**[20] an expression of despair.

They got on very well together. She used to sit in his office, to look after things in the Tivoli, to put down the accounts and pay the wages. And her rosy cheeks, her sweet, naive, radiant smile, were to be seen now at the office window, now in the **refreshment**[21] bar or behind the scenes of the theatre. And already she used to say to her acquaintances that the theatre was the chief and most important thing in life and that it was only through the drama that one could **derive**[22] true enjoyment and become **cultivated**[23] and humane.

"But do you suppose the public understands that?" she used to say. "What they want is a clown. Yesterday we gave *Faust Inside Out*[24], and almost all the boxes were empty; but if Vanitchka and I had been producing some vulgar thing, I assure you the theatre would have been **packed**[25]. Tomorrow Vanitchka and I are doing *Orpheus in Hell.* Do come."

And what Kukin said about the theatre and the actors she repeated. Like him she despised the public for their ignorance and their indifference to art; she took part in the **rehearsals**[26], she corrected the actors, she kept an eye on the behaviour of the musicians, and when there was an unfavourable **notice**[27] in the local paper, she **shed tears**[28], and then went to the editor's office to set things right.

The actors were fond of her and used to call her "Vanitchka and I," and "the darling"; she was sorry for them and used to lend

20. retain
   vt. 保持

21. refreshment
   n. 饮料；点心

22. derive
   vt. 获得

23. cultivated
   adj. 有修养（教养）
   的；高雅的

24. inside out
   彻底地

25. pack
   vt. 塞满

26. rehearsal
   n. 排演

27. notice
   n. 评论；短评

28. shed tears
   流泪

的心就甜蜜陶醉，毫无睡意。等天亮他回家时，她就轻轻地敲自己卧室的窗户，隔着窗帘只对他露出她的脸和一只肩膀，向他友好地微笑……

诗情画意，情真意切。

他向她求婚，于是他们就结了婚。他贴近看到了她的脖子和丰满的美肩，他举起双手，说道："你这宝贝儿！"

尽管他幸福，但因为结婚那天日夜下雨，他的脸上仍然保持着绝望的神情。

他们一起过得很好。她常常坐班，照看季沃里的业务，记账，发工钱。她红润的脸蛋，她可爱天真的满脸微笑，时而出现在售票窗口，时而出现在饮食部，时而出现在剧场后台。她过去常常对熟人说，戏剧是生活中最最重要的东西；只有通过戏剧，人才能得到真正的快乐，才会变得高雅和仁慈。

"可是，你认为观众明白这一点吗？"她常常说。"他们想要看的是小丑。昨天我们演出了《彻底的浮士德》，差不多全场的包厢都空着；可是，如果我和万尼奇卡换演一出庸俗的东西，我向你保证，剧院里倒会挤得满满的。明天，我和万尼奇卡要上演《俄耳浦斯在地狱》。请来看吧。"

库金说的有关戏剧和演员的话，她都要重复一遍。她像他一样瞧不起观众对艺术的无知和冷淡；她参加彩排，纠正演员的动作，监视乐师的行为；当本城报纸上发表对剧团不利的短评，她就流泪，然后跑到编辑部去摆平。

演员们喜欢她，常常叫她"我和万尼奇卡"与"宝贝儿"；她可怜他们，常常借给他们一小部分钱；如果

them small sums of money, and if they deceived her, she used to shed a few tears in private, but did not complain to her husband.

They got on well in the winter too. They took the theatre in the town for the whole winter, and let[29] it for short terms to a Little Russian company, or to a conjurer[30], or to a local dramatic society. Olenka grew stouter, and was always beaming with satisfaction, while Kukin grew thinner and yellower, and continually complained of their terrible losses, although he had not done badly all the winter. He used to cough at night, and she used to give him hot raspberry[31] tea or lime-flower[32] water, to rub him with eau de cologne[33] and to wrap him in her warm shawls.

"You're such a sweet pet!" she used to say with perfect sincerity, stroking[34] his hair. "You're such a pretty dear!"

Towards Lent[35] he went to Moscow to collect a new troupe[36], and without him she could not sleep, but sat all night at her window, looking at the stars, and she compared herself with the hens, who are awake all night and uneasy when the cock is not in the hen-house. Kukin was detained[37] in Moscow, and wrote that he would be back at Easter, adding some instructions about the Tivoli. But on the Sunday before Easter, late in the evening, came a sudden ominous[38] knock at the gate; some one was hammering on the gate as though on a barrel—boom, boom, boom! The drowsy[39] cook went flopping[40] with her bare feet through the puddles[41], as she ran to open the gate.

"Please open," said some one outside in a thick bass. "There is a telegram for you."

Olenka had received telegrams from her husband before, but this time for some reason she felt numb with terror. With shaking hands she opened the telegram and read as follows:

"IVAN PETROVITCH DIED SUDDENLY TO-DAY. AWAITING INSTRUCTIONS FOR FUNERAL TUESDAY."

29. let
　　vt. 出租
30. conjurer
　　n. 魔术师
31. raspberry
　　n. 悬钩子；覆盆子
32. lime-flower
　　n. 莱檬花
33. eau de cologne
　　n.（法）科隆香水
34. stroke
　　vt. 轻抚
35. Lent
　　n. 大斋期（从圣灰星期三到复活节的四十天，为纪念耶稣在荒野禁食）
36. troupe
　　n. 剧团
37. detain
　　vt. 耽搁；延迟
38. ominous
　　adj. 不祥的
39. drowsy
　　adj. 昏昏欲睡的
40. flop
　　vi. 脚步沉重地走
41. puddle
　　n. 水坑

他们骗了她，她常常暗自流泪，但不向丈夫诉苦。

冬天他们也过得很好。整整一冬，他们买下城里那座剧院，短期租给小俄罗斯剧团、魔术师或本地的戏剧社。奥莲卡越来越健壮，总是心满意足、喜气洋洋。库金却越来越面黄肌瘦，不断抱怨亏损严重，尽管整个冬天他做得不错。他夜里常常咳嗽，她常常给他喝覆盆子热茶和莱檬花汁，用科隆香水给他擦身，用她温暖的披肩裹住他。

"你真是可爱的宝贝儿！"她常常抚摸他的头发，非常诚恳地说。"你真是漂亮的宝贝儿！"

奥莲卡帮助丈夫打理剧社。

快到大斋节时，他前往莫斯科去请一个新剧团。没有他在身边，她就睡不着觉，而是整夜坐在窗边，望着星星；她把自己比作母鸡，公鸡不在窝里时，母鸡总是彻夜难眠，心神不定。库金有事滞留在莫斯科，写信说他到复活节才回来，还吩咐了有关季沃里的事儿。但是，在复活节前的那个星期天，夜深时分，突然传来了不祥的敲门声；有人在捶大门，就像在捶大桶一样——咚咚咚！昏昏欲睡的厨娘光着脚啪嗒啪嗒趟过水坑，跑去开门。

"请开门！"有人在门外用含混不清的男低音说。"有一封你们家的电报。"

奥莲卡以前曾经接到过丈夫的电报，但这次不知何故，她吓得目瞪口呆，两手颤抖着打开电报，念到了如下的电文：

"伊凡·彼得罗维奇今天突然去世。待星期二殡葬。"

It was signed by the **stage manager**[42] of the operatic company.

"My darling!" sobbed Olenka. "Vanka, my **precious**[43], my darling! Why did I ever meet you! Why did I know you and love you! Your poor heart-broken Olenka is alone without you!"

Kukin's funeral took place on Tuesday in Moscow, Olenka returned home on Wednesday, and as soon as she got indoors, she threw herself on her bed and sobbed so loudly that it could be heard next door, and in the street.

"Poor darling!" the neighbours said, as they crossed themselves. "Olga Semyonovna, poor darling! How she does **take on**[44]!"

Three months later Olenka was coming home from mass, **melancholy**[45] and in deep mourning. It happened that one of her neighbours, Vassily Andreitch Pustovalov, returning home from church, walked back beside her. He was the manager at Babakayev's, the timber merchant's. He wore a straw hat, a white waistcoat, and a gold watch-chain, and looked more a country gentleman than a man in trade.

"Everything happens as it is **ordained**[46], Olga Semyonovna," he said gravely, with a sympathetic note in his voice; "and if any of our dear ones die, it must be because it is the will of God, so we ought have **fortitude**[47] and bear it **submissively**[48]."

After seeing Olenka to her gate, he said good-bye and went on. All day afterwards she heard his **sedately**[49] dignified voice, and whenever she shut her eyes she saw his dark beard. She liked him very much. And apparently she had made an impression on him too, for not long afterwards an elderly lady, with whom she was only slightly acquainted, came to drink coffee with her, and as soon as she was seated at table began to talk about Pustovalov, saying that he was an excellent man whom one could thoroughly depend upon, and that any girl would be glad to marry him.

42. stage manager
   n. 舞台监督；现场导演

43. precious
   adj. 宝贵的；珍爱的

44. take on
   承担

45. melancholy
   adj. 忧郁的；愁思的

46. ordain
   vt. 注定

47. fortitude
   n. 坚韧

48. submissively
   adv. 顺从地

49. sedately
   adv. 镇静地；安详地

电报是歌剧团导演签的字。

"我的宝贝儿！"奥莲卡哭道。"万尼奇卡，我的爱人，我的亲人啊！为什么我跟你相遇啊！为什么我认识你、爱上你啊？你可怜心碎的奥莲卡没有你是多么孤单啊！"

库金的葬礼星期二在莫斯科举行，奥莲卡星期三回到家，一进门，就倒在床上，放声大哭，隔壁和街上都能听见。

"可怜的宝贝儿！"邻居们划着十字说。"奥尔佳·谢敏诺芙娜，可怜的宝贝儿！她怎么承受得了啊！"

三个月后，奥莲卡做完弥撒回家，忧郁哀伤。碰巧她的邻居瓦西里·安德烈伊奇·普斯托瓦洛夫也从教堂回家，走在她身边。他是巴巴卡耶夫木材场的经理。他戴着草帽，身穿白马甲，系着金表链，看上去与其说像生意人，不如说像乡绅。

丈夫去世了，奥莲卡该怎么办呢？

"万事乃天定，奥尔佳·谢敏诺芙娜，"他神情庄重地说，声音里带着同情的腔调。"如果我们的亲人去世，那一定是因为上帝的旨意，所以我们应该坚韧，顺从承受。"

他把奥莲卡送到大门口后，和她告别，接着赶路。之后，整整一天，她仿佛都听到他镇静威严的声音，她只要一闭眼就看到他的黑胡子。她非常喜欢他。而且显然她也给他留下了深刻印象，因为不久之后就有一位上了年纪、她只是稍微认识的太太到她家里来喝咖啡，一在桌边坐下，就开始谈起了普斯托瓦洛夫，说他是一个完全可靠的大好人，哪个姑娘都会乐意嫁给他。三天后，普斯托瓦洛夫也亲自上门。他没呆多久，大约只有

Three days later Pustovalov came himself. He did not stay long, only about ten minutes, and he did not say much, but when he left, Olenka loved him—loved him so much that she lay awake all night in a perfect fever, and in the morning she sent for the elderly lady. The match was quickly arranged, and then came the wedding.

Pustovalov and Olenka got on very well together when they were married.

Usually he sat in the office till dinner-time, then he went out on business, while Olenka took his place, and sat in the office till evening, making up accounts and booking orders.

"Timber gets dearer every year; the price rises twenty per cent," she would say to her customers and friends. "Only fancy we used to sell local timber, and now Vassitchka always has to go for wood to the Mogilev district. And the freight!" she would add, covering her cheeks with her hands in horror. "The freight!"

It seemed to her that she had been in the timber trade for ages and ages, and that the most important and necessary thing in life was timber; and there was something intimate and touching to her in the very sound of words such as "baulk[50]," "post," "beam," "pole," "scantling[51]," "batten[52]," "lath[53]," "plank," etc.

At night when she was asleep she dreamed of perfect mountains of planks and boards, and long strings of wagons, carting timber somewhere far away. She dreamed that a whole regiment[54] of six-inch beams forty feet high, standing on end, was marching upon the timber-yard; that logs, beams, and boards knocked together with the resounding crash of dry wood, kept falling and getting up again, piling themselves on each other. Olenka cried out in her sleep, and Pustovalov said to her tenderly: "Olenka, what's the matter, darling? Cross yourself!"

Her husband's ideas were hers. If he thought the room was too hot, or that business was slack[55], she thought the same.

50. baulk = balk
n. 横梁

51. scantling
n. 小梁

52. batten
n. 木条（铺室内地面的）

53. lath
n. 木板条；条板

54. regiment
n. 大量；一（大）批

55. slack
adj. 清淡的

十分钟，他也没多说，但当他离开时，奥莲卡就已经爱上了他——爱得是那么深，彻夜难眠，完全陷入了狂热之中，第二天早晨就派人去请那位上了年纪的太太。婚事很快敲定，随后就举行了婚礼。

结婚后，普斯托瓦洛夫和奥莲卡一块过得很好。

通常，他坐在办公室里直到午饭时间，饭后出去谈生意，奥莲卡接替他的位置，坐在办公室里算账、卖货，直到傍晚。

"木材年年看涨，价格涨了两成，"她常常对顾客和朋友们说。"试想一下，我们过去通常卖本地木材，现在瓦西奇卡总是不得不到莫吉廖夫区采办木材。还有运费啊！"她恐惧地用双手捂住脸，补充说道，"运费！"

她觉得自己仿佛已经做过很久很久的木材买卖，认为生活中最重要、最必需的东西就是木材；有什么"梁木"、"支柱"、"横梁"、"辕杆"、"小梁"、"木条"、"板条"、"厚板"等等，在她听来，这些词亲切动人。

夜里睡觉时，她梦见厚板和木板堆积如山，一长溜货车载着木材驶往远处的某个地方。她还梦见一大批六英寸粗、四十英尺高的梁木竖立起来，在木材场上大步行进；原木、梁木和木板碰撞在一起，发出干木撞击的回响声，时而倒下，时而又竖起，彼此堆在一块。奥莲卡在睡梦中大叫起来，普斯托瓦洛夫温柔地对她说："奥莲卡，怎么了，宝贝儿？在胸前画十字吧！"

丈夫怎么想，她就怎么想。如果他认为房间里太热或生意萧条，她也那么认为。丈夫不喜欢娱乐，节日呆

奥莲卡是一个尽心尽力的好女人。

Her husband did not care for entertainments, and on holidays he stayed at home. She did likewise.

"You are always at home or in the office," her friends said to her. "You should go to the theatre, darling, or to the circus."

"Vassitchka and I have no time to go to theatres," she would answer sedately. "We have no time for nonsense. What's the use of these theatres?"

On Saturdays Pustovalov and she used to go to the evening service; on holidays to early mass, and they walked side by side with softened faces as they came home from church. There was a pleasant **fragrance**[56] about them both, and her silk dress rustled agreeably. At home they drank tea, with **fancy bread**[57] and jams of various kinds, and afterwards they ate pie. Every day at twelve o'clock there was a **savoury**[58] smell of beet-root soup and of mutton or duck in their yard, and on **fast-days**[59] of fish, and no one could pass the gate without feeling hungry. In the office the **samovar**[60] was always boiling, and customers were **regaled with**[61] tea and **cracknels**[62]. Once a week the couple went to the baths and returned side by side, both red in the face.

"Yes, we have nothing to complain of, thank God," Olenka used to say to her acquaintances. "I wish every one were as **well off**[63] as Vassitchka and I."

When Pustovalov went away to buy wood in the Mogilev district, she missed him dreadfully, lay awake and cried. A young veterinary surgeon in the army, called Smirnin, to whom they had let their lodge, used sometimes to come in in the evening. He used to talk to her and play cards with her, and this entertained her in her husband's absence. She was particularly interested in what he told her of his home life. He was married and had a little boy, but was separated from his wife because she had been unfaithful to him, and now he hated her and used to send her forty roubles a month for the **maintenance**[64] of their son. And hearing of all this, Olenka sighed and shook her head. She was

56. fragrance
n. 香味，芬芳

57. fancy bread
花式面包

58. savoury
adj. 香喷喷的

59. fast day
n. 斋戒日

60. samovar
n. 俄国的一种茶壶

61. regale with
以……款待；使享受

62. cracknel
n. 薄饼干的一种；脆煎肉片

63. well off
adj. 富有的；处境好的

64. maintenance
n. 生活费；赡养费

在家里。她也呆在家里。

"你总是呆在家里或办公室里，"朋友们对她说。"宝贝儿，你应该去看戏，或者去看杂技。"

"我和瓦西奇卡没有时间去看戏，"她常常镇静地回答。"我们没有时间无聊。看那些戏有什么用呢？"

每逢星期六，她和普斯托瓦洛夫常常去做晚祷，遇到节日就去做早弥撒。他们从教堂出来回家时，并肩而行，脸上带着温和的神情。他们俩身上都有一股令人愉快的芳香，她的丝绸连衣裙发出悦耳的沙沙声。在家里，他们喝茶，吃花式面包和各种果酱，然后还吃馅饼。每天十二点，他们院子里会有一股甜菜汤、羊肉或鸭肉的香味，斋戒日则会有鱼的香味，所以无伦是谁路过大门口，都会垂涎欲滴。在办公室里，茶壶总是沸腾，他们招待顾客喝茶，吃脆饼干。夫妻俩每周去洗一次澡，并肩回来时，两人红光满面。

"是的，感谢上帝，我们没什么抱怨的，"奥莲卡常常对熟人说。"但愿每个人都像我和瓦西奇卡一样富有。"

奥莲卡全心全意帮助第二任丈夫打理木材生意。

每当普斯托瓦洛夫去莫吉廖夫区采办木材，她都非常想念他，伤心流泪，睡不着觉。军队里的一名年轻兽医斯米尔宁租住在她的家里，有时傍晚过来，跟她聊天、打牌，所以丈夫不在时，这让她非常开心。她尤其对他谈的他自己的家庭生活感兴趣。他结过婚，有一个小儿子，但他和妻子分居，因为她对他不忠，现在他还恨她，每月汇给她四十卢布，作为儿子的生活费。听到这些话，奥莲卡叹气，摇头，为他难过。

sorry for him.

"Well, God keep you," she used to say to him at parting, as she lighted him down the stairs with a candle. "Thank you for coming to cheer me up, and may the **Mother of God**[65] give you health."

And she always expressed herself with the same sedateness and dignity, the same reasonableness, **in imitation of**[66] her husband. As the veterinary surgeon was disappearing behind the door below, she would say: "You know, Vladimir Platonitch, you'd better **make it up**[67] with your wife. You should forgive her for the sake of your son. You may be sure the little fellow understands."

And when Pustovalov came back, she told him in a low voice about the veterinary surgeon and his unhappy home life, and both sighed and shook their heads and talked about the boy, who, no doubt, missed his father, and by some strange connection of ideas, they went up to the holy **ikons**[68], bowed to the ground before them and prayed that God would give them children.

And so the Pustovalovs lived for six years quietly and peaceably in love and complete harmony.

But behold! one winter day after drinking hot tea in the office, Vassily Andreitch went out into the yard without his cap on to see about sending off some timber, caught cold and was taken ill. He had the best doctors, but he grew worse and died after four months' illness. And Olenka was a widow once more.

"I've nobody, now you've left me, my darling," she sobbed, after her husband's funeral. "How can I live without you, in wretchedness and misery! Pity me, good people, all alone in the world!"

She went about dressed in black with long "**weepers**[69]," and gave up wearing hat and gloves **for good**[70]. She **hardly ever**[71] went out, except to church, or to her husband's grave, and led the life of a nun. It was not till six months later that she

Glossary

65. Mother of God
n. 圣母玛利亚

66. in imitation of
模仿

67. make it up
和解；讲和

68. ikon
n. 圣像

69. weeper
n. 服丧佩带物

70. for good
永远；永久

71. hardly ever
几乎从不；难得

"唉，上帝保佑你，"分别时，她举着蜡烛送他下楼，常常对他说。"谢谢你来让我开心，愿圣母玛利亚赐给你健康。"

她总是模仿丈夫的样子，表现得那样镇静威严、通情达理。兽医快走出楼下的门时，她常常说道："你知道，符拉季米尔·普拉托内奇，你最好跟妻子和好。你应该看在儿子的份上原谅她。你可以相信那小家伙心里明白。"

等到普斯托瓦洛夫回来时，她就把兽医和他那不幸的家庭生活低声讲给他听，两人就叹气，摇头，谈起那个男孩，说那孩子肯定想念父亲。后来，由于思想上的某种奇特联系，他们走到圣像前，跪下磕头，祈求上帝赐给他们孩子。

就这样，普斯托瓦洛夫夫妇在平静温和、相亲相爱、完美和谐中生活了六年。

可是，看哪！有一年冬天，瓦西里·安德烈伊奇在办公室喝过热茶后，没戴帽子出了门，到院子里派送木材，结果得了风寒，病倒了。她请来最好的医生给他看病，但他病得越来越重，四个月后他就撒手而去。奥莲卡又一次成了寡妇。

"你现在舍下我，我没有人了啊，我的亲人，"丈夫下葬后，她哭道。"没有你，我可怜巴巴可怎么过啊！好心的人们，可怜可怜我这个无依无靠的人吧！"

她穿上黑丧服，戴上长长的"黑面纱"，永远不再戴帽子和手套。除了上教堂或给丈夫上坟，她几乎从不出门，过着修女一样的生活。直到六个月后，她才摘掉

啊！命运真是捉弄人哪！善良干练的奥莲卡再次成为寡妇！

took off the weepers and opened the shutters of the windows. She was sometimes seen in the mornings, going with her cook to market for **provisions**[72], but what went on in her house and how she lived now could only be **surmised**[73]. People guessed, from seeing her drinking tea in her garden with the veterinary surgeon, who read the newspaper aloud to her, and from the fact that, meeting a lady she knew at the post-office, she said to her: "There is no proper veterinary inspection in our town, and that's the cause of all sorts of **epidemics**[74]. One is always hearing of people's getting **infection**[75] from the milk supply, or catching diseases from horses and cows. The health of **domestic animals**[76] ought to be as well cared for as the health of human beings."

She repeated the veterinary surgeon's words, and was of the same opinion as he about everything. It was evident that she could not live a year without some **attachment**[77], and had found new happiness in the lodge. In any one else this would have been **censured**[78], but no one could think ill of Olenka; everything she did was so natural. Neither she nor the veterinary surgeon said anything to other people of the change in their relations, and tried, indeed, to conceal it, but without success, for Olenka could not keep a secret. When he had visitors, men serving in his regiment, and she poured out tea or served the supper, she would begin talking of the **cattle plague**[79], of the foot and mouth disease, and of the municipal **slaughterhouses**[80]. He was dreadfully embarrassed, and when the guests had gone, he would seize her by the hand and hiss angrily: "I've asked you before not to talk about what you don't understand. When we veterinary surgeons are talking among ourselves, please don't put your word in. It's really annoying."

And she would look at him with astonishment and **dismay**[81], and ask him in alarm: "But, Voloditchka, what am I

72. provision
    n. 供应品（特指粮食与副食品）；杂货

73. surmise
    v. 猜测；推测

74. epidemic
    n. 时疫；流行病

75. infection
    n. 传染；感染

76. domestic animals
    n. 家畜

77. attachment
    n. 依恋；爱慕

78. censure
    v. 责难

79. cattle plague
    n. 牛瘟；牛疫

80. slaughterhouse
    n. 屠宰场

81. dismay
    n. 沮丧；惊慌

黑面纱，打开百叶窗。有时可以看到她早上跟厨娘一起到市场去买供应品，但现在她在家里情形怎样、如何生活，人们只能猜测。因为他们看到她在自家的花园里跟兽医一起喝茶，他给她大声念报，还因为她在邮局遇到一个认识的女士，就对那个女士说："我们城里根本没有正确的兽医检验，而这正是各种流行病的起因，总是听说人们因喝牛奶而染病，或者是从牛马身上染病。对家畜的健康应该像对人类的健康一样关心。"人们由此猜测纷纷。

兽医怎么说，她就怎么说，她对一切都和他持同一看法。显然，她要不爱什么人，连一年也活不下去，所以就在自己家的出租屋里找到了新的幸福。如果换了别人，这一定会受到责难，但对奥莲卡，谁也不会朝坏处想；她做的一切都是那么自然。她和兽医对别人都没有说过他们关系的变化，其实是设法隐瞒，但没有成功，因为奥莲卡守不住秘密。每当他有了客人——他团里的同行，她给他们沏过茶或上过晚饭，就常常谈论牛瘟、口蹄疫和本市的屠宰场。他局促不安，等客人们走后，他常常抓住她的手，生气地说："我早就要求过你不要谈你不懂的事儿！我们兽医之间交谈时，请你不要插话。这真让人恼火。"

她惊愕沮丧地望着他，惊恐地问道："可是，沃洛杰奇卡，我谈什么好呢？"

她眼含泪花抱住他，恳求他不要生气，然后他们俩都又高兴起来。

但是，这种幸福没有维持多久。兽医离去，随着军

奥莲卡既可爱又可怜，就像风中的芦苇一般。

to talk about?"

And with tears in her eyes she would embrace him, begging him not to be angry, and they were both happy.

But this happiness did not last long. The veterinary surgeon departed, departed for ever with his regiment, when it was transferred[82] to a distant place—to Siberia, it may be. And Olenka was left alone.

Now she was absolutely alone. Her father had long been dead, and his armchair lay in the attic, covered with dust and lame of one leg. She got thinner and plainer, and when people met her in the street they did not look at her as they used to, and did not smile to her; evidently her best years were over and left behind, and now a new sort of life had begun for her, which did not bear thinking about. In the evening Olenka sat in the porch, and heard the band playing and the fireworks popping in the Tivoli, but now the sound stirred no response. She looked into her yard without interest, thought of nothing, wished for nothing, and afterwards, when night came on she went to bed and dreamed of her empty yard. She ate and drank as it were unwillingly.

And what was worst of all, she had no opinions of any sort. She saw the objects about her and understood what she saw, but could not form any opinion about them, and did not know what to talk about. And how awful it is not to have any opinions! One sees a bottle, for instance, or the rain, or a peasant driving in his cart, but what the bottle is for, or the rain, or the peasant, and what is the meaning of it, one can't say, and could not even for a thousand roubles. When she had Kukin, or Pustovalov, or the veterinary surgeon, Olenka could explain everything, and give her opinion about anything you like, but now there was the same emptiness in her brain and in her heart as there was in her yard outside. And it was as harsh[83] and as bitter as wormwood[84] in the mouth.

Little by little the town grew in all directions. The road

---

82. transfer
vt. 调动

83. harsh
adj. 粗糙的；残酷的；气味令人生厌的

84. wormwood
n. 苦艾

队永远离开了，这次调到了一个遥远的地方——可能是西伯利亚。于是就剩下了奥莲卡孤身一人。

现在她完全孑然一身。她的父亲早已去世，他的扶手椅躺在阁楼上，布满灰尘，缺了一条腿。她越来越瘦，越来越不好看，所以人们在街上遇到她时，不像以往那样看着她，也不对她微笑了。显然，她最美好的岁月已经过去，留在了身后。现在她开始过起了一种新的生活，那种生活还是不忍去想。傍晚，奥莲卡坐在门廊上，听到乐队演奏，烟火在季沃里噼啪作响，但现在这种声音引不起任何反响。她百无聊赖地望着院子，什么也不想，什么也不盼；之后，当夜幕降临时，她就上床睡觉，梦见自己的空院子。她也吃也喝，好像是勉为其难。

最糟糕的是，她没有了任何见解。她看得见周围的事物，也明白看到的一切，但对那些事物却形不成任何看法，不知道该说什么。没有任何见解，这是多么可怕！比如，一个人看见一只瓶子，看见天在下雨，或者看见一个农民坐着货车走过，但说不出那只瓶子、那场雨、那个农民为什么存在、有什么意义，即使给她一千卢布，她也什么都说不出来。当初跟库金、普斯托瓦洛夫、兽医在一起时，奥莲卡什么都能解释，随便什么事儿她都说得出自己的见解，而现在她的脑海里和心里就像外面的院子一样空空荡荡。这令人生厌和不快，就像嘴里的苦艾似的。

渐渐地，这座城向四面八方扩展。公路变成了街道，季沃里和木材场的原址出现了一条条岔路口，建起了一座座新房子。时间过得真快啊！奥莲卡的房子变暗，屋顶生锈，货棚一边倾斜，整个院子长满了阔叶野

奥莲卡真是命运多舛的女人，两次成为寡妇，竟然连被大家都包容的情人也失去了！

became a street, and where the Tivoli and the timber-yard had been, there were new turnings and houses. How rapidly time passes! Olenka's house grew dingy[85], the roof got rusty, the shed sank on one side, and the whole yard was overgrown with docks[86] and stinging-nettles[87]. Olenka herself had grown plain and elderly; in summer she sat in the porch, and her soul, as before, was empty and dreary[88] and full of bitterness. In winter she sat at her window and looked at the snow. When she caught the scent of spring, or heard the chime[89] of the church bells, a sudden rush of memories from the past came over her, there was a tender[90] ache in her heart, and her eyes brimmed over with tears; but this was only for a minute, and then came emptiness again and the sense of the futility[91] of life. The black kitten, Briska, rubbed against her and purred[92] softly, but Olenka was not touched by these feline[93] caresses. That was not what she needed. She wanted a love that would absorb her whole being, her whole soul and reason—that would give her ideas and an object in life, and would warm her old blood. And she would shake the kitten off her skirt and say with vexation[94]: "Get along; I don't want you!"

And so it was, day after day and year after year, and no joy, and no opinions. Whatever Mavra, the cook, said she accepted.

One hot July day, towards evening, just as the cattle were being driven away, and the whole yard was full of dust, some one suddenly knocked at the gate. Olenka went to open it herself and was dumbfounded[95] when she looked out: she saw Smirnin, the veterinary surgeon, grey-headed, and dressed as a civilian. She suddenly remembered everything. She could not help crying and letting her head fall on his breast without uttering a word, and in the violence of her feeling she did not notice how they both walked into the house and sat down to tea.

"My dear Vladimir Platonitch! What fate has brought you?" she muttered, trembling with joy.

85. dingy
adj. 暗黑的；邋遢的

86. dock
n. 酸模；阔叶野草

87. stinging-nettle
n. 大荨麻

88. dreary
adj. 情绪低落的；乏味的

89. chime
n. 钟声

90. tender
adj. 多愁善感的；一触即痛的

91. futility
n. 无聊；无用

92. purr
v. 猫发出呜呜声

93. feline
adj. 猫的

94. vexation
n. 恼怒

95. dumbfound
v. 使目瞪口呆

草和大荨麻。奥莲卡自己也上了年纪，不好看了；夏天，她坐在走廊上，心里跟以前一样空洞乏味，充满苦涩。冬天，她坐在窗边看雪。当她闻到春天的芳香或听到教堂的钟声时，往事就会突然涌现在她的脑海里，心里隐隐作痛，眼泪盈眶，但这只有一分钟时间，随后便再度空落落的，感到生活无聊。黑猫布雷斯卡在她身边蹭来蹭去，柔声咪叫，但这种猫的爱抚打动不了奥莲卡。她需要的不是这个。她想要的是一种能吸引她整个生命、整个灵魂和理性的爱——那种给她思想、给她生活目标、温暖她年老血液的爱。她把黑猫从裙子上抖落，恼怒地说："走开，我不需要你！"

就这样，日复一日，年复一年，没有快乐，没有见解。厨娘玛芙拉说什么，她就认同什么。

七月的一个热天，将近傍晚时，牲口刚被赶走，整个院子到处是灰尘，有人突然来敲门。奥莲卡亲自去开门，向外望去，目瞪口呆，只见是兽医斯米尔宁，头发灰白，穿着便服。她突然想起了一切，禁不住痛哭失声，把头靠在他的胸口，一声不吭。她在激烈的情感中，没有注意到他们俩是怎么走进房子，怎么坐下喝茶的。

"我亲爱的符拉季米尔·普拉托内奇！是哪阵风把你吹来的？"她高兴得颤抖着喃喃说道。

"我要在这里永久住下来，奥尔佳·谢敏诺芙娜，"他告诉她说。"我已经退伍，为了我自己来这里定居，试试自己的运气。再说，我的儿子该上学了。他长大了。你知道，我跟妻子和好了。"

"她在哪里？"奥莲卡问。

奥莲卡是多好的女人啊！春夏秋冬，风霜雪雨，会泯灭她的生命之爱吗？

"I want to settle here for good, Olga Semyonovna," he told her. "I have resigned my post, and have come to settle down and try my luck on my own account. Besides, it's time for my boy to go to school. He's a big boy. I am reconciled with[96] my wife, you know."

"Where is she?' asked Olenka.

"She's at the hotel with the boy, and I'm looking for lodgings."

"Good gracious[97], my dear soul! Lodgings? Why not have my house? Why shouldn't that suit you? Why, my goodness, I wouldn't take any rent!" cried Olenka in a flutter[98], beginning to cry again. "You live here, and the lodge will do nicely for me. Oh dear! how glad I am!"

Next day the roof was painted and the walls were whitewashed, and Olenka, with her arms akimbo[99] walked about the yard giving directions. Her face was beaming with her old smile, and she was brisk[100] and alert as though she had waked from a long sleep. The veterinary's wife arrived—a thin, plain lady, with short hair and a peevish[101] expression. With her was her little Sasha, a boy of ten, small for his age, blue-eyed, chubby[102], with dimples[103] in his cheeks. And scarcely had the boy walked into the yard when he ran after the cat, and at once there was the sound of his gay, joyous laugh.

"Is that your puss[104], auntie?" he asked Olenka. "When she has little ones, do give us a kitten. Mamma is awfully afraid of mice."

Olenka talked to him, and gave him tea. Her heart warmed and there was a sweet ache in her bosom, as though the boy had been her own child. And when he sat at the table in the evening, going over his lessons, she looked at him with deep tenderness and pity as she murmured to herself: "You pretty pet! ...my precious! ...Such a fair little thing, and so clever."

"'An island is a piece of land which is entirely surrounded

"她和儿子住在旅馆，我来找房子。"

"天哪，我的亲人！找房子？何不住我的房子？有什么不适合你们的吗？啊，我的天哪，我不收任何房租！"奥莲卡不知如何是好，大声说道，说完又开始哭了起来，"你们住在这里，那个房子我住就行了。哎呀！我是多么高兴！"

第二天，房顶上漆，墙壁刷白，奥莲卡两手叉腰，在院子里走来走去发号施令。她的脸上露出了往日的愉快微笑，充满生机，行动轻快，仿佛刚从长眠中醒来一般。兽医的妻子到了——这个女人又瘦又丑，短头发，一脸不满的表情。跟她一起来的是小萨沙；他是个十岁的男孩，就年龄来说个子矮小，他胖墩墩的，蓝蓝的眼睛，脸颊上长着酒窝。男孩一走进院子，就追起了那只猫，马上传来了他欢天喜地的笑声。

"阿姨，这是你的猫吗？"他问奥莲卡。"等它下了小猫，请送给我们一只吧。妈妈非常害怕老鼠。"

奥莲卡对他说话，给他茶喝。她的心里暖融融的，感到既甜蜜又痛苦，好像这男孩是她自己的儿子。傍晚，他在桌边坐下，温习功课时，她带着深情和怜悯看着他，喃喃自语："你这漂亮的宝贝儿！……我的心肝宝贝！……这么漂亮、这么聪明的小东西。"

"'岛屿就是四面被水完全包围的一片陆地，'"他朗读道。

"岛屿就是一片陆地，"她重复道，这是她沉默多年和缺乏思想后第一次信心十足地发表意见。

现在她有了自己的见解。晚饭时，她跟萨沙的父母

作者再次写到奥莲卡的善良——她不仅接受了曾经的情人，而且接受了情人的妻子和儿子，为他们收拾房子，让他们一家住到自己家里。

by water,'" he read aloud.

"An island is a piece of land," she repeated, and this was the first opinion to which she gave utterance with positive **conviction**[105] after so many years of silence and **dearth**[106] of ideas.

Now she had opinions of her own, and at supper she talked to Sasha's parents, saying how difficult the lessons were at the high schools, but that yet the high school was better than a commercial one, since with a high-school education all careers were open to one, such as being a doctor or an engineer.

Sasha began going to the high school. His mother departed to Harkov to her sister's and did not return; his father used to go off every day to inspect cattle, and would often be away from home for three days together, and it seemed to Olenka as though Sasha was entirely abandoned, that he was not wanted at home, that he was being starved, and she carried him off to her lodge and gave him a little room there.

And for six months Sasha had lived in the lodge with her. Every morning Olenka came into his bedroom and found him fast asleep, sleeping noiselessly with his hand under his cheek. She was sorry to wake him.

"Sashenka," she would say mournfully, "get up, darling. It's time for school."

He would get up, dress and say his prayers, and then sit down to breakfast, drink three glasses of tea, and eat two large cracknels and a half a buttered roll. All this time he was hardly awake and a little ill-humoured **in consequence**[107].

"You don't quite know your fable, Sashenka," Olenka would say, looking at him as though he were about to set off on a long journey. "What a lot of trouble I have with you! You must work and do your best, darling, and obey your teachers."

"Oh, do leave me alone!" Sasha would say.

Then he would go down the street to school, a little figure,

105. conviction
   n. 深信；确信
106. dearth
   n. 缺乏
107. in consequence
   结果

亲交谈，说中学的功课真难，但中学比商校强，因为只要经过中学教育，各行各业都可以广开门路，比如当医生或工程师。

　　萨沙开始上中学。他的母亲动身去哈尔科夫她妹妹家，从此没再回来；他的父亲每天出门去给牲口看病，常常一去就是三天不在家。奥莲卡似乎觉得萨沙完全没人管，家里没人要他了，会被活活饿死，于是她就让他搬到她的房子，在那里给他收拾了一间小屋。

　　萨沙跟她在那个房间住了六个月。每天早晨，奥莲卡都走进他的卧室，发现他正在酣睡，手放在腮下静静地睡着。叫醒他，她也很难过。

　　"萨申卡，"她常常伤心地说，"起来，宝贝儿！该上学去了。"

　　他起床，穿衣，祷告，然后坐下吃早饭，喝三杯茶，吃完两大块脆饼干和半个黄油面包卷。这期间他几乎还没有醒来，因此脾气有点糟。

　　"你还没有完全熟悉那个寓言，萨申卡，"奥莲卡看着他说，好像他准备出远门一样。"我要为你操多少心啊！宝贝儿，你一定要学习，尽最大努力，要听老师的话。"

　　"噢，请别管我！"萨沙说。

　　随后，他就沿街上学。他身材矮小，头戴大帽子，肩背书包。奥莲卡常常静静地跟在他后面。

　　"萨申卡！"她在他后面叫道，接着会把一颗海枣或一块糖塞进他手里。他们走到学校所在的那条街时，他对后面跟着一个高大健壮的女人感到不好意思，就回

多么善良的女人！上帝会眷顾她吗？

wearing a big cap and carrying a **satchel**[108] on his shoulder. Olenka would follow him noiselessly.

"Sashenka!" she would call after him, and she would pop into his hand a **date**[109] or a **caramel**[110]. When he reached the street where the school was, he would feel ashamed of being followed by a tall, stout woman, he would turn round and say: "You'd better go home, auntie. I can go the rest of the way alone."

She would stand still and look after him fixedly till he had disappeared at the school-gate.

Ah, how she loved him! Of her former attachments not one had been so deep; never had her soul surrendered to any feeling so **spontaneously**[111], so disinterestedly, and so joyously as now that her maternal instincts were aroused. For this little boy with the dimple in his cheek and the big school cap, she would have given her whole life, she would have given it with joy and tears of tenderness. Why? Who can tell why?

When she had seen the last of Sasha, she returned home, contented and **serene**[112], brimming over with love; her face, which had grown younger during the last six months, smiled and beamed; people meeting her looked at her with pleasure. "Good-morning, Olga Semyonovna, darling. How are you, darling?"

"The lessons at the high school are very difficult now," she would relate at the market. "It's too much; in the first class yesterday they gave him a fable to learn by heart, and a Latin translation and a problem. You know it's too much for a little chap."

And she would begin talking about the teachers, the lessons, and the school books, saying just what Sasha said.

At three o'clock they had dinner together; in the evening they learned their lessons together and cried. When she put him to bed, she would stay a long time making the Cross over him and murmuring a prayer; then she would go to bed and dream of

108. satchel
　　n. 书包

109. date
　　n. 海枣；枣椰子

110. caramel
　　n.（果味）块糖

111. spontaneously
　　adv. 自然地；本能地

112. serene
　　adj. 沉静的；安详的

过头说："您最好回家去吧，阿姨。剩下的路我可以一个人走了。"

她站在那里一动不动，定定地望着他的背影，直到他走进校门不见踪影。

啊，她是多么爱他！她以前的爱恋从来没有这么深过；她从来没有这样自发、这样无私、这样快乐地放任自己的感情，因为她的母性本能已被唤醒。为了这个头戴学生帽、脸上有酒窝的小男孩，她愿意献出她的整个生命，她愿意带着喜悦和温柔的眼泪奉献出来。为什么？谁能告诉这是为什么呢？

奥莲卡的母性光辉光照人间。

她把萨沙送到学校后，就沉静地走回家去，心满意足，踏踏实实，满腔热爱。她的脸在过去的六个月中变得越来越年轻，总是带着微笑，喜气洋洋；碰见她的人都愉快地看着她。"早上好，亲爱的奥尔佳·谢敏诺芙娜！你好啊，宝贝儿？"

"现在中学的功课真难，"她常常在市场上说。"太过分了；昨天第一节课他们就让他背会一则寓言，译一篇拉丁文，解一道题。你晓得这对一个小家伙太过分了。"

她开始谈论老师、功课、课本，说的正是萨沙说过的话。

三点钟，他们一起吃午饭，傍晚一起学习功课，一起哭。她让他上床睡觉后，常常久久地在他胸前画十字，低声祷告；然后，她也上床睡觉，梦想到了遥远朦胧的将来，那时萨沙将会完成学业，成为一名医生或工程师，将会拥有自己的大房子，买了马和马车，结婚生子……她睡着后，还在想着这件事，眼泪从她紧闭的眼睛

that far-away misty future when Sasha would finish his studies and become a doctor or an engineer, would have a big house of his own with horses and a carriage, would get married and have children.... She would fall asleep still thinking of the same thing, and tears would run down her cheeks from her closed eyes, while the black cat lay purring beside her: "Mrr, mrr, mrr."

Suddenly there would come a loud knock at the gate.

Olenka would wake up breathless with alarm, her heart **throbbing**[113]. Half a minute later would come another knock.

"It must be a telegram from Harkov," she would think, beginning to tremble from head to foot. "Sasha's mother is sending for him from Harkov.... Oh, mercy on us!"

She was in despair. Her head, her hands, and her feet would turn chill, and she would feel that she was the most unhappy woman in the world. But another minute would pass, voices would be heard: it would turn out to be the veterinary surgeon coming home from the club.

"Well, thank God!" she would think.

And gradually the load in her heart would **pass off**[114], and she would feel at ease. She would go back to bed thinking of Sasha, who lay sound asleep in the next room, sometimes crying out in his sleep: "I'll give it you! Get away! Shut up!"

113. throb
v.（心脏等急速地）
跳动，悸动

114. pass off
逐渐消失

里流出来，总是顺着她的脸颊滚下；与此同时，那只黑猫躺在她身边总会发出愉快的"喵，喵，喵"的叫声。

突然，门口传来了响亮的敲门声。

奥莲卡醒来，吓得大气都不敢喘，心怦怦直跳。半分钟后，又传来了敲门声。

"这一定是从哈尔科夫发来的电报，"她想，开始浑身颤抖。"萨沙的母亲从哈尔科夫派人来叫他了……噢，可怜可怜我们吧！"

她陷入了绝望之中，头、手和脚顿时冰凉，感到她是世界上最不幸的女人。但是，又过了一分钟，就传来了说话声：原来是兽医从俱乐部回家来了。

"啊，谢天谢地！"她想。

渐渐地，她心里没有了负担，轻松自在。她躺回床上想着萨沙，萨沙正在隔壁房间酣睡，有时在梦中大声喊："我揍你！滚开！住嘴！"

契诃夫不愧为天才作家！他将人性剖析得如此明彻。

名篇赏析

　　有时，人的命运不掌握在自己的手里，就像奥莲卡这个善良干练的女人一样——她两次找到心爱的人，并全力帮助丈夫发展，受到人们的好评，但命运之神还是两次从她手里夺走她的丈夫！后来她又倾心于斯米尔宁，尽管以后斯米尔宁带来了他的妻子和儿子，奥莲卡并没有醋意大发，而是全力地帮助他们，把自己的房子无代价地给他们居住。特别是当小萨沙失去父母后，奥莲卡完全承担下来对小萨沙的照顾——她终于从小萨沙那里又获得了一份滋润。奥莲卡对萨沙无微不至的关怀照顾，更进一步表现了奥莲卡的动人心魄的善良。奥莲卡把这个跟自己没有任何血缘关系的萨沙，完全当成了自己的孩子——甚至比自己的孩子还要关怀。我们不得不对奥莲卡竖起大拇指，并且在心理为她祝福，期望上天给予她幸福。

　　无论在什么情况下，人都不能失去起码的善良，不能丧失生活的勇气；要深信命运之神是会眷顾每个善良的好人的。像奥莲卡这样的人，实在是我们社会的"宝贝儿"！

Sinclair Ross

part
01 *September Snow*

九月雪

姓名	辛克莱·罗斯
出生日期	1908年1月22日
出生地	加拿大萨斯喀彻温省舍尔布鲁克附近
性别	男

成就和特色

　　加拿大著名作家。他最著名的长篇小说是《我和我的房子》；最著名的短篇小说是《上漆的门》、《一片麦田》和《中午时分的灯》。他的写作风格具有加拿大本土作家的独特风格，粗犷而又细腻，加上技法娴熟的结构和精准传神的自然风光的描写，令读者耳目一新，啧啧称奇。

写作背景

　　丈夫威尔放牧，妻子爱丽娜做家务。虽然生活艰辛，但他们相亲相爱。然而，就在九月雪的这一天，威尔在与风雪寒冷搏斗了一昼夜后，却永远失去了自己的爱妻爱丽娜。作者没有用任何风花雪月的语言来写威尔夫妇的相亲相爱，而是把他的爱都贯穿在了语言和动作行为的细节描写上。

1. drab
   adj. 单调乏味的；淡褐色的

2. inert
   adj. 呆滞的

3. at large
   自由；不受拘束

4. blizzard
   n. 雪暴；暴风雪

5. barb
   n. 动物触须

6. spatter
   n. 飞溅；滴落

01

September Snow

All day there had been rain. It swept down from the hills in drizzling, smoky sheets that made a lineless blend of sky and prairie. The **drab**[1] yellow stubble-fields lay suddenly **inert**[2], oppressed by the clouds and wetness. Night came early, a wind with it, and the rain thickened.

On the way home from town Will tried to trot the horses, but the tugging roads and the big rims of mud on the wagon wheels held them to a walk. He was afraid of snow and anxious to get the cattle up to the stable before dark. They were running **at large**[3] now that harvest was over and the fields stripped; without shelter they would drift all night with the storm. It would kill the late calves. He had seen wild **blizzards**[4] in September.

By the time he drove into the yard the snow was beginning; fine **barbs**[5] of sleet that felt like prickly hairs against the skin; now and then the soft **spatter**[6] of a big, spongy flake. At the sound of the wagon Eleanor came to the door and called that supper was ready. "I've got to get the cattle," he shouted back. She slammed the door, opened it again. "But it's dark now anyway—why can't you have supper first?" Her voice had been like that of late—high-pitched and irritable. The baby coming, he told himself; another couple of weeks she'll be herself again.

He was cold; it was nearly seven hours since he had eaten; but the threat of a storm made him indifferent to himself and eager to be away for the cattle. He hesitated a minute in the stable, his fingers on Bess's bridle; and then, because the baby

九月雪

雨整整下了一天。淅淅沥沥，烟雾蒙蒙，从小山上横扫下来，将天空和草原连成一体，分不清东南西北。在乌云与潮气的压迫下，秋收后单调黄色的布满茬儿的田地突然显得死气沉沉。夜幕早早就降临了，风随之而来，雨下得更紧了。

从镇子回家的路上，威尔想策马小跑，但黏糊糊的路面和车轮上的大圈泥浆使它们举步维艰。他既害怕下雪，又心急火燎，想在天黑前将牛群赶进牛棚。当前收割已经结束，田野里光秃秃一片，牛群到处乱跑，没有避雨的地方，它们会整夜在暴风雨中游荡。这样会把晚生的牛犊冻死。九月份出现狂暴风雪，他可是亲眼见过的。

等他驾车走进院子时，雪已经开始下了起来；细小的冰雨像鬃毛一样刺扎着他的皮肤；不时还落下大片大片海绵状的、软软的雪花。听到马车声，爱丽娜走到门口大声说道，晚饭已经准备好了。"我得去把牛找回来，"他大声应着。她砰地关上门，紧接着又打开来。"先吃饭吧，反正天已经黑了！"她的声音近来老是这样——又烦躁又刺耳。他心里说，这是因为她快生孩子了，再过两个星期她就会恢复正常的。

他很冷；他已经快七个小时没吃东西了；但是，暴风雪的威胁使他顾不上自己，一心只想着去找牛群。他

was only a week or ten days away, he ran impatiently to the house.

It was a difficult meal. He was on edge, anxious about the cattle; while Eleanor, instead of appreciating, as he felt she should, the he was delaying on her account, asked **fretfully**[7] why he had stayed so long in town. His nerves were already **taut**[8]; it was **exasperating**[9] to have to start telling her about the muddy roads. He let his voice rise irritably, then, catching himself leaned across the table. "Eleanor—you're sure you're all right?"

She nodded, but started to whimper. "I wish you wouldn't go—all you think about is crop and cows. It's dark—you may be away again for hours."

He stared at her blankly, bewildered. This was their first year; she knew as well as he what a struggle it was to keep out of debt. "But I'm selling the **steers**[10] next week. If they're out all night running with the storm they'll lose weight."

"I know." There was a sudden limpness in her voice. "It's the wind, that's all—waiting for you and watching it get dark." She stood up, keeping her eyes away from him, and went to the door. "Look how it's snowing — you'll never find them anyway."

He glanced over her shoulder, grabbed his cap and coat, then looked down at her and stopped short, helpless. "I won't be long—you're sure you don't mind?"

He wheeled, **plunged**[11] outside. The wind was high; the wet snow slapped on his face like soft, strong wings, **clogging**[12] his eyes and nostrils. He saddled the mare without taking time to light a lantern, and giving her free rein to pick her way, rode south, the wind in his back. The snow beneath and around him made it seem he was riding on the top of a cloud. It was getting colder and Will had only a pair of canvas gloves that he had used in the harvest. He kept changing hands to hold the reins, shoving first one and then the other into his pockets where his legs warmed them a little. Then his body too began to chill, for

7. fretfully
  adv. 焦躁地；不安地

8. taut
  adj. 绷紧的

9. exasperate
  vt. 使恼火

10. steer
  n. 阉牛；菜牛

11. plunge
  vi. 冲入；闯进

12. clog
  vt. 堵塞；使凝结

在牛棚里迟疑了一会儿，手指搭在贝丝的辔头上；转念又想她十天八天就要生孩子了，便不耐烦地跑进了屋。

这是一顿难熬的晚饭。他紧张不安，担心着牛群，爱丽娜却不领情，他本以为她会的，因为他是因为她才耽搁的，而她却絮叨地问他为何在镇上呆得那么久。他的神经已经绷紧；还得向她解释道路是怎样泥泞，真让人窝火。他烦躁地提高了嗓音，但又克制住了，将身体倾过桌子，问道："爱丽娜——你肯定你没事吧？"

她点点头，却又开始呜咽起来。"但愿你不要走——你就知道庄稼和奶牛。天黑了——你可能又要外出几个小时。"

他茫然地盯着她，很是为难。这是他们结婚后的第一年，她和他一样清楚，要做到不欠债有多难。"可下星期我要卖这些菜牛。要是让它们整夜在风雪中乱跑，会掉膘的。"

"我知道。"她的声音突然软了下来。"只是刮着大风——我一直在等着你，看着天黑下来。"她站起来，眼光一直避开，不看他，走到门口。"看，雪下得多大——恐怕你也没法找到它们。"

他从她身后瞥了一眼，迅速抓过帽子和外套，然后俯视着她，突然站住，一副无奈的神情。"我去去就来——你肯定不会介意吧？"

他转过身，冲了出去。风很大；湿雪打在他的脸上，有如柔软有力的翅膀，堵住了他的眼睛和鼻孔。他摸黑给母马装上马鞍，就放开缰绳，让马择路南下，自己背向着风。雪在他脚下和四周飞舞，使他仿佛走在云端。天更冷了，威尔只戴着一双收割时用过的帆布手套。他两手交替执缰，替换着把一只手插入裤袋，靠腿的温度温暖手。不久，他的身体也开始发冷，因为他只

一个"软"字将妻子对他的担忧表现得淋漓尽致。夫妻间的关爱之情体现得是多么充分！

he was wearing just a **smock**[13] and raincoat. He bent low over the saddle, shivering, peering into the snowy darkness, every few seconds imagining he saw black shapes in front of him.

Just as he had hoped, the cattle were at the fence, heads pushed far over the wire, tails to the wind. Bess came alertly to life, she kept making sudden dashes at the cattle, **grazing**[14] her teeth along their **rumps**[15]. Bess biting wheeling, staggering— but the cattle were numb with cold, and only knotted themselves and huddled tight against the fence. Sometimes they half-turned, or made a stiff, side-wise jump, but none of them would face the wind and snow. Even when Will rode close and kicked them in the ribs or shoulder, they only sidled along the fence a few feet, or made a half-timid **lunge**[16] with their horns in the direction of Bess. His temper flared, and not having a whip with him, he struck Bess with his doubled fist.

Will **reined in**[17] Bess. He **dismounted**[18], one hand on Bess's bridle. With a jerk of her head Bess pulled the bridle out of his hand, swung away and disappeared into the night.

He lay in a minute. As he struggled to his feet his anger kept him from realizing his **predicament**[19]. Doggedly determined to try again to move the cattle, he climbed through the fence and ran along in front of them, striking them in the face and shouting. But they resisted stupidly and only huddled closer to the fence. He gave up finally, **clammy**[20] with sweat and **cringing**[21] before the wind, then, passive and spent, he stumbled on **stolidly**[22].

He stumbled onto one of his straw-stacks at last. The wind fell away abruptly; there was a sudden calm, the whistle of the storm remote. He lay a long time in a kind of **stupor**[23]. Out of the wind it was not cold, and after his struggle with the storm, the hush and ease of shelter brought a sense of physical contentment that **lulled**[24] like a drug. The warmth, however, was only because of his escape from the wind; presently he began to shiver again, chilled by his sweat-damp clothing. He sat erect, started to

13. smock
    n. 工作服；罩衫

14. graze
    vt. 擦磨

15. rump
    n. 兽的臀部

16. lunge
    n. 猛冲

17. rein in
    勒缰绳使马止步

18. dismount
    v. 下马

19. predicament
    n. 困境、险境

20. clammy
    adj. 冷湿的

21. cringe
    vi. 畏缩

22. stolidly
    adv. 感觉迟钝地

23. stupor
    n. 昏迷

24. lull
    vt. 使缓和；使平静

穿了一件工作服和一件雨衣。他趴在马鞍上，冻得瑟瑟发抖，凝视着飘雪的夜空，每隔几秒钟就想象着自己看到前面有几条黑影。

正如他期望的那样，牛群在栅栏旁，头伸过铁丝，屁股对着风。贝丝活跃起来，它一次次冲向牛群，用牙齿轻触牛的臀部。贝丝又是咬，又是转，又是晃——但是，牛已经冻僵了，只是靠着栅栏拼命挤成一团。有时它们半侧过身子，或是僵硬地侧跳一下，但没有一头牛愿意面对风雪。即使威尔骑着马来到它们跟前踢它们的肋部或肩部，它们也只是侧身沿着栅栏挪几步或是胆小地用犄角朝贝丝的方向晃一晃。他脾气上来了，手里没拿鞭子，就握紧拳头捶打贝丝。

威尔勒紧缰绳，令贝丝止步，跳下马背，一手拉着贝丝的辔头。贝丝突然甩头把缰绳从他手中挣脱，一溜烟地跑掉，消失在了夜幕之中。

他在地上静静地躺了一分钟。当他挣扎着站起来时，愤怒使他忘记了自己处境的危险。他顽固地想再设法驱赶牛群，他钻过铁丝栅栏，跑到它们前面，一边迎面打它们，一边大声吆喝。但是，它们愚蠢地负隅顽抗，只是更加靠近栅栏挤作一团。最后，他放弃了，浑身汗湿，迎风畏缩，尔后情绪低落，筋疲力尽，呆头呆脑，蹒跚离去。

最后，他踉跄着撞在他自己家的一个草垛上。风骤然而止；突然间，一切都平静了，暴风雨的呼啸声远去了。他恍恍惚惚地在那里躺了很长一段时间。没有风，天就不冷了。在同风暴拼搏之后，这避风处的宁静和舒适给他一种肉体上的满足，像麻醉品一样让他安静下来。然而，这温暖只是因为他避开了风；不一会儿，他就又打起了冷战，汗湿的衣服使他感到冰冷。他坐立起

这里既有比喻，又有夸张，没有真正的生活体验是写不出这样真实感人的场景的。

tear out a hollow for himself in the straw.

He **tunnelled into**[25] it, **lengthwise**[26], feet first, kicking and **burrowing**[27] until he could stretch his legs. And now the warmth was real, but wide awake from the effort it had cost him to pull out the straw he began to think of Eleanor, and to feel troubled and even guilty because he was lying here comfortable and idle. Her face came back to him, the strange flash in her eyes and her tight mouth. She would be waiting for him, pacing through the house, window to window, trying to peer out, afraid he might be lost. Sometimes a woman did queer things when she was expecting a baby. She might even start out to look for him, or try to make her way to a neighbour's.

Towards morning he dozed. When he woke the wind had died; there was a pale, early light. The snow-swept landscape lay horizonless, merging into a low, **shaggy**[28] sky, colourless and blank, without balance or **orientation**[29]. For a few seconds he looked at it stupidly, puzzled; then, remembering the cattle and the storm, he crept out uneasily from his shelter.

He set off at a stiff, dull walk. The buildings were only a mile away, suspended in the empty blur of sky and snow with an aloof, unfamiliar **detachment**[30] that chilled and dispirited him. It was hard walking. When he reached the buildings Bess came out of the cattle shed, still with the saddle and bridle on, and started to paw in front of the stable. He swung towards her, intending to let her inside, but glanced towards the house and stopped abruptly. The kitchen door was open; there was a drift across it, two feet above the threshold. He stood weak and dizzy a moment, then recovered swiftly and explained: Eleanor hadn't shut the door properly; it needed a strong push to make the lock catch. Bess **whinnied**[31]. He half-turned towards her—hesitated—bolted across the yard to the house.

The snow was mounded right across the kitchen, curled up like a wave against the far wall, piled on table and chairs. Even on the stove—the fire must have been out for hours. He shivered

25. tunnel into
    挖掘

26. lengthwise
    adv. 横向地

27. burrow
    vi. 掘洞

28. shaggy
    adj. 有杂乱毛发形云
    彩的

29. orientation
    n. 定向；定位

30. detachment
    n. 冷淡

31. whinny
    vi. 马嘶

来，开始给自己在草垛中掏一个洞。

他双脚朝前，横钻进草洞里，踢踢掏掏直到能展开腿。现在的确是暖和了。但是，掏草垛花的劲使他完全清醒了，他想起了爱丽娜，感到心烦意乱，甚至有些内疚，因为他舒适懒散地躺在这里。爱丽娜的面容在他眼前晃动，双眼闪耀着异样光芒，嘴唇紧闭。爱丽娜一定在等他，在屋里走来走去，从一个窗户到另一个窗户，企图瞧见外面，害怕他会迷路。有时怀孕的女人会做出违反常规的事情。她甚至可能出门来找他，或者试图穿过雪地到邻居家去。

天快亮时，他进入了梦乡。一觉醒来，风已经息了，露出了早晨苍白的光亮。大雪扫过的大地无边无际，与有乱云的、低沉的天空融成一体，灰白空旷，缺少平衡和方向感。他迟钝而困惑地看了几秒钟；接下来想起了牛群和暴风雪，他心神不安地从草垛里爬出来。

他迈着僵硬迟缓的步子出发了。到自家的房子大约有一英里，它们悬在空旷模糊的天空和雪地之间，一副陌生的冷淡和漠然的面孔使他心寒和沮丧。这是一段艰难的路程。当他到家时，母马贝丝从牲口棚走出来，仍配着马鞍和辔头，在牛棚前用蹄子刨着地。他转向母马，想让它进去；当他的目光掠向房子时，他突然停了下来。只见厨房门开着，里边积了一大堆雪，超出门槛两英尺。他一阵头晕，无力地站在那里，随后很快恢复了常态，暗自解释道，是爱丽娜没关好门；撞上门锁得费好大劲儿。母马嘶叫起来。他半转向它——犹豫了一下——闪电般穿过院子奔向房子。

雪在厨房里堆满了一地，靠着远处墙边旋成了波浪形，堆在了桌椅上，甚至火炉上——火一定熄灭好几个小时了。他踏进去时，打了个冷战。"爱丽娜！"他叫

生活的艰辛并没有泯灭他对妻子的爱和思念，也没有泯灭他对妻子的担忧。

as he stepped inside. "Eleanor!" he called, "Do you hear, Eleanor? Where are you?"

There was a little moaning sound in answer, and he sprang across the kitchen and into the bedroom. She was on the bed, half-undressed, her face twisted into a kind of grin, the forehead shining as if the skullbones were trying to burst through the skin. He knelt beside her, shook her, then sprang up and ran back to the kitchen. He would have to get a fire going—and the snow out and the door closed. She moaned again. A doctor first—a woman—

He ran to the stable and caught Bess, and with his fists and heels beat her crazily to a gallop over the treacherous drifts. It was a mile to the neighbours. He burst into the house, motioning wildly in the direction he had come. "Eleanor—she's having her baby—the house is full of snow."

They drove him away from her, out of the house altogether. Her mother was there now. By noon they had the doctor. No one spoke to Will. He worked in the stable. He climbed onto the stacks of oat sheaves beside the stable and shook off the melting snow. The cattle were coming home; he could see them from here, a long, broken straggle[32] in the distance.

About three o'clock they took him to Eleanor. She was white, her eyes closed, but the ugly look of pain had gone. He sat still beside her, not understanding. Finally the doctor had to tell him she had just died. Then a faint, jagged[33] little saw of sound, the baby started to cry. He felt a twinge of recognition. He seemed to be listening to the same plaintiveness[34] and protest that had been in Eleanor's voice of late. An impulse seized him to see and hold his baby; but just for a minute longer he stood there, looking out across the sunspangled[35] snow, listening.

---

32. straggle
   n. 散乱的一群人或物

33. jagged
   adj. 参差不齐的

34. plaintiveness
   n. 悲哀；哀伤

35. sunspangled
   adj. 阳光灿烂的

道。"你听到了吗，爱丽娜？你在哪里？"

好像有一丝微弱的呻吟声在回答。他跳过厨房，进入卧室。爱丽娜躺在床上，衣服半脱，脸部扭曲，呲牙咧嘴，额头发光，好像颅骨要从头皮里爆裂出来似的。他跪在爱丽娜身边，摇着她，接着跃身跳起，跑回厨房，他得生上火——把雪弄出去，把门关上。她又呻吟起来。先找医生叫一个女帮手——

这一连串动作将他对妻子的关爱、担忧表现得淋漓尽致。

他跑向牲口棚，抓住贝丝，疯狂地用拳头和脚后跟踢打，使它在危机四伏的雪地上飞驰。到邻居家有一英里路。他冲进房子，狂乱地指着他来的方向。"爱丽娜——她在生孩子——房子里灌满了雪。"

她们把他从爱丽娜身边赶开，赶出了房子。现在丈母娘也在那里了。到中午时分，她们找来了医生。没人和威尔说话。他在牲口棚里干活，他爬到牛棚外的燕麦捆垛上，抖掉正在融化的雪。牛群正往回走，他从这里能看到它们，在远处一支长长的零乱队伍。

大约下午3点钟，她们把威尔带到爱丽娜跟前。爱丽娜脸色惨白，双目闭合，但她面部那难看的痛苦表情已经没有了。威尔一动不动地坐在爱丽娜身边，不明白是怎么回事。最后，医生不得不告诉他爱丽娜已经死了。接着，出现一种微弱、参差、拉锯一般的声音，是婴儿开始哭了起来。他心中感到一阵熟悉的剧痛。他听到的似乎正是爱丽娜近来嗓音中的哀怨和抗议。他一阵冲动，要去看他的孩子，将孩子抱在怀里；但他只是在那里多站了一会儿，目光越过阳光灿烂的积雪，注视远方，倾听着。

名篇赏析

　　小说写了一对在艰辛中生活的夫妇，丈夫威尔放牧，妻子爱丽娜做家务。虽然生活艰辛，但他们相亲相爱。然而就在九月雪的这一天，威尔在与风雪寒冷搏斗了一昼夜后，却永远失去了自己的爱妻爱丽娜。作者没有用任何风花雪月的语言来写威尔夫妇的相亲相爱，而是把他的爱都贯穿在了语言和动作行为的细节描写上。小说就这样通过这些语言和动作行为的描写，为读者展现了这一对夫妇在大风雪灾难中的相亲相爱。结尾处，妻子爱丽娜在大风雪中生产时失去了生命，但新生儿的啼哭声还是为威尔今后的生活涂上了一抹灿烂的色彩。

Sinclair Ross

02 *The Lamp at Noon*

中午时分的灯

姓名	辛克莱·罗斯
出生日期	1908年1月22日
出生地	加拿大萨斯喀彻温省舍尔布鲁克附近
性别	男

成就和特色

　　加拿大著名作家。他最著名的长篇小说是《我和我的房子》；最著名的短篇小说是《上漆的门》、《一片麦田》和《中午时分的灯》。他的写作风格具有加拿大本土作家的独特风格，粗犷而又细腻，加上技法娴熟的结构和精准传神的自然风光的描写，令读者耳目一新，啧啧称奇。

写作背景

　　小说以大草原为背景，描写草原人的生活斗争。罗斯以传奇色彩的优美笔法将内外景融为一体，外景反射出人物的内心世界。小说描写的"灯"象征着男主人公保罗的希望。

02

The Lamp at Noon

1. demented
   adj. 疯狂的
2. keen
   vi. 哀鸣；哭丧
3. respite
   n. 暂缓
4. impenetrable
   adj. 无法穿透的
5. granary
   n. 谷仓；粮仓
6. obscure
   vt. 遮掩；使暗淡
7. topple
   vt. 摇摇欲坠；颠覆
8. rift
   n. 裂缝
9. tattered
   adj. 衣衫褴褛的；破破烂烂的
10. wizened
    adj. 干瘪的；皱巴巴的
11. diffused
    adj. 散射的；分散的
12. immobility
    n. 一动不动；固定静止

A little before noon she lit the lamp. **Demented**[1] wind fled **keening**[2] past the house: a wail through the eaves that died every minute or two. Three days now without **respite**[3] it had held. The dust was thickening to an **impenetrable**[4] fog.

She lit the lamp, then for a long time stood at the window motionless. In dim, fitful outline the stable and oat **granary**[5] still were visible; beyond, **obscuring**[6] fields and landmarks, the lower of dust clouds made the farmyard seem an isolated acre, poised aloft above a somber void. At each blast of wind it shook, as if to **topple**[7] and spin hurtling with the dust-reel into space.

From the window she went to the door, opening it a little, and peering toward the stable again. He was not coming yet. As she watched there was a sudden **rift**[8] overhead, and for a moment through the **tattered**[9] clouds the sun raced like a **wizened**[10] orange. It shed a soft, **diffused**[11] light, dim and yellow as if it were the light from the lamp reaching out through the open door.

She closed the door, and going to the stove, tried the potatoes with a fork. Her eyes all the while were fixed and wide with a curious **immobility**[12]. It was the window. Standing at it, she had let her forehead press against the pane until the eyes were strained apart and rigid. Wide like that they had looked out to the deepening ruin of the storm. Now she could not close them.

中午时分的灯

临近中午时，她点着了灯。狂风疾驰，一路哀鸣，掠过屋顶消逝而去。那是一种透过屋檐每隔一两分钟消逝的哀鸣声。已经连续刮了三天三夜。飞尘越来越厚，形成了一阵无法穿越的浓雾。

她点亮灯后，好一阵子站在窗前，一动不动。在昏暗的沙尘中，马厩和燕麦谷仓断断续续的轮廓依稀可见；稍远处，下压的一团团尘云遮住了田野和路标，使农家院看上去就像一块孤零零的荒地，镇定自若，漂浮在阴郁的虚空之中。每一阵大风袭来，它都随风飘摆，仿佛摇摇欲坠，随着席卷而来的飞尘一路飞奔，旋入天空。

她离开窗户，走向门口，打开一条门缝，眯眼张望马厩那边。他还没有回来。这时，她看到头顶上空突然出现了一道裂缝，太阳透过一道道散碎的云隙一路奔跑，就像干瘪的橘子似的。阳光微弱散淡，暗黄色的光犹如开门时从门口照出的灯光。

她关上门，走向炉灶，用叉子试了试土豆，眼睛始终圆睁凝视，样子奇怪，一动不动。是那扇窗户。之前，她站在窗边时，前额紧贴在玻璃上朝外看，直瞪得两眼发酸，紧张僵硬。她一直那样瞪着两眼，紧盯着窗

三天三夜遮天蔽日的黄沙和需要点灯的中午。作品一开始对于恶劣环境的描述，使读者不禁开始担心起主人公的命运。

恶劣的风沙天气中，他关注的是生存的田野和耕作的马匹。

The baby started to cry. He was lying in a homemade crib over which she had arranged a tent of muslin. Careful not to disturb the folds of it, she knelt and tried to still him, whispering huskily in a singsong voice that he must hush and go to sleep again. She would have liked to rock him, to feel the comfort of his little body in her arms, but a fear had obsessed[13] her that in the dust-filled air he might contract[14] pneumonia. There was dust sifting everywhere. Her own throat was parched with it. The table had been set less than ten minutes, and already a film was gathering on the dishes. The little cry continued, and with wincing, frightened lips she glanced around as if to find a corner where the air was less oppressive. But while the lips winced, the eyes maintained their wide, immobile stare. "Sleep," she whispered again. "It's too soon for you to be hungry. Daddy's coming for his dinner."

He seemed a long time. Even the clock, still a few minutes off noon, could not dispel[15] a foreboding[16] sense that he was longer than he should be. She went to the door again—and then recoiled slowly to stand white and breathless in the middle of the room. She mustn't. He would only despise her as if she ran to the stable looking for him. There was too much grim[17] endurance in his nature ever to let him understand the fear and weakness of a woman. She must stay quiet and wait. Nothing was wrong. At noon he would come—and perhaps after dining stay with her awhile.

Yesterday, and again at breakfast this morning, they had quarreled bitterly. She wanted him now, the assurance of his strength and nearness, but he would stand aloof, wary, remembering the words she had flung at him in her anger, unable to understand it was only the dust and wind that had driven her.

Tense, she fixed her eyes upon the clock, listening. There

13. obsess
   vt. 使心神不宁；纠缠
14. contract
   vt. 感染；患上
15. dispel
   vt. 驱散；消除
16. foreboding
   adj. 不祥之兆的；预感的
17. grim
   adj. 冷酷的；恐怖的

外沙尘暴造成的日益严重的破坏。现在她的眼睛都合不上了。

　　婴儿开始哭了起来。他睡在他们自制的婴儿床里，她在小床上方罩了一层细薄棉布。她怕抖动棉布上的褶子时掉下灰尘，跪在床边哄孩子，声音沙哑地轻轻哼着，想哄孩子安睡。她多想把孩子抱在怀里摇晃，感受他的小小身体给她带来的安慰，却又担心得要命，生怕孩子会在这浮尘弥漫的空气中染上肺炎。灰尘无孔不入，她自己的喉咙都被灰尘糊住了。桌子刚摆好不到十分钟，但盘子上已经落了一层薄尘。孩子轻声哭个不停。她嘴角惊恐地抽搐着，环顾四周，好像在找一个能透气的角落。不过，尽管她嘴角抽搐，但眼睛还是大睁，一眨不眨。"睡吧，"她又轻声说道。"现在还早，你不可能是饿了，爸爸很快就回来吃午饭了。"

　　看上去他得很长时间才能回来。尽管钟表还有几分钟才到正午，但还是无法驱散她心头的不祥预感；他比平时回来得要晚。她再次走到门口，随后又慢慢退到屋子中央，站在那里，脸色苍白，呼吸急促。她绝不能去。她跑到马厩找他，只能让他瞧不起。他过于冷酷刚强，根本不了解女人的恐惧和柔弱。她必须安静地呆在那里等。没事儿。中午他会回来，说不定午饭后还会陪她一会儿。

　　昨天和今天早上吃饭时，夫妻俩一直都在激烈争吵。现在她需要他，需要他的强健有力和陪伴在身边带来的安慰，但他却站得远远的，神情漠然，小心翼翼，念叨着她在气头上冲他说的那些话，根本不明白那只是被这漫天灰尘和肆虐狂风逼的。

　　她紧张地盯着时钟，侧耳倾听。外面刮着两股风，

恶劣的风沙天气中，她关注的是丈夫能早点回家。

were two winds: the wind in flight, and the wind that pursued. The one sought refuge in the eaves, **whimpering**[18], in fear; the other assailed it there, and shook the eaves apart to make it flee again. Once as she listened this first wind sprang into the room, **distraught**[19] like a bird that has felt the graze of **talons**[20] on its wing; while furious the other wind shook the walls, and the **thudded**[21] tumbleweeds against the window till its **quarry**[22] glanced away again in fright. But only to return—to return and quake among the feeble eaves, as if in all this dust-mad wilderness it knew no other **sanctuary**[23].

Then Paul came. At his step she hurried to the stove, intent upon the pots and frying pan. "The worst wind yet," he ventured, hanging up his cap and smock. "I had to light the lantern in the tool shed, too."

They looked at each other, then away. She wanted to go to him, to feel his arms supporting her, to cry a little just that he might soothe her, but because his presence made the **menace**[24] of the wind seem less, she gripped herself and thought, "I'm in the right. I won't give in. For his sake, too, I won't."

He washed, hurriedly, so that a few dark welts of dust remained to **indent**[25] upon his face a **haggard**[26] strength. It was all she could see as she wiped the dishes and set the food before him: the strength, the grimness, the young Paul growing old and hard, **buckled**[27] against a desert even grimmer than his will. "Hungry?" she asked, touched to a **twinge**[28] of pity she had not intended. "There's dust in everything. It keeps coming faster than I can clean it up."

He nodded. "Tonight, though, you'll see it go down. This is the third day."

18. whimper
    vi. 幽怨；呜咽
19. distraught
    adj. 心烦意乱的；
    发狂的
20. talon
    n. 猛禽的爪子
21. thudded
    adj. 砰地落下的
22. quarry
    n. 猎物
23. sanctuary
    n. 避难所
24. menace
    n. 威胁；恐吓
25. indent
    vi. 留凹痕于
26. haggard
    adj. 憔悴的；野性的
27. buckle
    vi. 抗争；紧扣
28. twinge
    n. （通常指不快的）
    一阵强烈情感

一股是在前面逃跑的风，另一股是在后面追赶的风。逃跑的风躲在屋檐里惊恐地呜咽着，追赶的风不停地向屋檐发起攻击，晃开屋檐的缝隙，迫使逃跑的风继续逃。有一次，她听到逃跑的风惊慌失措地闯入房间，就像一只小鸟感觉到翅膀已经擦到了老鹰爪一般。而此时追赶的风愤怒地摇晃墙壁，卷起风滚草噼里啪啦抽打窗户，直至猎物再次惊逃。但是，逃跑的风无处可去，只能返回——返回到并不结实的屋檐下瑟瑟抖动，好像在风尘肆虐的整个荒原中根本找不到其他避难所。

描写形象生动，捕捉生活细节十分老到。比兴手法运用自如，令人信服。

这时，保罗回来了。听到脚步声，她赶忙跑到灶边，一心一意在煮锅和煎锅上忙碌起来。"从未见过这么大的风，"他一边挂帽子和外衣，一边试着跟她说话，"在工具棚里，我也得点着灯。"

他们对视了一下，又移开了目光。她本想扑到他的怀里，感受他怀抱的安慰，哭上一小会儿，让他哄哄自己。不过，他回来了，狂风也就没有那么可怕了，她控制住自己的感情，心想："我有理，不会屈服，就是冲他，我也不会屈服。"

他匆匆洗了洗脸，还有几道灰印没有洗净，这使他的脸上显出一种野性的坚韧。她在他面前擦干盘子、摆放食物时所能看到的是保罗的坚韧、保罗的顽强和曾经年轻的保罗日渐苍老，也日渐刚强，在拼命跟甚至比他的意志还顽强的沙漠化土地抗争。"饿吗？"她问，这时突然莫名地心疼起了保罗。"到处是灰尘。不等我清理干净，就又积了新灰尘。"

他点了点头。"不过，今晚你就会看见风会下去的。这都是第三天了。"

She looked at him in silence a moment, and then as if to herself muttered **broodingly**[29], "Until the next time. Until it starts again."

There was a dark timbre of resentment in her voice now that boded another quarrel. He waited, his eyes on her **dubiously**[30] as she mashed a potato with her fork. The lamp between them threw strong lights and shadows on their faces. Dust and drought, earth that betrayed alike his labor and his faith, to him the struggle had given sternness, an impassive courage. Beneath the whip of sand his youth had been effaced. Youth, zest, **exuberance**[31]—there remained only a harsh and clenched **virility**[32] that yet became him, that seemed at the cost of more engaging qualities to be fulfillment of his inmost and essential nature. Whereas to her the same debts and poverty had brought a plaintive **indignation**[33], a nervous dread of what was still to come. The eyes were hollowed, the lips **pinched**[34] dry and colorless. It was the face of a woman that had aged without maturing, that had loved the little vanities of life, and lost them **wistfully**[35].

"I'm afraid, Paul," she said suddenly. "I can't stand it any longer. He cries all the time. You will go, Paul—say you will. We aren't living here—not really living—"

The pleading in her voice now, after its shrill bitterness yesterday, made him think that this was only another way to persuade him. Evenly he answered, "I told you this morning, Ellen; we keep on right where we are. At least I do. It's yourself you're thinking about, not the baby."

This morning such an accusation would have stung her to rage; now, her voice swift and panting, she pressed on, "Listen, Paul—I'm thinking of all of us—you, too. Look at the sky—and

29. broodingly
　　adv. 沉思地；若有所思地
30. dubiously
　　adv. 疑惑地
31. exuberance
　　n. 激昂；激情
32. virility
　　n. 男子汉气概
33. indignation
　　n. 愤慨；愤怒
34. pinch
　　vi. 紧闭；压紧
35. wistfully
　　adv. 渴望地；望眼欲穿地

她看了保罗一会儿，接着好像是若有所思地自个儿咕哝了一句："直到下一次。直到大风再次刮起。"

她的话里有一丝幽怨，预示着他们又要争吵。他等着，两眼一副困惑的样子，看着她用叉子捣碎土豆。那盏油灯摆在两人中间，把强烈的光线和阴影投射在他们的脸上。对他来说，与这些风沙、干旱，还有同样背叛他的劳动和信念的土地的抗争，赋予了他坚韧刚毅的性格；这是一种处之泰然的勇气。在风沙的鞭笞下，他的青春已经逝去。青春、热情和激情都已消逝，剩下的只有那种咬紧牙关硬挺下去的男子汉气概，而这与他非常相称，但代价是这好像代替了原来会使他本性完美的一些更吸引人的品质。然而，对她来说，同样的债务和贫穷给她带来的却是哀伤引起的愤怒，一种对于不知道未来还会发生什么的紧张导致的恐惧。她眼睛深陷，嘴唇紧闭，没有血色。这是一张尚未成熟便已衰老的女性的脸庞。她爱慕生活中的小小虚荣，但却在满怀渴望当中失去了它们。

"保罗，我怕，"她突然说道，"我再也受不了了。孩子整天都在哭。保罗，离开这里吧，你说你愿意。我们不能生活在这里，这样的日子真不叫生活——"

昨天吵闹之后，保罗认为，她此刻这种恳求的语气只是换了一种方式劝他离开。他心平气和地回答："埃伦，我今天早上已经对你说过了，我们就呆在这里，至少我不会离开。你是在为你自己考虑，而不是为孩子。"

要是换成今天早上，这种指责会让她火冒三丈。现在，她只是急促地喘气。她语声快速短促，坚持自己的观点："听着，保罗，我是为我们一家人着想，也是为你着想。看看这天空，再看看你的田地。你看不见吗？

丈夫在与恶劣环境抗争的过程中变得粗鲁执拗，郁郁寡欢；妻子在恐怖的环境中渴望丈夫的保护，思虑孩子的未来。离开还是留下就成为夫妻争吵的理由。

your fields. Are you blind? **Thistles**[36] and tumbleweeds—it's a desert, Paul. You won't have a straw this fall. You won't be able to feed a cow or a chicken. Please, Paul, say we'll go away—"

"Go where?" His voice as he answered was still remote and even, inflexibly in unison with the narrowed eyes, and the great hunch of muscle-knotted shoulder. "Even as a desert it's better than sweeping out your father's store and running his errands. That's all I've got ahead of me if I do what you want."

"And here—" she faltered. "What's ahead of you here? At least we'll get enough to eat and wear when you're sweeping out his store. Look at it—, you fool. Desert—the lamp lit at noon—"

"You'll see it come back," he said quietly. "There's good wheat in it yet."

"But in the meantime—year after year—can't you understand, Paul? We'll never get them back—"

He put down his knife and fork and leaned toward her across the table. "I can't go, Ellen. Living off your people—**charity**[37]—stop and think of it. This is where I belong. I've no trade or education. I can't do anything else."

"Charity!" she repeated him, letting her voice rise in derision. "And this—you call this independence! Borrowed money you can't even pay the interest on, seed from the government—grocery bills—doctor bills—"

"We'll have crops again," he persisted. "Good crops—the land will come back. It's worth waiting for."

"And while we're waiting, Paul!" It was not anger now, but a kind of sob. "Think of me—and him. It's not fair. We have our lives, too, to live."

"And you think that going home to your family—taking

36. thistle
   n. 蓟草
37. charity
   n. 施舍；救济

只有蓟草和风滚草，都成沙漠了，保罗。今年秋天，你将会颗粒无收，连喂一头奶牛或一只鸡的东西都收不到。保罗，求你了，我们离开这里吧——"

"去哪里？"他的声音好像是从很远很远的地方传来，但极其平和，与他眯起的眼睛和肩上高高凸起的肌肉非常相称。"即使生活在沙漠里，也比为你父亲打扫商店、替你父亲跑腿强得多。我要是按照你说的做，以后就只能做这些了。"

"在这里——"她顿了一下，"在这里，以后会有什么呢？你打扫父亲的商店，我们至少可以吃得饱穿得暖。看看这里，你这傻瓜。这里是沙漠，中午都要点着灯。"

"土地会恢复的，"他平静地说，"小麦还会有好收成。"

"但在那一天到来之前，一年年就这样过去了，你不明白吗，保罗？一年一年就这样一去不复返了。"

他放下刀叉，身子探向坐在饭桌对面的妻子。"我不会走的，埃伦。依靠你的家人生活就等于是乞求救济施舍。停下好好想想吧，我只属于这里。我没有手艺，没有文化，别的什么都干不了。"

"救济！"她重复着他的话，大声指责。"那么，这种日子呢？你把这种日子叫作自力更生！你连借款的利息都还不清，买种子欠政府的钱，欠便利店的钱，欠医生的钱——"

"我们还会有收成，"他坚持说，"会有好收成，土地会恢复，值得等。"

"就这样等待啊，保罗！"现在，埃伦不再愤怒，而是呜咽着说。"你替我，也替孩子想想啊，这对我们不公平。我们也要过自己的生活。"

"那你认为回到你的家人那里，带着你的丈夫回

尽管在恶劣环境中经受土地对他们的一次次背叛和欺骗，但丈夫仍然选择对土地的信任和期待，仍然顽强地选择继续等待、继续耕种。

The Lamp at Noon 中午时分的灯　　55

your husband with you—"

"I don't care—anything would be better than this. Look at the air he's breathing. He cries all the time. For his sake, Paul. What's ahead of him here, even if you do get crops?"

He clenched his lips a minute, then, with his eyes hard and **contemptuous**[38], struck back, "As much as in town, growing up a pauper. You're the one who wants to go, Ellen—it's not for his sake. You think that in town you'd have a better time—not so much work—more clothes—"

"Maybe—" she dropped her head defenselessly. "I'm young still. I like pretty things."

There was silence now—a deep fastness of it enclosed by rushing wind and creaking walls. It seemed the yellow lamplight cast a hush upon them. Through the haze of dusty air the walls **receded**[39], dimmed, and came again. At last she raised her head and said listlessly, "Go on—your dinner's getting cold. Don't sit and stare at me. I've said it all."

The spent quietness in her voice was harder even than her anger to endure. It **reproached**[40] him, against his will insisted that he see and understand her a lot. To **justify**[41] himself he tried, "I was a poor man when you married me. You said you didn't mind. Farming's never been easy, and never will be."

"I wouldn't mind the work or the skimping if there was something to look forward to. It's the hopelessness—going on— watching the land blow away."

"The land's all right," he repeated. "The dry years won't last forever."

"But it's not just dry years, Paul!" The little sob in her voice gave way suddenly to a ring of **exasperation**[42]. "Will you never see? It's the land itself—the soil. You've plowed and

38. contemptuous
adj. 轻蔑的；鄙视的
39. recede
vi. 逐渐退缩；退隐
40. reproach
vt. 责备；申斥
41. justify
vt. 证明……有理；
为……辩护
42. exasperation
n. 恼怒；愤怒

去……"

"我不在乎，随便什么，都会比这强。看孩子呼吸的是什么样的空气，他整天哭个不停。保罗，看在孩子的分上。即使你真能收庄稼，在这里孩子又会有什么未来呢？"

他抿着嘴唇，过了一会儿用严厉鄙夷的眼神盯着妻子，反驳道，"回到城里又能咋样，他只能长成一个穷小子。埃伦，是你自己想走，这不是为孩子着想。你认为在城里你的日子会好过些，你可以少做家务，还可以买更多的衣服——"

"也许吧，"她垂下了头，不再辩护。"我还年轻，喜欢漂亮的东西。"

两个人都不吭声了，陷入了深深的沉默，周围是呼啸而来的风声和墙壁发出的嘎吱声，仿佛黄色的灯光给他们施下了沉默的魔咒。透过弥漫着灰尘的空气望去，墙壁渐渐远去，越发模糊，然后又变得清晰起来。最后，她抬起头来，有气无力地说："吃饭吧，饭都凉了。别坐在那里盯着我，我要说的都说完了。"

她声音透出的疲惫宁静甚至比她的怒火更让人受不了。这种宁静是在责怪他，坚持让他违心地明白和理解她的命运。于是，他为自己申辩道："你嫁给我时，我就是个穷小子。你说过你不在乎。种地本来就不是轻松的事儿，将来也不会轻松。"

"如果生活有盼头，我并不在乎辛劳，省吃俭用。可是，现在的生活只有绝望——，一直下去——，眼看着风把土地吹走。"

"土地不是问题，"他重复说道，"干旱不会一直持续下去。"

"这不仅仅是干旱的问题，保罗！"她原本有点呜咽的声音突然变为狂怒。"你还不明白吗？问题在于

环境能改造人，也能毁灭人，不同的心态必然会产生不同的结果。丈夫和妻子关注的是不同的层面。

harrowed[43] it until there's not a root of fibre left to hold it down. That's why the soil drifts—that's why in a year or two there'll be nothing left but the bare clay. If in the first place you farmers had taken care of your land—if you hadn't been so greedy for wheat every year—"

She had taught school before she married him, and of late in her anger there had been a kind of **disdain**[44], an attitude almost of **condescension**[45], as if she no longer looked upon the farmers as her equals. He sat still, his eyes fixed on the yellow lamp flame, and seeming to know how her words had hurt him, she went on softly, "I want to help you, Paul. That's why I won't sit quiet while you go on wasting your life. You're only thirty— you owe it to yourself as well as me."

Still he sat, with his lips drawn and white and his eyes on the lamp flame. It seemed indifferent now, as if he were ignoring her, and stung to anger again she cried, "Do you ever think what my life is? Two rooms to live in—once a month to town, and nothing to spend when I get there. I'm still young—I wasn't brought up this way."

Stolidly[46] he answered, "You're a farmer's wife now. It doesn't matter what you used to be, or how you were brought up. You get enough to eat and wear. Just now that's all that I can do. I'm not to blame that we've been dried out five years."

"Enough to eat!" she laughed back shrilly, her eyes all the while fixed expressionless and wide. "Enough salt pork—enough potatoes and eggs. And look—" Springing to the middle of the room, she thrust out a foot for him to see the scuffed old slipper. "When they're completely gone, I suppose you'll tell me I can go barefoot—that I'm a farmer's wife—that it's not your fault we're dried out—"

"And look at these—" He pushed his chair away from the table now to let her see what he was wearing. "**Cowhide**[47]—

43. harrow
    vt. 耙地
44. disdain
    n. 蔑视；鄙视
45. condescension
    n. 屈尊；纡尊降贵
46. stolidly
    adv. 不动声色地；
    冷淡地
47. cowhide
    n. 牛皮

土地本身，是土壤。你们又是犁地又是耙地，一直弄到地里连固定土壤的草根都没留下，那才是土壤飘走的原因——这才是为什么一两年后地里会什么都留不下，只会剩下赤裸裸的黏土。如果你们这帮农民当初悉心照料这片土地，如果你们不是每年都贪求小麦——"

跟他结婚前，她教过书，而且最近在她的愤怒当中夹杂着一种蔑视，那是一种近乎屈尊的态度，好像她再也不将这些农民视为跟自己平等。他坐在那里，一动不动，眼睛盯着油灯黄色的火苗。她好像知道她的话对他造成了怎样的伤害，便又轻声说道："保罗，我想帮你，不能坐视你浪费生命。你才三十岁，那样不仅对我有必要，对你自己也有必要。"

他一动不动坐在那里，耷拉着苍白的嘴唇，盯着灯上的火苗，好像对她说的话无动于衷，好像根本不理睬她。她又被激怒了，开始愤怒地喊道："你想过我过的是什么日子吗？两间屋子，一个月进一次城，而且去了也没钱买东西。我还年轻，我不是在这种环境中长大的。"

生活的艰辛使相爱的夫妻产生了分歧。

他不动声色地说："你现在嫁给了农民。你以前过的是什么样的生活，以什么样的方式长大，都不重要了。现在我所能做的就是让你吃得上穿得上。干旱五年又不是我的错。"

"吃够！"她尖声笑起来，一直圆睁着无神的眼睛。"咸猪肉、土豆和鸡蛋，都吃够。你看——"她跳到屋子中央，抬起一只脚给他看磨破的旧拖鞋。"拖鞋磨破了，你大概会让我光脚吧，因为我嫁给了农民，因为干旱不是你的错——"

"那你看看这些——"他一下子从桌边推开椅子，让她看自己脚上穿的鞋，"牛皮做的，硬得像木板，不过我的脚磨起了厚茧，都感觉不到脚上的鞋了。"

比喻贴切。

The Lamp at Noon 中午时分的灯 **59**

hard as boards—but my feet are so **calloused**[48] I don't feel them anymore."

Then hurriedly he stood up, ashamed of having tried to match her hardship with his own. But frightened now as he reached for his smock she pressed close to him. "Don't go yet. I brood and worry when I'm left alone. Please, Paul—you can't work on the land anyway."

"And keep on like this?" Grimly he buttoned his smock right up to his throat. "You start before I'm through the door. Week in and week out—I've troubles enough of my own."

"Paul—please stay—" The eyes were **glazed**[49] now, distended a little as if with the **intensity**[50] of her dread and pleading. "We won't quarrel anymore. Hear it! I can't work—I just stand still and listen—"

The eyes frightened him, but responding to a kind of instinct that he must **withstand**[51] her, that it was his self-respect and manhood against the **fretful**[52] weakness of a woman, he answered unfeelingly, "I'm here safe and quiet—you don't know how well off you are. If you were out in it—fighting it—swallowing it—"

"Sometimes, Paul, I wish I were. I'm so caged—if I could only break away and run. See—I stand like this all day. I can't relax. My throat's so tight it aches—"

Firmly he loosened his smock from the **clutch**[53] of her hands. "If I stay we'll only keep on like this all afternoon. Tomorrow when the wind's down we can talk over things quietly." Then, without meeting her eyes again he swung outside, and doubled low against buffets of the wind, fought his way slowly toward the stable. There was a deep hollow calm within, a vast darkness engulfed beneath the tides of moaning wind.

48. calloused
   adj. 有茧子的；粗硬的
49. glazed
   adj. 呆滞无神的
50. intensity
   n. 强烈；强度
51. withstand
   vt. 反抗；抵挡
52. fretful
   adj. 烦躁的
53. clutch
   n. 紧抓；控制

说到这里，他急忙站起身，为自己跟妻子比较谁更艰难而惭愧。他伸手去拿外套。她感到害怕，往他身边靠了靠，"先别出去。我一个人在家时总是胡思乱想，担心这个担心那个。保罗，求你了，反正你也不能到田里干什么活。"

　　"那就这么跟你吵下去吗？"他毫不动心地扣着外套纽扣，扣得严严实实，一直扣到下巴。"我还没进门，你就开始了。一连几周都是这样，我自己的麻烦已经够多了。"

　　"保罗——求求你留下来。"她的眼睛呆滞无神，好像因为极度恐惧，又因为急于恳求，圆睁的眼睛有点虚肿。"我们不会再争吵了。听听外边！我什么都做不了，就那么呆站着，听着——"

　　她的眼神让他害怕，但基于一种本能反应——他一定不能对她让步，这是男人的自尊和成熟与女人反复无常的弱点的斗争，所以他硬着心肠说："这里既安全又安静，你都不知道你的日子有多么好过。你要是到外面大风里，跟风沙抗争，吞咽风沙——"

　　"保罗，有时我真希望能到外面去，觉得自己像笼中鸟一样。要是我能挣脱出去逃跑该有多好啊。你看，我整天就这样站着，放松不下来。我的嗓子发紧、疼痛——"

　　他坚定地把外套从她紧抓着的两只手里挣脱开来。"我留下来，我们就会整个下午都吵个没完。明天风小点时，我们再冷静地好好谈谈吧。"说完，他连看都没看她一眼，就转身出去了。他深深地猫下腰，迎着阵阵狂风，艰难缓慢地朝马厩走去。马厩里有一种深深的空空的平静，一片黑茫茫淹没在狂风的一阵阵呜咽声中。他站在那里，一时喘不过气，因为风暴的戛然而止和四周裹身而来

暴虐的风沙使土地连年颗粒无收，但丈夫执着地坚守着没有希望的土地，女人就成为被放逐的孤魂，对未来无望的等待，对丈夫安危的担心，对孩子未来的牵挂，对恶劣环境的不堪忍受，一切都使她发狂、发疯。

The Lamp at Noon 中午时分的灯　　**61**

He stood breathless a moment, hushed almost to a stupor by the sudden **extinction**[54] of the storm and the incredible stillness that enfolded him. It was a long, far-reaching stillness. The first dim stalls and **rafters**[55] led the way into cavernlike obscurity, into vaults and recesses that extended far beyond the stable walls. Nor in these first quiet moments did he forbid the illusion, the sense of release from a harsh, familiar world into one of immeasurable peace and darkness. The **contentious**[56] mood that his stand against Ellen had roused him to, his **tenacity**[57] and clenched despair before the **ravages**[58] of wind, it was ebbing now, losing itself in the cover of darkness. Ellen and the wheat seemed remote, unimportant. At a whinny from the bay mare, Bess, he went forward and into her stall. She seemed grateful for his presence and thrust her nose deep between his arm and body. They stood a long time thus, comforting and assuring each other.

For soon again the first deep sense of quiet and peace was shrunken to the battered shelter of the stable. Instead of release or escape from the assaulting wind, the walls were but a feeble stand against it. They creaked and sawed as if the fingers of a giant hand were tightening to collapse them; the empty loft **sustained**[59] a pipelike cry that rose and fell but never ended. He saw the dust-black sky again, and his fields blown smooth with drifted soil.

But always, even while listening to the storm outside, he could feel the tense and **apprehensive**[60] stillness of the stable. There was not a hoof that clumped or shifted, not a rub of halter against **manger**[61]. And yet, though it had been a strange stable, he would have known, despite the darkness, that every stall was filled. They, too, were all listening.

From Bess he went to the big gray **gelding**[62], Prince.

---

54. extinction
   n. 消灭；消失
55. rafter
   n. 椽木
56. contentious
   adj. 好争论的；好斗的
57. tenacity
   n. 不屈不挠；坚韧
58. ravage
   n. 劫掠后的破坏；毁坏
59. sustain
   vt. 持续（发出）
60. apprehensive
   adj. 令人忧虑的
61. manger
   n. 马槽
62. gelding
   n. 骟马

的莫名寂静，几乎让他神情恍惚。这是一种漫长深邃的寂静。最初隐约看到的马厩隔栏和橡木向里延伸，通向山洞般朦胧的马厩，又通向远远超出四壁的拱形棚顶和墙壁的凹处向外延伸。在这最初的寂静时刻，他并没有阻止自己产生这种幻觉，这是一种摆脱残酷而熟悉的现实世界、进入无限宁静而黑暗的世界后才会有的轻松感。与埃伦抗衡，激起了他的好斗情绪；他在狂风造成的毁坏面前表现出的是不屈不挠和咬紧牙关的绝望，而现在这一切都渐渐退去，在黑幕的掩盖下渐渐消失了。埃伦和小麦似乎都是非常遥远的事儿，根本不重要了。听到红鬃马贝丝一声嘶鸣，他向前走去，来到了贝丝的隔栏里。贝丝好像非常感激他的到来，把鼻子深深地埋到他的腋下。他们就这样站了很久，不断地安抚着对方。

作者观察生活细致入微，语言表达极具张力。

　　没过多久，他最初深深感受到的平和与宁静渐渐消失了，只剩下破损的庇护所——马厩。四周墙壁并没有摆脱或逃过狂风的进攻，只是一道软弱无力的屏风，像被紧紧攥在巨人的手指间，吱嘎作响，出现裂痕；空空的草料棚不停地发出类似管子里发出的呜呜声，时高时低，没完没了。他看到了黑压压的天空，又看到了自己田地上疏松的土壤被风吹走后，剩下的光秃秃一片。

　　但是，从始到终，即使在听着外面的风暴声时，他也能感觉到马厩里面寂静的令人紧张的忧虑。没有马蹄重重踏在地上或移动的声音，也没有马笼头刮蹭食槽的响声。不过，即使这是一个奇怪的马厩，尽管其中一片漆黑，他也明白每个棚栏都不是空的。它们也都在倾听风声。

　　他离开贝丝，来到灰色高大的骟马王子面前。王子已经二十岁了，两侧肋骨凸出，臀部的骨头高高突起。

Prince was twenty years old, with rib-grooved sides, and high, protruding hipbones. Paul ran his hand over the ribs, and felt a sudden shame, a sting of fear that Ellen might be right in what she said. For wasn't it true—nine years a farmer now on his own land, and still he couldn't even feed his horses? What, then, could he hope to do for his wife and son?

There was much he planned. And so vivid was the future of his planning, so real and constant, that often the actual present was but half felt, but half endured. Its difficulties were lessened by a confidence in what lay beyond them. A new house for Ellen, new furniture, new clothes. Land for the boy—land and still more land—or education, whatever he might want.

But all the time was he only a blind and stubborn fool? Was Ellen right? Was he **trampling on**[63] her life, and throwing away his own? The five years since he married her, were they to go on repeating themselves, five, ten, twenty, until all the brave future he looked forward to was but a stark and **futile**[64] past?

She looked forward to no future. She had no faith or dream with which to make the dust and the poverty less real. He understood suddenly. He saw her face again as only a few minutes ago it had begged him not to leave her. The darkness around him now was as a slate on which her lonely terror limned itself. He went from Prince to the other horses, combing their manes and forelocks with his fingers, but always still it was her face before him, its staring eyes and twisted suffering. "See, Paul—I stand like this all day. I just stand still—my throat's so tight it aches—"

And always the wind, the creak of walls, the wind lipless wailing through the loft. Until at last as he stood there, staring into the livid face before him, it seemed that this scream of wind was a cry from her **parched**[65] and frantic lips. He knew it

63. trample on
    践踏；蹂躏
64. futile
    adj. 徒劳无益的；
    没有出息的
65. parched
    adj. 干裂的；干渴的

保罗用手抚摸着王子的肋骨，突然感到一阵惭愧，痛苦地意识到埃伦的话好像很有道理。不是吗？一个在这片土地上辛苦耕作了九年的农民，甚至连自己的马都喂不饱。那还能指望他为妻儿做什么呢？

他有许多计划设想。这些对未来的设想是那样清晰逼真，又那样频繁出现，所以他对现实生活往往是一半在感觉，一半在忍受。现实生活中的种种苦难因他对未来的信心而变小。为埃伦建一座新房子，买些新家具，添些新衣服；为儿子置办土地，越来越多的土地，或者让儿子接受良好的教育，提供他想要的一切。

可是，难道他一直都是一个盲目固执的傻瓜吗？埃伦是对的吗？他是不是在践踏埃伦的生活，同时也毁了自己的生活呢？他们结婚的这五年生活，以后是不是还会继续这样过下去呢？会不会是五年、十年、二十年，直到他期待的一切灿烂的未来变成一无所获徒劳无益的过去呢？

理想与现实使保罗矛盾纠结却又内心不甘。

她的生活没有盼头。她缺乏能让眼前的沙尘和贫困显得不那么真实的信念与梦想。突然，他明白了一切，眼前又出现了几分钟前埃伦恳求他不要离开她时的样子。现在，他四周的黑暗像一块石板，上面刻着她的孤独与恐惧。他离开王子，走到其他几匹马跟前，用手指头梳理着它们的鬃毛和额毛，但眼前始终浮现出埃伦的脸庞，一双凝视的眼睛和扭曲的痛苦表情。"保罗，你看，我整天都这样站着。我就这样静静站着，我的喉咙发紧、疼痛——"

风没完没了地刮着，墙壁嘎吱作响，风穿过阁楼时呜呜狂号。直到最后，他站在那里呆望着面前那张苍白

couldn't be, he knew that she was safe within the house, but still the wind persisted as a woman's cry. The cry of a woman with eyes like those that watched him through the dark. Eyes that were mad now—lips that even as they cried still pleaded, "See, Paul —I stand like this all day. I just stand still—so caged! If I could only run!"

He saw her running, pulled and driven headlong by the wind, but when at last he returned to the house, compelled by his anxiety, she was walking quietly back and forth with the baby in her arms. Careful, despite his concern, not to reveal a fear or weakness that she might think **capitulation**[66] to her wishes, he watched a moment through the window, and then went off to the tool shed to mend harness. All afternoon he stitched and riveted. It was easier with the lantern lit and his hands occupied. There was a wind whining high past the tool shed too, but it was only wind. He remembered the arguments with which Ellen had tried to persuade him away from the farm, and one by one he defeated them. There would be rain again—next year or the next. Maybe in his ignorance he had farmed his land the wrong way, seeding wheat every year, working the soil till it was lifeless dust— but he would do better now. He would plant clover and alfalfa, breed cattle, acre by acre and year by year restore to his land its fiber and **fertility**[67]. That was something to work for, a way to prove himself. It was ruthless wind, blackening the sky with his earth, but it was not his master. Out of his land it had made a wilderness. He now, out of the wilderness, would make a farm and home again.

Tonight he must talk with Ellen. Patiently, when the wind was down, and they were both quiet again. It was she who had told him to grow **fibrous**[68] crops, who had called him an

66. capitulation
    n. 投降；妥协
67. fertility
    n. 肥沃；丰产
68. fibrous
    adj. 含纤维的；长须根的

的面孔，仿佛这风的呼啸声就是从她干裂紧张的嘴唇之间发出的一种呼叫。尽管他知道这不可能，也知道妻子安然呆在家里，但狂风呼啸依然像是女人的哭喊。女人哭喊，眼睛仿佛是透过黑暗盯着他看。一时间，那双眼睛疯狂起来，她一边哭，一边恳求他："你看，保罗，我整天都这样站着。我就静静地站着，像一只笼中鸟！要是我能逃跑，该多好啊！"

　　他的眼前出现了她奔跑的情景，被大风推着直向前跑。然而，当他忧心忡忡终于回到住处时，却看到她正抱着孩子安静地在屋里来回走动。尽管他关心她，但他却小心翼翼，唯恐露出恐惧和脆弱，这样就会让她以为他屈从了她的想法。于是，他只是透过窗户看了她一会儿，随后到工具棚里修补马具。整个下午，他又是缝又是铆。挂灯点着，手里忙着，时间就容易打发了。工具棚外也刮起了一阵漫天大风，但那只不过是风。他想着埃伦说服他离开农场的种种理由，他却一一推翻了。天还会下雨，明年不下雨，后年也会下雨。也许因为无知导致他没有按正确方法耕种这片土地，一年年只种植小麦，直到土壤成了毫无生命力的沙土。但是，他现在会做得好些了。他将会种上三叶草和苜蓿，饲养牛群，一亩亩一年年恢复土地的植被和肥力。那值得劳作，是一种证明自己的方式。无情的大风扬起他土地上的泥土，遮天蔽日，但却无法主宰他的意志。狂风把他的土地变成了荒原，而现在他又要将这片荒原变成他的农场和家园。

　　今晚他必须跟埃伦谈谈。到时大风平息，他们俩也都会安静下来。她曾经告诉他要种植长须根的作物。当他在夏天休耕期还耕种小麦时，她说他是个无知的傻

修辞手段运用娴熟，使作品更添魅力和色彩。

ignorant fool because he kept on with summer fallow and wheat. Now she might be **gratified**[69] to find him acknowledging her wisdom. Perhaps she would begin to feel the power and **steadfastness**[70] of the land, to take a pride in it, to understand that he was not a fool, but working for her future and their son's.

And already the wind was slackening. At four o'clock he could sense a lull. At five, straining his eyes from the tool shed doorway, he could make out a neighbor's buildings half a mile away. It was over—three days of **blight**[71] and **havoc**[72] like a **scourge**[73]—three days so bitter and so long that for a moment he stood still, unseeing, his senses idle with a numbness of relief.

But only for a moment. Suddenly he emerged from the numbness; suddenly the fields before him struck his eyes to **comprehension**[74]. They lay black, naked. Beaten and mounded, smooth with dust as if a sea in gentle swell had turned to stone. And though he had tried to prepare himself for such a scene, though he had known since yesterday that not a blade would last the storm, still now, before the utter waste **confronting**[75] him, he sickened and stood cold. Suddenly like the fields he was naked. Everything that had **sheathed**[76] him a little from the realities of existence: vision and purpose, faith in the land, in the future, in himself—it was all rent now, all stripped away. "Desert," he heard her voice begin to sob. "Desert, you fool—the lamp lit at noon!"

In the stable again, measuring out their feed to the horses, he wondered what he would say to her tonight. For so deep were his instincts of loyalty to the land that still, even with the images of his betrayal stark upon his mind, his concern was how to withstand her, how to go on again and justify himself. It had not occurred to him yet that he might or should **abandon**[77] the land. He had lived with it too long. Rather was his impulse to

69. gratify
    vt. 使满足；使满意
70. steadfastness
    n. 执着；坚定不移
71. blight
    n. 荒芜
72. havoc
    n. 破坏
73. scourge
    n. 灾祸
74. comprehension
    n. 理解；明白
75. confront
    vt. 面对；面临
76. sheathe
    vt. 覆盖；包裹
77. abandon
    vt. 放弃；抛弃

瓜。现在看到保罗承认了她的智慧，她应该感到满意了。说不定她将开始感受到土地的力量和执着，开始为土地感到骄傲，并开始明白他并不是傻瓜，而是一个为了妻儿的未来操劳的男子汉。

风渐渐减弱。四点钟时，他能感觉到风快停了。到五点钟，他站在工具房门口瞪大眼睛向外看时，都看得见半英里外邻居的房舍了。风停了。三天多的摧残和破坏就像一场浩劫。三天时间是那么痛苦漫长，结果他静静地站了一会儿，浑然不觉，伴随着解脱带来的麻木，茫然无措。

不过，这只是一时的现象。突然，他从麻木中醒过来；眼前的田地突然让他明白了什么。农田黑黢黢，光秃秃的。连续遭到大风的肆虐，田里沙土成堆，沙尘填平了整块田地，就像微微起伏的大海变成了一块大石头。尽管对眼前的这种景象他早就尽量做好了心理准备，尽管从昨天起他就知道不会有一棵小麦能幸免于这场风暴，但现在面对眼前这片彻底的荒原，他还是心灰意冷，手脚冰凉。一时间，他觉得自己像这片光秃秃的土地一样赤裸。原来他还包裹着一层保护衣，将他从现实生活稍微遮挡。而这层保护衣——曾经抱有的幻想、坚持的目标和对土地、对自己和对未来的信心现在土崩瓦解，从他身上剥离开来。"沙漠，"他耳边又响起了埃伦的抽泣声。"沙漠！你这傻瓜——中午都要点着灯！"

点题。呼应。极具传奇特色。

回到马厩后，他一边把饲料分给每匹马，一边考虑晚上跟妻子谈些什么。尽管他心里显然出现了反叛的迹象，但因为他依然本能地深深忠诚于这片土地，所以他关心的还是如何把妻子留在家里，再继续耕种并证明自

defend it still—as a man defends against the scorn of strangers even his most worthless kin.

He fed his horses, then waited. She too would be waiting, ready to cry at him, "Look now—that crop that was to feed and clothe us! And you'll still keep on! You'll still say 'Next year—there'll be rain next year'!"

But she was gone when he reached the house. The door was open, the lamp blown out, the crib empty. The dishes from their meal at noon were still on the table. She had perhaps begun to sweep, for the broom was lying in the middle of the floor. He tried to call, but a terror clamped upon his throat. In the wan, returning light it seemed that even the deserted kitchen was straining to whisper what it had seen. The tatters of the storm still whimpered through the eaves, and in their moaning told the desolation of the miles they had **traversed**[78]. On tiptoe at last he crossed to the adjoining room; then at the threshold, without even a glance inside to satisfy himself that she was really gone, he wheeled again and plunged outside.

He ran a long time—distraught and **headlong**[79] as a few hours ago he had seemed to watch her run—around the farmyard, a little distance into the pasture, back again blindly to the house to see whether she had returned—and then at a stumble down the road for help.

They joined him in the search, rode away for others, spread calling across the fields in the direction she might had been carried by the wind—but nearly two hours later it was himself who came upon her. Crouched down against a drift of sand as if for shelter, her hair in matted **strands**[80] around her neck and face, the child clasped tightly in her arms.

The child was quite cold. It had been her arms, perhaps, too

78. traverse
   vt. 穿过；横穿
79. headlong
   adv. 一头向前冲地
80. strand
   n. （头发）缕

己是对的。直到现在，保罗还从未想过有可能或应该放弃这片土地。他跟土地一起生活的时间太久了，因此保护土地几乎成为一种本能的冲动，就像男人在一个并不亲近的亲属遭到陌生人嘲笑时也会挺身而出一样。

他喂好马，然后等待该回家的时刻。她也会在等着，正准备冲他喊叫："看看吧，看看你准备靠它让我们吃饱穿暖的庄稼吧！可你还要坚持下去！你还会说：'明年——明年就会下雨'！"

然而，他回到家时，她已经走了。门开着，灯刮灭了，婴儿床空空的。午饭用过的盘子还放在桌上。她大概开始打扫了，因为扫帚就放在屋子中央的地上。他想喊她，但恐惧使他喉咙发紧。外边渐渐亮起，在微弱的光线中，甚至空荡荡的厨房仿佛也在诉说曾经发生的一切。狂风卷来的破布条透过屋檐的缝隙哀号，诉说所到之处的荒凉景象。最后，他蹑手蹑脚走到另一间屋的门口，不用跨进门槛，也不用寻找，就知道她真的已经走了，便猛地转过身，冲了出去。

他跑了好久，心慌意乱，向前直奔，就像几小时前他似乎曾望见埃伦那样奔跑。他绕着整个农田跑一圈，向牧场里跑一小会儿，又盲目地跑回家，想看看埃伦是否已经回家——随后跌跌撞撞沿路跑去救援。

大家都出来帮忙寻找，有的骑马去叫人帮忙，在田里分头呼喊埃伦的名字，沿着她可能被风刮走的方向寻找。差不多两小时后，还是他自己找到了她。她正蹲靠在一个小沙丘边，像是在避风。打成结的头发贴在脸上和脖子上，她怀里紧抱着孩子。

孩子已经很冷了。也许是她在慌乱中没有用双臂保

尽管保罗对土地也曾怀疑、沮丧、失望，但依然保持着对恶劣环境下这片土地的热爱、坚守和忠诚。

拟人手法，借物喻人。

The Lamp at Noon 中午时分的灯   71

frantic to protect him, or the **smother**[81] of dust upon his throat and lungs. "Hold him," she said as he knelt beside her. "So— with his face away from the wind. Hold him until I tidy my hair."

Her eyes were still wide in an immobile stare, but with her lips she smiled at him. For a long time he knelt transfixed, trying to speak to her, touching fearfully with his fingertips the dust-grimed cheeks and eyelids of the child. At last she said, "I'll take him again. Such clumsy hands—you don't know how to hold a baby yet. See how his head falls forward on your arm."

Yet it all seemed familiar—a **confirmation**[82] of what he had known since noon. He gave her the child, then, gathering them up in his arms, struggled to his feet, and turned toward home.

It was evening now. Across the fields a few spent clouds of dust still shook and fled. Beyond, as if through smoke, the sunset **smoldered**[83] like a distant fire.

He walked with a long dull stride, his eyes before him, heedless of her weight. Once he glanced down and with her eyes she still was smiling. "Such strong arms, Paul—and I was so tired with carrying just him."

He tried to answer, but it seemed that now the dusk was drawn apart in breathless waiting, a finger on its lips until they passed. "You were right, Paul," her voice came whispering, as if she too could feel the hush. "You said tonight we'd see the storm go down. So still now, and the sky burning—it means tomorrow will be fine."

81. smother
   n. 窒息
82. confirmation
   n. 证实
83. smolder
   vi. 闷烧；阴燃

护好他，也许是孩子喉咙和肺里的灰尘窒息所致。"抱着孩子，"当他跪在她身边时，她说，"这样，别让他的脸迎着风。先抱他一会儿，等我把头发整理一下。"

她的眼睛仍然瞪得大大的，一眨不眨，但嘴角却对他露出一丝微笑。好一阵子，他都一直跪在那里，呆若木鸡，想对她说点什么，胆怯地用指尖触摸这孩子满是灰尘的脸颊和眼皮。最后，她说："我来抱吧。看你笨手笨脚的，还不会抱孩子。你瞧，孩子的头都耷拉到你的胳膊上了。"

而这一切好像都很熟悉，证实了从中午起他内心确信的一切。他把孩子递给妻子，然后把她和孩子一块抱起，挣扎着站起来，向家走去。

现在是傍晚时分。田地那边还有几小股风沙在仓皇逃奔。远处模糊，仿佛笼罩在烟雾之中，夕阳像是在远方闷燃的一堆火。

他缓慢地大步前行，眼睛直视前方，注意不到她的重量。有一次，他低头看了她一眼，她两眼仍然含笑地对他说："胳膊真有劲儿，保罗——我抱着孩子真累。"

他想回答什么，但此刻仿佛黄昏都被拉到一边屏住呼吸等待着，等候他们过去。"你说得对，保罗，"她轻声说道，似乎也感觉到了这片沉寂。"你说过今晚风暴会过去。现在风息了，天空在燃烧——这意味着明天是个晴天。"

对环境的恐惧、对未来的渴望、对儿子的担心，迫使女人做出逃跑的决定，逃离那黄沙蔽日，连中午都要点灯照明的生息地，结果却是孩子被弥漫的黄沙和母亲紧紧的拥抱窒息。

名篇赏析

　　人类，作为世界上的一种造物，无论忍受多少来自外部和内部的磨难，总能顽强不屈地生存下去。自然的无情与暴戾，生活的悲苦与单调，都无法战胜人们生存下去的勇气，停息的风沙和火红的天空预示着希望的来临。开始的中午点灯意在反衬自然环境的恶劣，生存条件的艰辛。结尾的中午灯灭蕴含的是夫妻宽容，不仅仅是狂风过去带来的亮丽晴天。

Guy de Maupassant

part 01

The Prisoners

俘 虏

姓名	居伊·德·莫泊桑
出生日期	1850年8月5日
出生地	法国西北部诺曼底省狄埃卜城
性别	男

成就和特色

　　短篇小说之王，十九世纪下半叶法国优秀的批判现实主义作家。莫泊桑是法国文学史上短篇小说创作数量最大、成就最高的作家，三百余篇短篇小说的巨大创作量在十九世纪文学中绝无仅有；他的短篇描绘的生活面极为广泛，实际上构成了十九世纪下半叶法国社会一幅全面的风俗画；更重要的是，他把现实主义短篇小说的艺术提高到了一个前所未有的水平，他在文学史上的重要地位主要就是由他短篇小说的成就奠定的。

写作背景

　　这个故事的真正核心是法国村姑智斗德国兵，同样也是故事最精彩的部分。后面法国军官的参与，只是这场斗争的补充。贝蒂娜却是小说所有人物中最聪明、最勇敢、最机智的人。

The Prisoners

There was not a sound in the forest save the indistinct, **fluttering**[1] sound of the snow falling on the trees. It had been snowing since noon; a little fine snow, that covered the branches as with frozen moss, and spread a silvery covering over the dead leaves in the ditches, and covered the roads with a white, **yielding**[2] carpet, and made still more **intense**[3] the boundless silence of this ocean of trees.

Before the door of the forester's dwelling a young woman, her arms bare to the elbow, was chopping wood with a hatchet on a block of stone. She was tall, slender, strong—a true girl of the woods, daughter and wife of a forester.

A voice called from within the house: "We are alone tonight, Berthine; you must come in. It is getting dark, and there may be Prussians or wolves about."

"I've just finished, mother," replied the young woman, splitting as she spoke an **immense**[4] log of wood with strong, **deft**[5] blows, which expanded her chest each time she raised her arms to strike. "Here I am; there's no need to be afraid; it's quite light still."

Then she gathered up her sticks and logs, piled them in the **chimney corner**[6], went back to close the great **oaken**[7] shutters, and finally came in, drawing behind her the heavy bolts of the door.

Her mother, a wrinkled old woman whom age had **rendered**[8] timid, was spinning by the fireside. "I am uneasy,"

1. flutter
   vi. 飘动；颤动
2. yielding
   adj. 柔软的
3. intense
   adj. 强烈的
4. immense
   adj. 巨大的；（口）
   非常好的
5. deft
   adj. 敏捷的；熟练的
6. chimney corner
   n. 炉角
7. oaken
   adj. 橡木制的
8. render
   vt. 使得；致使

俘 虏

　　除了雪落在树上的轻微颤动声，森林里没有一点声音。雪从中午起就一直下着；细细的小雪落在树枝上，树枝就像覆盖了一层冰冻的苔藓似的，给坑洼里的枯叶普遍盖上了一层银被，给道路铺上了一层雪白柔软的地毯，使这无边无际的茫茫林海越发沉寂了。

雪景描写为后面普鲁士军人迷路作铺垫。

　　在看林人的房门前，一个露出胳膊肘的年轻女人正用斧头在一块石头上劈柴。她高大、苗条、健壮——是名副其实在森林里长大的姑娘，她的父亲和丈夫都是看林人。

　　房子里有一个声音喊道："贝蒂娜，今晚就我们两个人；你必须进来。天快要黑了，说不定附近会有普鲁士人或狼。"

　　"妈妈，我这就劈完了，"年轻女人一边动作熟练用劲劈一根大圆木，一边答道。她每举起双臂劈一下，就挺挺胸。"我就来；不必害怕，天还没有完全黑。"

　　随后，她收拾起大大小小的劈柴，把它们堆放在炉角，返身去关橡木做的大百叶窗，最后才进来插上沉重的门闩。

　　她的母亲，一个满脸皱纹的老妇人，正在炉边纺

she said, "when your father's not here. Two women are not much good."

"Oh," said the younger woman, "I'd cheerfully kill a wolf or a Prussian if it came to that." And she glanced at a heavy revolver hanging above the hearth.

Her husband had been called upon to serve in the army at the beginning of the Prussian invasion, and the two women had remained alone with the old father, a keeper named Nicolas Pichon, sometimes called Long-legs, who refused **obstinately**[9] to leave his home and **take refuge in**[10] the town.

This town was Rethel, an ancient stronghold built on a rock. Its inhabitants were **patriotic**[11], and had made up their minds to resist the invaders, to **fortify**[12] their native place, and, if need be, to stand a **siege**[13] as in the good old days. Twice already, under Henri IV and under Louis XIV, the people of Rethel had distinguished themselves by their heroic defence of their town. They would do as much now, by gad! or else be **slaughtered**[14] within their own walls.

They had, therefore, bought cannon and rifles, organized a militia, and formed themselves into **battalions**[15] and companies, and now spent their time drilling all day long in the square. All—bakers, grocers, butchers, lawyers, carpenters, booksellers, chemists—took their turn at military training at regular hours of the day, under the **auspices**[16] of Monsieur Lavigne, a former **noncommissioned**[17] officer in the dragoons, now a draper, having married the daughter and inherited the business of Monsieur Ravaudan, Senior.

He had taken the rank of commanding officer in Rethel, and, **seeing that**[18] all the young men had gone off to the war, he had enlisted all the others who were in favor of resisting an attack. Fat men now **invariably**[19] walked the streets at a rapid pace, to reduce their weight and improve their breathing, and

9. obstinately
   adv. 顽固地；倔强地
10. take refuge in
   避难到……
11. patriotic
   adj. 爱国的；有爱国心的
12. fortify
   vt. 在……设要塞；在……建防御工事
13. siege
   n. 围攻
14. slaughter
   vt. 残杀；屠杀
15. battalion
   n. （陆军的）营
16. auspice
   n. （常用复）主办；赞助
17. noncommissioned
   adj. 未授军官衔的；军士的
18. seeing that
   因为
19. invariably
   adv. 总是

线，她上了年纪，胆子也小了。"你爹不在这里，我心神不安。两个女人不大好啊。"

"噢，"年轻女人说，"要是狼或普鲁士人来这里，我一定会杀个不亦乐乎。"说完，她瞅了瞅挂在壁炉上方的大左轮手枪。

她的丈夫在普鲁士人刚开始入侵时就参了军，就剩下母女俩和老父亲，老父亲名叫尼古拉·毕雄，别人有时叫他"长腿"，他死活不愿离开家到城里去避难。

这座城市就是雷泰尔，是一座建在岩石上的古老要塞。那里的居民具有爱国热忱，早已下定决心抵抗侵略者，构筑防御工事，如有必要，会像古时候那样，成功抵御围攻。在亨利四世和路易十四世统治时期，雷泰尔人曾经两次以英勇保卫城市而著名。如今他们也一定会这样做！否则就会遭到屠城。

所以，他们购置了枪炮，组织了民兵，并编排成营和连，现在一天到晚在广场上操练。所有人——面包师、杂货商、屠夫、律师、木匠、书商、药剂师——在拉维涅先生的指挥下轮流在规定时间进行军事训练，拉维涅先生从前在龙骑兵队里当过士官，现在是布料商，娶了老拉沃当先生的女儿，并继承了他的店铺。

他当上了雷泰尔的指挥官，因为所有的年轻人都已经上了战场，所以他就征召了所有其余愿意抵抗进攻的人。现在身体肥胖的人总是快步走在街上，为的是减肥和增加肺活量；体力欠佳的人为了增强臂力提起了重物。

独特的话语勾勒出她豪放勇敢的性格。

weak men carried weights to strengthen their muscles.

And they awaited the Prussians. But the Prussians did not appear. They were not far off, however, for twice already their scouts had **penetrated**[20] as far as the forest dwelling of Nicolas Pichon, called Long-legs.

The old keeper, who could run like a fox, had come and warned the town. The guns had been got ready, but the enemy had not shown themselves.

Long-legs' dwelling served as an outpost in the Aveline forest. Twice a week the old man went to the town for **provisions**[21] and brought the citizens news of the outlying district.

On this particular day he had gone to announce the fact that a small **detachment**[22] of German **infantry**[23] had halted at his house the day before, about two o'clock in the afternoon, and had left again almost immediately. The noncommissioned officer in charge spoke French.

When the old man set out like this he took with him his dogs—two powerful animals with the jaws of lions—as a safeguard against the wolves, which were beginning to get fierce in this season, and he left directions with the two women to **barricade**[24] themselves securely within their dwelling as soon as night fell.

The younger feared nothing, but her mother was always **apprehensive**[25], and repeated continually: "We'll **come to grief**[26] one of these days. You see if we don't!"

This evening she was more nervous than ever. "Do you know what time your father will be back?" she asked.

"Oh, not before eleven, for certain. When he dines with the commandant he's always late."

And Berthine was hanging her pot over the fire to warm

20. penetrate
   vt. 穿过；渗入
21. provision
   n. 供应品（特指粮食与副食品）
22. detachment
   n. 分遣队
23. infantry
   n. 步兵
24. barricade
   vt. 遮蔽住；关闭
25. apprehensive
   adj. 担心的；恐惧的
26. come to grief
   遭难；出事

他们就这样等着普鲁士人。但是，普鲁士人没有出现。不过，他们离得并不远，因为他们的侦察兵已经穿过森林两次，一直走到了号称"长腿"的尼古拉·毕雄的护林房。

这个能跑得像狐狸一样快的老看林人已经事先把消息通知了城里。大炮严阵以待，但敌人没有露面。

"跑得像狐狸一样快"为后面的故事埋下伏笔。

"长腿"的房子充当设在阿韦林森林里的前哨。为了采购食物，也为了把边远地区的消息带给城里的居民，老人每周进城两次。

这一天，他去了城里，要报告前一天下午两点左右，一小队德国步兵在他家里停留，后来几乎马上就开拔了。带队的士官说的是法国话。

老人这样出发时，随身带着他的狗——两条强壮的狮子嘴大狗，以防有狼，因为狼在这个季节开始变得非常凶残，所以他临行前嘱咐妻女，天一黑，她们就要关好门呆在家里。

年轻的女儿什么也不怕，但她的母亲总是提心吊胆，不断重复说："最近我们一定会遭难的。不遭难才怪！"

这天傍晚，她比往常更加心神不安。"你知道你爹几点回来吗？"她问。

母亲的慌乱更彰显了女儿的冷静。

"噢，十一点前肯定回不来。他和指挥官一起吃饭，总是很晚。"

贝蒂娜把锅挂在火上热汤，这时她留心听到一个声音从烟囱传来，突然站住不动了。"有人在树林里走

the soup when she suddenly stood still, listening attentively to a sound that had reached her through the chimney. "There are people walking in the wood," she said; "seven or eight men at least."

The terrified old woman stopped her spinning wheel, and gasped: "Oh, my God! And your father not here!"

She had scarcely finished speaking when a succession of violent blows shook the door.

As the women made no reply, a loud, **guttural**[27] voice shouted: "Open the door!"

After a brief silence the same voice repeated: "Open the door or I'll break it down!"

Berthine took the heavy revolver from its hook, slipped it into the pocket of her skirt, and, putting her ear to the door. "Who are you?" demanded the young woman. "What do you want?"

"The detachment that came here the other day," replied the voice. "My men and I have lost our way in the forest since morning. Open the door or I'll break it down!"

The forester's daughter had no choice; she shot back the heavy bolts, threw open the **ponderous**[28] shutter, and perceived in the **wan**[29] light of the snow six men, six Prussian soldiers, the same who had visited the house the day before.

"What are you doing here at this time of night?" she asked **dauntlessly**[30].

"I lost my **bearings**[31]," replied the officer; "lost them completely. Then I recognized this house. I've eaten nothing since morning, nor my men either."

"But I'm quite alone with my mother this evening," said Berthine.

"Never mind," replied the soldier, who seemed a decent sort of fellow. "We won't do you any harm, but you must give us

27. guttural
   adj. 粗嘎的；喉音的
28. ponderous
   adj. 沉重的
29. wan
   adj. 苍白的；暗淡的
30. dauntlessly
   adv. 无所畏惧地；大胆地
31. bearing
   n. 方位

动，"她说。"至少有七八个人。"

大惊失色的老太太停止了纺轮，气喘吁吁地说："噢，我的上帝！你爹不在家呀！"

她的话还没有说完，就传来了一连串激烈的砸门声。

母女俩没有应声，这时一个粗嘎的声音大声喊道："开门！"

一阵短暂的沉默之后，同样的声音又喊道："开门，不然我就要砸门了！"

贝蒂娜从钩子上摘下那支大左轮手枪，塞进裙子口袋，随后把耳朵贴到门上。"你是谁？"年轻女人厉声问道。"你想要什么？"

"是前几天来过这里的小分队，"那个声音答道。"从早上起，我和手下就在树林里迷路了。开门，不然我就要砸门了！"

看林人的女儿别无选择；她马上抽开沉重的门闩，拉开厚重的百叶窗，然后看到了光线暗淡的雪地里有六个人，六个普鲁士士兵，就是前一天来过的那伙人。

"晚上这个时候你到这里来干什么？"她无所畏惧地问道。

贝蒂娜临危不乱，镇定从容，为后文打下了伏笔。

"我迷失了方位，"军官答道。"完全迷失了方位。随后，我认出了这座房子。从早上起，我还没有吃东西，我的手下也没有。"

"可是，今晚只有我和妈妈，"贝蒂娜说。

"不用担心，"那个听上去好像正派的军人答道。"我们不会伤害你们，但你必须给我们弄点吃的。我们

something to eat. We are nearly dead with hunger and fatigue."

Then the girl moved aside. "Come in," she said.

They entered, covered with snow, their helmets sprinkled with a creamy-looking **froth**[32], which gave them the appearance of **meringues**[33]. They seemed utterly worn out.

The young woman pointed to the wooden benches on either side of the large table. "Sit down," she said, "and I'll make you some soup. You certainly look tired out, and no mistake." Then she bolted the door afresh. She put more water in the pot, added butter and potatoes; then, taking down a piece of bacon from a hook in the chimney corner, cut it in two and slipped half of it into the pot.

The six men watched her movements with hungry eyes. They had placed their rifles and helmets in a corner and waited for supper, as well behaved as children on a school bench.

The old mother had resumed her spinning, casting from time to time a **furtive**[34] and uneasy glance at the soldiers. Nothing was to be heard save the humming of the wheel, the crackling of the fire, and the singing of the water in the pot.

But suddenly a strange noise—a sound like the harsh breathing of some wild animal sniffing under the door—startled the occupants of the room.

The German officer sprang toward the rifles. Berthine stopped him with a gesture, and said, smilingly: "It's only the wolves. They are like you—**prowling**[35] hungry through the forest."

The **incredulous**[36] man wanted to see with his own eyes, and as soon as the door was opened he perceived two large grayish animals disappearing with long, swinging trot into the darkness.

He returned to his seat, muttering: "I wouldn't have believed it!"

32. froth
    n. 泡沫
33. meringue
    n.（盛冰淇淋、水果的）蛋白酥皮筒（卷）；蛋白饼糕
34. furtive
    adj. 偷偷摸摸的；鬼鬼祟祟的
35. prowl
    vi.（野兽等）潜行（以觅食）
36. incredulous
    adj. 怀疑的；不轻信的

又饿又困，快要死了。"

于是，姑娘退开一步。"进来吧，"她说。

他们进来了，浑身落满了雪，钢盔上撒了一层奶油一样的泡沫，看上去像蛋白酥皮卷似的，他们都像是筋疲力尽了。

年轻女人指着大桌两边的木头长凳。"坐下吧，"她说。"我去给你们做些汤。你们看上去肯定是累得够呛，没错，"随后，她又插上门闩。她在锅里添了更多水，加了黄油和土豆，接着从炉角的钩子上取下了一块熏肉，切成两半，一半放进了锅里。

六个人饥肠辘辘眼巴巴看着她的一举一动。他们已经把步枪和钢盔放在了一个墙角，等着吃饭，规矩得就像坐在学校长凳上的孩子一样。

老母亲又纺起纱来，不时地向那些士兵不安地偷偷瞥上一眼。除了纺轮的嗡嗡声、炉火的噼啪声和水在锅里的响声，什么也不听到。

但突然，一个奇怪的声音把屋里的人都吓了一跳，听上去像是一只野兽在门下呼哧呼哧喘气的声音。

德国军官纵身跳向步枪。贝蒂娜打了个手势拦住他，微笑着说："那不过是狼。它们像你们一样饥肠辘辘在森林里走来走去。"

那个人将信将疑，想亲眼看看，他一打开门，就看见两只浅灰色的大野兽晃着大步消失在了黑暗中。

他回到座位上，咕哝道："我不敢相信真是这么回事！"

这并非年轻女人的合作，而是她的欲擒故纵之计，作者并没有交待她的心理，采用的写作手法也是"欲擒故纵"。

And he waited quietly till supper was ready.

The men **devoured**[37] their meal **voraciously**[38], with mouths stretched to their ears that they might swallow the more. Their round eyes opened at the same time as their jaws, and as the soup coursed down their throats it made a noise like the gurgling of water in a rainpipe.

The two women watched in silence the movements of the big red beards. The potatoes seemed to be **engulfed**[39] in these moving **fleeces**[40].

But, as they were thirsty, the forester's daughter went down to the cellar to draw them some **cider**[41]. She was gone some time. The cellar was small, with an arched ceiling, and had served, so people said, both as prison and as hiding-place during the Revolution. It was approached by means of a narrow, winding staircase, closed by a trap-door at the farther end of the kitchen.

When Berthine returned she was smiling mysteriously to herself. She gave the Germans her jug of cider. Then she and her mother supped apart, at the other end of the kitchen.

The soldiers had finished eating, and were all six falling asleep as they sat round the table. Every now and then a forehead fell with a thud on the board, and the man, awakened suddenly, sat upright again.

Berthine said to the officer: "Go and lie down, all of you, round the fire. There's lots of room for six. I'm going up to my room with my mother."

And the two women went upstairs. They could be heard locking the door and walking about overhead for a time; then they were silent.

The Prussians lay down on the floor, with their feet to the fire and their heads resting on their rolled-up cloaks. Soon all six

37. devour
    vt.（尤指动物）吞
    吃；狼吞虎咽
38. voraciously
    adv. 贪婪地
39. engulf
    vt. 卷入；吞没
40. fleece
    n. 似羊毛物；羊毛
41. cider
    n. 苹果酒

接下来，他便静静等候，直到晚饭做好。

这帮人狼吞虎咽吃了起来，为了尽可能吞得更多，嘴巴都张到了耳朵根，圆溜溜的眼睛像嘴巴一样同时张开，汤流进喉咙发出的响声，就像落水管里汩汩的水声。

母女俩默默地看着这些大红胡子的一举一动。一块块土豆像是被吞进了那些蠕动的毛丛里。

而当他们口渴时，看林人的女儿就下到地窖里去给他们取苹果酒。她去了一段时间。地窖很小，带着拱形天花板，据说在大革命时期曾经做过牢房，也做过藏身处，人通过一道狭窄蜿蜒的梯子可以走进去，地窖出口在厨房尽头，一块活板门盖在上面。

贝蒂娜回来时，暗自露出了神秘的微笑。她把那罐苹果酒交给了德国人。随后，她和母亲离开，到厨房另一头吃晚饭。

这个微笑的小细节暗示出贝蒂娜已想到对付他们的方法。作者将细节打磨得很精致，行文中不露痕迹。

这些兵吃完饭，六个人围坐在桌边打起了瞌睡。不时会有一个人的额头砰地瞌在桌上，这个人会突然醒来，又坐直身体。

贝蒂娜对军官说："你们所有人都到炉边躺下吧。地方大，容得下六个人。我和母亲上我的屋里去。"

随后，母女俩就上楼去了。他们可以听见她们锁上了门，听见她们在楼上走动了一阵，随后她们就没有了声音。

普鲁士人都躺在了地板上，脚对着火，头枕着卷起的外衣。不久，六个人便发出了响亮的鼾声，不间断地发出六种不同的调。

snored loudly and **uninterruptedly**[42] in six different **keys**[43].

They had been sleeping for some time when a shot rang out so loudly that it seemed directed against the very wall's of the house. The soldiers rose hastily. Two—then three—more shots were fired.

The door opened hastily, and Berthine appeared, barefooted and only half dressed, with her candle in her hand and a scared look on her face.

"There are the French," she stammered; "at least two hundred of them. If they find you here they'll burn the house down. For God's sake, hurry down into the cellar, and don't make a sound, whatever you do. If you make any noise we are lost."

"We'll go, we'll go," replied the terrified officer. "Which is the way?"

The young woman hurriedly raised the small, square trap-door, and the six men disappeared one after another down the narrow, winding staircase, feeling their way as they went.

But as soon as the **spike**[44] of the last helmet was out of sight Berthine lowered the heavy oaken lid—thick as a wall, hard as steel, furnished with the **hinges**[45] and bolts of a prison cell —shot the two heavy bolts, and began to laugh long and silently, possessed with a mad longing to dance above the heads of her prisoners.

They made no sound, inclosed in the cellar as in a strong-box, obtaining air only from a small, iron-barred vent-hole.

Berthine lighted her fire again, hung the pot over it, and prepared more soup, saying to herself: "Father will be tired to-night."

Then she sat and waited. The heavy **pendulum**[46] of the clock swung to and fro with a **monotonous**[47] tick.

Every now and then the young woman cast an impatient

---

42. uninterruptedly
    adv. 不间断地；连续地
43. key
    n. 调
44. spike
    n. 穗；尖峰
45. hinge
    n.（门、盖等的）铰链；合页
46. pendulum
    n. 钟摆；摇锤
47. monotonous
    adj. 单调的

他们睡了一段时间，突然一声枪响，枪声非常响亮，似乎是正对着屋墙打的。那些士兵慌忙站起。枪声又响了两下……三下……接着更多。

门匆忙打开，贝蒂娜赤着脚，走了出来，衣服都没穿齐，手里端着蜡烛，脸上露出了恐惧的神情。

"法国人来了，"她结结巴巴地说。"至少有两百人。一旦他们在这里发现你们，就会烧掉这座房子。看在上帝面上，赶快下地窖，千万别弄出任何响声。一旦你们弄出声来，我们就都没命了。"

这是贝蒂娜的计策，她完美的表演不仅骗过了普鲁士人，也骗过了读者。

"我们这就下，我们这就下，"神情恐惧的军官答道。"从哪里下？"

年轻女人赶忙揭起了那块四方小活门，六个人一个接一个沿着蜿蜒狭窄的楼梯摸索下去，不见了踪影。

但一看最后一顶钢盔尖不见了，贝蒂娜就赶紧放下了那块沉重的橡木盖——厚似墙、硬如钢，装有监狱牢房那样的铰链和插销——插上了两道沉重的插销。她带着一种想要在这群俘虏的头顶跳舞的狂喜，默默地笑了好久。

计策初步成功之后，贝蒂娜仍然保持沉着冷静。

他们没有出声，关在地窖，就像关进保险箱一样，只能从一个装有铁栅的小通风孔获得空气。

贝蒂娜再次燃起了炉火，把锅挂在火上，一边重新做汤，一边自言自语："父亲今晚一定很累。"

随后，她坐下来等着。挂钟沉重的钟摆来回摆动，发出单调的嘀嗒声。

年轻女人不时急躁地瞥一眼挂钟，那目光好像是

glance at the dial[48]—a glance which seemed to say: "I wish he'd be quick!"

But soon there was a sound of voices beneath her feet. Low, confused words reached her through the masonry[49] which roofed the cellar. The Prussians were beginning to suspect the trick she had played them, and presently the officer came up the narrow staircase, and knocked at the trap-door. "Open the door!" he cried.

"What do you want?" she said, rising from her seat and approaching the cellarway[50].

"Open the door!"

"I won't do any such thing!"

"Open it or I'll break it down!" shouted the man angrily.

She laughed. "Hammer away, my good man! Hammer away!"

He struck with the butt-end[51] of his gun at the closed oaken door. But it would have resisted a battering ram[52].

The forester's daughter heard him go down the stairs again. Then the soldiers came one after another and tried their strength against the trap-door. But, finding their efforts useless, they all returned to the cellar and began to talk among themselves.

The young woman heard them for a short time, then she rose, opened the door of the house; looked out into the night, and listened.

A sound of distant barking reached her ear. She whistled just as a huntsman would, and almost immediately two great dogs emerged from the darkness, and bounded to her side. She held them tight, and shouted at the top of her voice: "Hullo, father!"

A far-off voice replied: "Hullo, Berthine!"

She waited a few seconds, then repeated: "Hullo, father!"

The voice, nearer now, replied: "Hullo, Berthine!"

48. dial
n.（钟表的）钟面，表盘
49. masonry
n. 砖石建筑；石造建筑
50. cellarway
n. 通往地窖的路
51. butt-end
n. 平头端；大头
52. battering ram
（破门用的）撞杆；大木槌

说：“但愿他快点！”

但是，不久她的脚下就传来了说话声。模糊不清的低声说话透过地窖的石砌拱顶传到了她的耳朵里。普鲁士人开始渐渐猜到了她搞的计策；很快，那个军官爬上狭窄的楼梯，敲起了活板门。“开门！”他喊道。

“你想要什么？”贝蒂娜说着，从座位上站起来，走近地窖口。

“开门！”

“我不会开的！”

“开门，不然我就要砸它！”那个人愤怒地说。

她笑出了声。“砸吧，好小子！你就砸吧！”

他用枪托砸起了关闭的橡木门。不过，它一定会顶住枪托的撞击。

看林人的女儿听到他又下了楼梯。随后，那些士兵一个接一个来用力撞门。但是，他们发现是在白费力气后，就又回到了地窖，开始商谈起来。

年轻女人听到他们商谈了一小段时间，随后她站起来，打开屋门，望着外面的夜空，侧耳倾听。

远处一阵狗叫声传到了她的耳朵里。她像猎人一样吹起了口哨，两条大狗随即便从黑暗中出现，跳到了身边。她紧紧地抱住它们，放开嗓子喊道：“喂，爸爸！”

远处一个声音回答：“喂，贝蒂娜！”

她等了几秒钟，然后又喊道：“喂，爸爸！”

那个声音越来越近，回答道：“喂，贝蒂娜！”

贝蒂娜的笑流露出她对自己计策的信心，还有她的沉着和无畏。

"Don't go in front of the vent-hole!" shouted his daughter. "There are Prussians in the cellar!"

Suddenly the man's tall figure could be seen to the left, standing between two tree trunks. "Prussians in the cellar?" he asked anxiously. "What are they doing?"

The young woman laughed. "They are the same as were here yesterday. They lost their way, and I've given them free lodgings in the cellar." She told the story of how she had alarmed them by firing the revolver, and had shut them up in the cellar.

The man, still serious, asked: "But what am I to do with them at this time of night?"

"Go and fetch Monsieur Lavigne with his men," she replied. "He'll take them prisoners. He'll be delighted."

Her father smiled. "So he will be delighted."

"Here's some soup for you," said his daughter. "Eat it quick, and then be off."

The old keeper sat down at the table, and began to eat his soup, having first filled two plates and put them on the floor for the dogs.

The Prussians, hearing voices, were silent.

Long-legs set off a quarter of an hour later, and Berthine, with her head between her hands, waited.

The prisoners began to make themselves heard again. They shouted, called, and beat furiously with the butts of their **muskets**[53] against the rigid trap-door of the cellar. Then they fired shots through the vent-hole, hoping, no doubt, to be heard by any German detachment which chanced to be passing that way.

The forester's daughter did not stir, but the noise irritated and **unnerved**[54] her. Blind anger rose in her heart against the

53. musket
n. 步枪
54. unnerve
vt. 使紧张

"不要走通风口前，"他的女儿喊道。"地窖里有普鲁士人！"

只见那个人的高大身影突然出现在了左边，站在两个树干之间。"普鲁士人在地窖里？"他担心地问道。"他们在干什么？"

年轻女人笑出了声。"他们就是昨天来过这里的那几个人。他们迷了路，我让他们免费住在地窖里。"她把她怎样开火恐吓他们，又怎样把他们关进地窖的经过讲了一遍。

那个人仍然一脸严肃，问道："可是，夜里这么晚了，我拿他们怎么办？"

"去叫拉维涅先生和他的队伍来，"她答道。"他可以把他们抓起来。他一定会非常高兴。"

她的父亲露出了微笑。"他一定会非常高兴。"

"我给你做了汤，"他的女儿说。"赶快吃了再走。"

老看林人在桌边坐下来，先把两只盘子盛满汤，放在地上喂那两条狗，然后才开始喝汤。

普鲁士人听到说话声，都不作声了。

长腿一刻钟后出发了，贝蒂娜两手抱头等待着。

那些俘虏又开始说话了。他们呼喊、叫嚷、怒气冲冲地用枪托撞击地窖上那块牢不可破的活板门。随后，他们从通风口放了几枪，无疑是希望碰巧在此经过的德国小分队听到。

看林人的女儿没有动，但这声音让她恼怒和紧张。

贝蒂娜的计策此时才完全交待出来，她在控制着整个事情的发展。

prisoners; she would have been only too glad to kill them all, and so silence them. Then, as her impatience grew, she watched the clock, counting the minutes as they passed.

Her father had been gone an hour and a half. He must have reached the town by now. She **conjured up**[55] a vision of him telling the story to Monsieur Lavigne, who grew pale with emotion, and rang for his servant to bring him his arms and uniform. She fancied she could hear the drum as it sounded the call to arms. Frightened faces appeared at the windows. The citizen-soldiers emerged from their houses half dressed, out of breath, **buckling**[56] on their belts, and hurrying to the commandant's house.

Then the troop of soldiers, with Long-legs at its head, set forth through the night and the snow toward the forest.

She looked at the clock. "They may be here in an hour." A nervous impatience possessed her. The minutes seemed **interminable**[57]. Would the time never come?

At last the clock marked the moment she had fixed on for their arrival. And she opened the door to listen for their approach. She perceived a shadowy form creeping toward the house. She was afraid, and cried out. But it was her father.

"They have sent me," he said, "to see if there is any change in the state of affairs."

"No—none."

Then he gave a shrill whistle. Soon a dark mass loomed up under the trees; the advance guard, composed of ten men.

"Don't go in front of the vent-hole!" repeated Long-legs at intervals.

And the first arrivals pointed out the much-dreaded vent-

---

55. conjure up
   想象；推想
56. buckle
   vi. 扣住；扣紧
57. interminable
   adj. 无限的；冗长的

她心里对这些俘虏腾起了无名之火；她真想把他们统统杀死，这样就可以让他们安静了。之后，她越来越急躁，望着墙上的挂钟，一分钟一分钟数着过去的时间。

◀ 此刻的恼怒和紧张，让贝蒂娜这个人物显得更加真实。

她的父亲已经走一个半小时了。他现在一定已经到了城里。她仿佛看到了他把事情经过告诉拉维涅先生的情景，拉维涅先生因情绪激动而脸色发白，拉铃让仆人给他拿武器和军服。她仿佛听到了召集拿起武器的鼓声。一张张惊恐的面孔出现在各家窗口。那些民兵气喘吁吁走出家门，衣服还没有穿好，一边扣皮带，一边朝指挥官家里跑去。

随后，队伍由长腿领头，穿过黑夜和积雪，向森林开拔。

她看着挂钟。"他们说不定一小时候就到这里了。"她感到焦躁不安。每一分钟都好像无限漫长。那个时刻再也不会来了吗？

最后，时钟指向了她确定他们到来的那个时刻。她打开门，倾听他们走近的声音，只见有个人影悄悄地向房子走来。她吓得大声呼喊。原来是她的父亲。

"他们派我，"他说，"来看看事态有没有什么变化。"

"没有……一点也没有。"

◀ 派看林人探路显露了军官的沉稳，但从另一个角度讲，也暴露了他们的畏缩，因为一旦情况有变，老看林人将会牺牲。

这时，他打了一声尖利的口哨。很快，一团黑影就从树下慢慢走上前来；是十个人组成的前哨。

"不要走在通风口前，"长腿不时重复说道。

前面先到的人把那个让人万分恐惧的通风口指给后

hole to those who came after.

At last the main body of the troop arrived, in all two hundred men, each carrying two hundred **cartridges**[58].

Monsieur Lavigne, in a state of intense excitement, posted them in such a fashion as to surround the whole house, save for a large space left vacant in front of the little hole on a level with the ground, through which the cellar **derived**[59] its supply of air.

Monsieur Lavigne struck the trap-door a blow with his foot, and called: "I wish to speak to the Prussian officer!"

The German did not reply.

"The Prussian officer!" again shouted the **commandant**[60].

Still no response. For the space of twenty minutes Monsieur Lavigne called on this silent officer to surrender with **bag and baggage**[61], promising him that all lives should be spared, and that he and his men should be **accorded**[62] military honors. But he could **extort**[63] no sign, either of consent or of defiance. The situation became a puzzling one.

The citizen-soldiers kicked their heels in the snow, slapping their arms across their chest, as cabdrivers do, to warm themselves, and gazing at the vent-hole with a growing and childish desire to pass in front of it.

At last one of them took the risk—a man named Potdevin, who was fleet of limb. He ran like a deer across the zone of danger. The experiment succeeded. The prisoners gave no sign of life.

A voice cried: "There's no one there!"

And another soldier crossed the open space before the dangerous vent-hole. Then this **hazardous**[64] sport developed into a game. Every minute a man ran swiftly from one side

58. cartridge
   n. 子弹
59. derive
   vt. 获得
60. commandant
   n. 指挥官
61. bag and baggage
   adv. 完全地
62. accord
   vt. 给予
63. extort
   vt. 逼（供）；勒索
64. hazardous
   adj. 危险的；冒险的

到的人注意。

最后，部队的主力都到齐了，一共是两百人，每人带了两百发子弹。

拉维涅先生万分激动，布置他们把房子团团围住，只有和地面水平、供地窖通风的小孔前面留下了一大片空地。

拉维涅先生用脚跺了跺活板门，喊道："我希望跟普鲁士军官说话！"

德国人没有回应。

"普鲁士军官！"指挥官又喊道。

还是没有回应。拉维涅先生用了二十分钟时间要求这个沉默的军官彻底投降，同时答应他，不伤害任何人的生命，给予军人应有的荣誉。但是，他既无法得到同意的表示，也无法得到挑衅的表示。情况变得让人莫名其妙。

为了取暖，民兵们像马车夫那样在雪地里跺着脚，用胳膊拍打胸脯，同时盯着通风口，想从通风口前跑过的欲望像孩子一样越来越强烈。

比喻贴切，细节真实。

最后，其中一个人冒起了这个险，这个人名叫波特万，身手敏捷，像鹿一样跑过那个危险区域。这个尝试取得了成功。那些俘虏没有露出任何生命的迹象。

一个声音喊道："那里没有人！"

随后，又一个民兵穿过了这个危险的通风口的开阔地。接着，这个危险的运动就变成了一场游戏。每过一

to the other, like a boy playing baseball, kicking up the snow behind him as he ran. They had lighted big fires of dead wood at which to warm themselves, and the figures of the runners were **illumined**[65] by the flames as they passed rapidly from the camp on the right to that on the left.

Some one shouted: "It's your turn now, Maloison."

Maloison was a fat baker, whose **corpulent**[66] person served to point many a joke among his comrades.

He hesitated. They **chaffed**[67] him. Then, nerving himself to the effort, he set off at a little, **waddling**[68] gait, which shook his fat **paunch**[69] and made the whole detachment laugh till they cried.

"Bravo, bravo, Maloison!" they shouted for his encouragement.

He had accomplished about two-thirds of his journey when a long, crimson flame shot forth from the vent-hole. A loud **report**[70] followed, and the fat baker fell, face forward to the ground, uttering a frightful scream.

No one went to his assistance. Then he was seen to drag himself, groaning, on all fours through the snow until he was beyond danger, when he fainted.

He was shot in the upper part of the thigh.

After the first surprise and fright were over they laughed at him again.

But Monsieur Lavigne appeared on the threshold of the forester's dwelling. He had formed his plan of attack. He called in a loud voice, "I want Planchut, the plumber, and his workmen."

Three men approached.

"Take the **eaves troughs**[71] from the roof."

In a quarter of an hour they brought the commandant thirty

65. illumine
vt. 照亮
66. corpulent
adj. 肥胖的
67. chaff
vt. 戏弄；开玩笑
68. waddle
v. 蹒跚而行；摇摆
行走
69. paunch
n. 腹，大肚子
70. report
n. 爆炸声
71. eaves trough
n. 落水管

分钟，就有一个人从一边飞跑到另一边，就像男孩打垒球一样，跑动时在身后踢起雪。为了取暖，他们点起枯枝，燃起了几大堆火，民兵们从营地右边飞跑到营地左边，他们跑动的身影被火光照亮。

有个人喊道："现在该你了，马洛瓦松。"

马洛瓦松是一个肥胖的面包师，他的过于肥胖常常引起战友们的笑话。

他犹豫不决。有人取笑他。于是，他鼓起勇气，迈着小小的摇摆步伐出发了，这种步伐晃动着他的大肚子，引得全体队员哈哈大笑，眼泪都笑了出来。

"加油，加油，马洛瓦松！"他们叫喊着给他鼓劲。

他跑了大约三分之二的路程时，一道长长的红色火焰从通风口里射了出来。紧接着，传来一声响亮的爆炸，胖面包师发出了一声可怕的尖叫，面朝前扑倒在地。

没有人跑去救他。随后，只见他一边呻吟，一边拖着身体爬过雪地，等一爬过危险地段，他就晕倒了。

他的大腿上半部中了一枪。

最初的吃惊和惊慌过后，他们又取笑起了他。

但是，拉维涅先生来到了看林人的房门前。他已经想出了作战计划。他声音响亮地喊道："我要管子工普朗许和他的工人们过来。"

三个人走到近前。

"把房顶上的落水管取下来。"

一刻钟后，他们给指挥官送来了三十码长的落水管。

胖子的笨拙和其他士兵的冷漠，更反衬出贝蒂娜的英勇机智。

yards of pipes.

Next, with infinite **precaution**[72], he had a small round hole drilled in the trap-door; then, making a **conduit**[73] with the **troughs**[74] from the pump to this opening, he said, with an air of extreme satisfaction, "Now we'll give these German gentlemen something to drink."

A shout of frenzied admiration, mingled with **uproarious**[75] laughter, burst from his followers. And the commandant organized **relays**[76] of men, who were to **relieve**[77] one another every five minutes. Then he commanded: "Pump!"

And, the pump handle having been set in motion, a stream of water trickled throughout the length of the piping, and flowed from step to step down the cellar stairs with a gentle, gurgling sound.

They waited.

An hour passed, then two, then three.

The commandant, in a state of feverish **agitation**[78], walked up and down the kitchen, putting his ear to the ground every now and then to discover, if possible, what the enemy were doing and whether they would soon **capitulate**[79].

The enemy was astir now. They could be heard moving the casks about, talking, splashing through the water.

Then, about eight o'clock in the morning, a voice came from the vent-hole, "I want to speak to the French officer."

Lavigne replied from the window, taking care not to put his head out too far: "Do you surrender?"

"I surrender."

"Then put your rifles outside."

A rifle immediately **protruded**[80] from the hole, and fell into the snow, then another and another, until all were

72. precaution
    n. 警惕
73. conduit
    n. 导管
74. trough
    n. 槽;水槽
75. uproarious
    adj. 喧嚣的;喧闹的
76. relay
    n. 接替人员,替班
77. relieve
    vt. 换班
78. agitation
    n. 激动不安;焦虑
79. capitulate
    vi. 投降;认输
80. protrude
    v. 伸出

接下来，指挥官小心翼翼地在活板门上钻了一个小圆孔，用落水管做导管从抽水泵里向这个圆孔里抽水，他兴高采烈地说："现在，我们要给这些德国先生喝点东西。"

他的手下爆发出了疯狂的叫好声和喧闹的笑声。随后，指挥官组织替换人员，他们要五分钟换一次班。接着，他命令道："抽水！"

于是，泵把手开始摇动，一股细流顺着落水管流动着，发出轻轻的潺潺声一节一节流进了地窖。

他们等待着。

一个小时过去了，两个小时、三个小时过去了。

指挥官坐立不安，在厨房里走来走去，不时把耳朵贴在地上，想尽可能发现敌人正在做什么，他们是否会马上投降。

敌人骚动起来了。可以听见他们到处移动木桶的声音、说话声、溅着水走过的声音。

后来，早上八点钟左右，通风口传来一个声音："我要和法国军官谈话。"

拉维涅小心翼翼，不把头伸得过远，从窗口回应道："你投降吗？"

"我投降。"

"那把枪都放在外面。"

一支步枪马上从通风口伸出来，落在了雪地里，随后是第二支、第三支，直到所有的枪都扔了出来。先前那个

克敌制胜有时并不需要刀光剑影、枪炮齐鸣。

disposed of[81]. And the voice which had spoken before said: "I have no more. Be quick! I am drowned."

"Stop pumping!" ordered the commandant.

And the pump handle hung motionless.

Then, having filled the kitchen with armed and waiting soldiers, he slowly raised the oaken trap-door.

Four heads appeared, soaking wet, four fair heads with long, sandy hair, and one after another the six Germans emerged— scared, shivering and dripping from head to foot.

They were seized and bound. Then, as the French feared a surprise, they set off at once in two convoys[82], one in charge of the prisoners, and the other conducting[83] Maloison on a mattress borne on poles.

They made a triumphal entry into Rethel.

Monsieur Lavigne was decorated[84] as a reward for having captured a Prussian advance guard, and the fat baker received the military medal for wounds received at the hands of the enemy.

81. dispose of
    处理；除掉
82. convoy
    n. 护送队
83. conduct
    vt. 管理；带领
84. decorate
    vt. 授勋

声音说道："我再也没有了。快点！我要淹死了。"

"停止抽水！"指挥官命令道。

于是，泵把手停住不动了。

接着，等持枪等待的民兵站满厨房后，指挥官才慢慢地掀起了橡木活板门。

四颗脑袋——四颗浅黄长发的脑袋——露了出来，湿淋淋的。六个德国人一个接一个走了出来——神情恐惧，瑟瑟发抖，从头到脚滴着水。

他们全被抓住，捆了起来。法国人恐有意外，分成两队马上出发，一队负责押解俘虏，另一队用几根辕杆载着床垫抬着马洛瓦松。

他们胜利回到了雷泰尔。

拉维涅先生因俘获普鲁士的一支先头部队而被授予勋章，胖面包师也因被敌人打伤而得了一枚军功章。

小说结尾看似自然，实际上充满了讽刺意味。

名篇赏析

　　这是一篇精彩的战斗传奇故事。之所以用战斗，是因为它称不上是战争。这个故事的真正核心是法国村姑智斗德国兵，同样也是故事最精彩的部分。后面法国军官的参与，只是这场斗争的补充。但在小说的立意上，法国军官们的故事并不是画蛇添足或可有可无。小说最后写到法国军官获得了勋章，受伤的胖面包师也获得了勋章。而这场战斗中最关键的人物——看林人的女儿贝蒂娜却只字未提，当然也没有被授予任何勋章。贝蒂娜却是小说所有人物中最聪明、最勇敢、最机智的人。小说的讽刺意味到这里就昭然若揭了。但是，作者在文字中却没有轻易流露出这种意味。这种巧妙的笔法用中国的成语概括就是"羚羊挂角，无迹可寻"。

Edgar Allan Poe

01 The Masque of the Red Death
红死魔的假面舞会

姓名	埃德加·爱伦·坡
出生日期	1809年1月19日
出生地	美国波士顿
性别	男

成就和特色

　　美国著名作家、文艺评论家、侦探小说鼻祖、恐怖小说大师、科幻小说先驱之一。他的小说风格怪异离奇，充满恐怖气氛，语言和形式精致优美、内容多样。1841年，他发表的《莫格街谋杀案》被公认为最早的侦探小说。他把神秘和恐怖的文学发展到了前所未有的程度，他的神秘故事、侦探小说以及恐怖故事中的冥界气氛，在美国文学中无与伦比，在任何时代都独一无二。受到他影响的主要作家有柯南·道尔、儒勒·凡尔纳、罗伯特·路易斯·斯蒂文森、希区柯克等。

写作背景

　　贵族们为躲避蔓延的红死魔病，在栖身的城堡中肆意狂欢。戴着假面的红死魔渗入城堡的舞会，开始收割四散逃窜的亡灵。

01

The Masque of the Red Death

The "Red Death" had long **devastated**[1] the country. No **pestilence**[2] had ever been so fatal, or so hideous. Blood was its **Avatar**[3] and its seal—the redness and the horror of blood. There were sharp pains, and sudden dizziness, and then **profuse**[4] bleeding at the **pores**[5], with **dissolution**[6]. The scarlet stains upon the body and especially upon the face of the victim, were the pest ban which shut him out from the aid and from the sympathy of his fellow-men. And the whole seizure, progress and termination of the disease, were the incidents of half an hour.

But the Prince Prospero was happy and dauntless and **sagacious**[7]. When his **dominions**[8] were half depopulated, he summoned to his presence a thousand **hale**[9] and light-hearted friends from among the knights and dames of his court, and with these retired to the deep seclusion of one of his **castellated**[10] abbeys. This was an extensive and magnificent structure, the creation of the prince's own **eccentric**[11] yet **august**[12] taste. A strong and lofty wall girdled it in. This wall had gates of iron. The courtiers, having entered, brought furnaces and massy hammers and welded the bolts. They resolved to leave means neither of **ingress**[13] or egress to the sudden impulses of despair or of frenzy from within. The abbey was amply **provisioned**[14]. With such precautions the courtiers might bid defiance to **contagion**[15]. The external world could take care of itself. In the meantime it was folly to grieve, or to think. The prince had provided all the appliances of pleasure. There were **buffoons**[16], there were **improvisatori**[17], there were ballet-dancers, there

1. devastate
   vt. 蹂躏
2. pestilence
   n. 瘟疫
3. avatar
   n. 化身
4. profuse
   adj. 极其丰富的；大量的
5. pore
   n. 毛孔
6. dissolution
   n. 死亡
7. sagacious
   adj. 精明的
8. dominion
   n. 疆土；版图
9. hale
   adj. 强壮的；健壮的
10. castellated
    adj. 城堡形的
11. eccentric
    adj. 古怪的
12. august
    adj. 庄严的；有气势的；威严的
13. ingress
    n. 入口处
14. provision
    vt. 向……供应
15. contagion
    n. 传染病；蔓延
16. buffoon
    n. 小丑
17. improvisatori
    n. （意）即兴；即席

红死魔的假面舞会

　　"红死魔"已经蹂躏这个国家很久了。从来没有瘟疫这样致命、这样骇人。鲜血是它的化身和标志——鲜血的红色和恐怖。有剧烈的疼痛，有突然的眩晕，随后是毛孔大量出血而死。受害者身上——尤其是脸上出现猩红斑点，就是亲朋好友无法救助和同情他的红死病禁令。这种病从感染、发病到死亡整个过程也就是半小时的事儿。

作品开篇便充满了恐怖骇人的气氛。

　　但是，普洛斯彼罗君主快乐、大胆而精明。当他领地上的人死了一半时，他把从宫廷男女爵士中挑出的一千名身体健壮、无忧无虑的拥护者召到面前，带着他们隐居到一座偏僻幽深城堡风格的修道院。这是一个宽阔宏伟的建筑，按照君主自己古怪而尊贵的品位建成。四周围着一道坚固的高墙。高墙有两扇铁门。这些朝臣进来后，就带来熔炉和巨大铁锤焊住了门闩。他们决心破釜沉舟，不留退路，以防因绝望或疯狂而产生的想出去的冲动。修道院里储备充足。因为这些预防措施，所以那些朝臣就蔑视传染病的蔓延。外面的世界自己能够照顾自己。在这种时候去忧心忡忡是庸人自扰。君主早就做好了寻欢作乐的一切安排。有小丑，有即兴表演，

were musicians, there was Beauty, there was wine. All these and security were within. Without was the "Red Death."

It was toward the close of the fifth or sixth month of his seclusion, and while the pestilence raged most furiously abroad, that the Prince Prospero entertained his thousand friends at a masked ball of the most unusual magnificence.

It was a voluptuous[18] scene, that masquerade. But first let me tell of the rooms in which it was held. There were seven—an imperial suite. In many palaces, however, such suites form a long and straight vista, while the folding doors slide back nearly to the walls on either hand, so that the view of the whole extent is scarcely impeded[19]. Here the case was very different; as might have been expected from the duke's love of the bizarre. The apartments were so irregularly disposed[20] that the vision embraced but little more than one at a time. There was a sharp turn at every twenty or thirty yards, and at each turn a novel effect. To the right and left, in the middle of each wall, a tall and narrow Gothic window looked out upon a closed corridor which pursued the windings of the suite. These windows were of stained glass whose color varied in accordance with the prevailing[21] hue of the decorations of the chamber into which it opened. That at the eastern extremity was hung, for example, in blue—and vividly blue were its windows. The second chamber was purple in its ornaments and tapestries, and here the panes were purple. The third was green throughout, and so were the casements. The fourth was furnished and lighted with orange—the fifth with white—the sixth with violet. The seventh apartment was closely shrouded in black velvet tapestries that hung all over the ceiling and down the walls, falling in heavy folds upon a carpet of the same material and hue. But in this chamber only, the color of the windows failed to correspond with the decorations. The panes here were scarlet —a deep blood color. Now in no one of the seven apartments was there any lamp or candelabrum[22], amid the profusion of golden ornaments that lay scattered to and fro or depended from the roof. There was no light of any kind emanating from[23] lamp

18. voluptuous
   adj. 骄奢淫逸的
19. impede
   vt. 妨碍；阻碍
20. dispose
   vt. 布置
21. prevailing
   adj. 主要的
22. candelabrum
   n. 枝状烛台或灯台；
   烛架
23. emanate from
   发出；发源于

有芭蕾舞演员，有音乐家，有美女，还有美酒。墙里应有尽有、平安无事。墙外则是"红死魔"的天下。

隐居快五六个月时，外面的瘟疫最猖獗，普洛斯彼罗君主举办了一场最不寻常的化装舞会，招待那些追随者。

那个假面舞会，真是一个骄奢淫逸的场面。但是，首先让我讲述一下举行舞会的那些房间。共有七个房间——那是一个富丽堂皇的套房。然而，在许多宫殿里，这种套房只要把折叠门向左右两边差不多推到墙边，就可以形成一个又长又直的通道，因此整个套房几乎一览无余。这里的情况却截然不同，因为君主别出心裁，所以可想而知。这些房间布置极不规则，一次只能看到一个地方。每隔二三十码，就有一个急转弯，每个转弯都是一幅奇观。左右两边每道墙壁中间都是又高又窄的哥特式窗户，窗外是一条环绕这个套房的密封回廊。这些窗户都装有彩色玻璃，色彩各异，但和打开的各个房间装饰的主色调一致。比如，最东边的那个房间悬挂着蓝色饰物——而且窗户呈鲜蓝色。第二个房间的装饰和挂毯呈紫色，这里的窗玻璃也是紫色。第三个房间全部是绿色，窗扉也是绿色。第四个房间家具和光线都是橘黄色——第五个房间是白色——第六个房间是紫罗兰色。第七个房间从天花板到四面墙壁都被黑天鹅绒帷幔盖得密不透风，褶皱层层叠叠沉甸甸地落在布料和色调相同的同是黑天鹅绒地毯上。但是，只有这个房间里的窗户色彩与室内装饰不相协调。这里的窗玻璃是猩红色——浓重的血色。在这七个房间里，到处摆着

修道院成了普洛斯彼罗君主带领他的朝臣与红死魔斗争的堡垒，坚固的围墙让他们蔑视红死魔的蔓延。

or candle within the suite of chambers. But in the corridors that followed the suite, there stood, opposite to each window, a heavy tripod, bearing a brazier of fire, that projected its rays through the tinted glass and so glaringly illumined the room. And thus were produced a multitude of gaudy[24] and fantastic appearances. But in the western or black chamber the effect of the fire-light that streamed upon the dark hangings through the blood-tinted panes, was ghastly in the extreme, and produced so wild a look upon the countenances[25] of those who entered, that there were few of the company bold enough to set foot within its precincts[26] at all.

It was in this apartment, also, that there stood against the western wall, a gigantic clock of ebony. Its pendulum swung to and fro with a dull, heavy, monotonous clang; and when the minute-hand made the circuit of the face, and the hour was to be stricken, there came from the brazen lungs of the clock a sound which was clear and loud and deep and exceedingly musical, but of so peculiar a note and emphasis that, at each lapse of an hour, the musicians of the orchestra were constrained to pause, momentarily, in their performance, to harken to the sound; and thus the waltzers perforce[27] ceased their evolutions; and there was a brief disconcert of the whole gay company; and, while the chimes[28] of the clock yet rang, it was observed that the giddiest grew pale, and the more aged and sedate[29] passed their hands over their brows as if in confused revery or meditation. But when the echoes had fully ceased, a light laughter at once pervaded[30] the assembly; the musicians looked at each other and smiled as if at their own nervousness and folly, and made whispering vows, each to the other, that the next chiming of the clock should produce in them no similar emotion; and then, after the lapse of sixty minutes, (which embrace three thousand and six hundred seconds of the Time that flies,) there came yet another chiming of the clock, and then were the same disconcert and tremulousness[31] and meditation as before.

But, in spite of these things, it was a gay and magnificent revel. The tastes of the duke were peculiar. He had a fine eye for colors and effects. He disregarded the decora of mere fashion.

24. gaudy
    adj. 华而不实的
25. countenance
    n. 面容；脸色
26. precinct
    n. 区域；范围
27. perforce
    adv. 必然地
28. chime
    n. 钟声
29. sedate
    adj. 安静的；稳重的
30. pervade
    vt. 遍及
31. tremulousness
    n. 发抖；胆小

或挂着的琳琅满目金碧辉煌的饰物中，却没有一盏灯，也没有一个烛台。整套房间里，没有任何灯光和烛光。但是，在围绕套房的回廊里，每扇窗跟前都立着一张三脚支架，上面放着一盆火，光线透过彩色玻璃照进来，将房间照得闪闪发亮。因此，房间里产生了一种绚丽斑斓、光怪陆离的奇异景象。但是，在西屋或黑屋里，火光透过血红色的玻璃落在黑色帷幔上的效果可怕到了极点，凡是进屋的人无不吓得魂飞魄散，所以胆敢涉足那个房间的人寥寥无几。

同样也是在这个房间，靠西墙立着一座巨大的黑檀木钟。钟摆来回晃动，响声乏味、沉重、单调。当分针在表面上转完一圈报点时刻来临时，巨钟的黄铜腔里就发出报时声，那声音清晰、响亮、深沉，非常悦耳，但音调和重音又非常奇特；结果每过一个小时，管弦乐队的乐师们都不得不暂停演奏，倾听钟声；因此，那些跳华尔兹的人必然停止旋转；狂欢的人群都出现了一阵短暂的慌乱；当钟声还在敲响时，即使最轻浮的人也都脸色煞白，上了年纪和沉着稳重的人都以手抚额，仿佛陷入了迷惑的幻想或沉思之中。但当回荡的钟声完全停止时，人群中又马上充满了轻松的欢笑。乐师们面面相觑，微微一笑，好像是笑自己的神经过敏和愚蠢举止；他们还相互低声发誓，下次钟声响起时，不会产生类似的情绪；随后，六十分钟（那包含着飞逝而过的三千六百秒）过后，钟声再次响起，于是又出现了像先前那样的慌乱、颤抖和沉思。

但尽管如此，整个化装舞会仍不失为一场穷奢极欲的欢宴。君主的品位非常奇特。他对色彩和视觉效果

举行舞会的那七个房间和那座巨大的黑檀木钟都具有体现主题的意象。

The Masque of the Red Death 红死魔的假面舞会

His plans were bold and fiery, and his conceptions glowed with barbaric lustre. There are some who would have thought him mad. His followers felt that he was not. It was necessary to hear and see and touch him to be sure that he was not.

He had directed, in great part, the moveable embellishments[32] of the seven chambers, upon occasion of this great fete[33]; and it was his own guiding taste which had given character to the masqueraders. Be sure they were grotesque. There were much glare and glitter and piquancy[34] and phantasm—much of what has been since seen in *Hernani*. There were arabesque[35] figures with unsuited limbs and appointments[36]. There were delirious fancies such as the madman fashions. There was much of the beautiful, much of the wanton, much of the bizarre, something of the terrible, and not a little of that which might have excited disgust. To and fro in the seven chambers there stalked, in fact, a multitude of dreams. And these—the dreams—writhed in and about, taking hue from the rooms, and causing the wild music of the orchestra to seem as the echo of their steps. And, anon, there strikes the ebony[37] clock which stands in the hall of the velvet. And then, for a moment, all is still, and all is silent save the voice of the clock. The dreams are stiff-frozen as they stand. But the echoes of the chime die away—they have endured but an instant—and a light, half-subdued laughter floats after them as they depart. And now again the music swells, and the dreams live, and writhe[38] to and fro more merrily than ever, taking hue from the many tinted windows through which stream the rays from the tripods. But to the chamber which lies most westwardly of the seven, there are now none of the maskers who venture; for the night is waning away; and there flows a ruddier light through the blood-colored panes; and the blackness of the sable drapery appals[39]; and to him whose foot falls upon the sable[40] carpet, there comes from the near clock of ebony a muffled peal[41] more solemnly emphatic than any which reaches their ears who indulge in the more remote gaieties of the other apartments.

32. embellishment
    n. 装饰；布置
33. fete
    n. 庆祝；节日
34. piquancy
    n. 活泼有趣
35. arabesque
    adj. 奇特的；复杂难懂的
36. appointment
    n. （复）家具；设备
37. ebony
    adj. 乌木制的；黑檀的
38. writhe
    v. 扭动
39. appal
    v. 惊骇
40. sable
    adj. 黑貂皮的；黑的
41. peal
    n. 隆隆声；响亮的钟声

独具慧眼。他对仅仅时尚的装饰不屑一顾。他的构想大胆热烈，他的构思闪耀着原始的光辉。有人会认为他疯了。他的追随者并不这样认为。要确信君主的确没疯，那必须叫他说话，与他见面，同他接触。

　　为了举办这次盛大的庆祝会，七个房间的活动装饰大部分都由他亲自指点；而正是他个人的情趣嗜好使舞会参加者的化装各具特色。他们的确是奇形怪状。真是耀眼绚丽，活泼有趣，如梦似幻——大都是在《爱尔那尼》里见过的场景。到处都是肢体与面具不相称的光怪陆离的轮廓。到处都是狂乱的幻景，只有疯子才想得出来。其中有许多美妙的东西，有许多放荡的东西，有许多奇异的东西，有的让人害怕，还有许多让人厌恶。事实上，是一群梦中人在这七个房间里昂首阔步走来走去。这些人——这些梦中人——带着那些房间的色彩扭进扭出，引得乐队奏起了疯狂的音乐，仿佛是他们脚步的回声。不久，立在天鹅绒帷幔遮盖的房间里的黑檀木钟又敲响了。于是，一时间，除了钟声，万籁俱寂，悄无声息。这些梦中人站在那里僵住了。但是，等回荡的钟声渐渐消失——它们只持续了一会儿——随着钟声远去，人群中就响起了略为压抑的轻笑声。于是，音乐再次扬起，那些梦中人又活跃起来，扭来扭去，比先前更加欢快。三脚支架火盆里发出的光线透过五光十色的窗户色彩变幻。但是，现在参加假面舞会的人谁也不敢进七个房间中最西边的那间，因为夜渐渐深了；透过血红色的窗户泻进一片更红的光；黑沉沉的帷幔令人惊骇；对踏上黑地毯的人来说，近处传来的黑檀木钟发出的沉

Hernani 爱尔那尼（法国作家雨果创作的五幕韵文正剧，剧本表现了强烈的反封建精神，在艺术上打破了古典主义关于悲喜剧的界限，全面运用了对照原则，显示出丰富多彩的风格，堪称浪漫主义戏剧的代表作）。作者在此提到浪漫主义戏剧《爱尔那尼》有其深意。

But these other apartments were densely crowded, and in them beat feverishly the heart of life. And the revel went whirlingly on, until at length there commenced the sounding of midnight upon the clock. And then the music ceased, as I have told; and the evolutions of the waltzers were quieted; and there was an uneasy cessation[42] of all things as before. But now there were twelve strokes to be sounded by the bell of the clock; and thus it happened, perhaps that more of thought crept, with more of time, into the meditations of the thoughtful among those who revelled[43]. And thus too, it happened, perhaps, that before the last echoes of the last chime had utterly sunk into silence, there were many individuals in the crowd who had found leisure to become aware of the presence of a masked figure which had arrested the attention of no single individual before. And the rumor of this new presence having spread itself whisperingly around, there arose at length from the whole company a buzz, or murmur, expressive of disapprobation[44] and surprise—then, finally, of terror, of horror, and of disgust.

In an assembly of phantasms such as I have painted, it may well be supposed that no ordinary appearance could have excited such sensation. In truth the masquerade license of the night was nearly unlimited; but the figure in question had out-Heroded[45] Herod, and gone beyond the bounds of even the prince's indefinite decorum[46]. There are chords in the hearts of the most reckless which cannot be touched without emotion. Even with the utterly lost, to whom life and death are equally jests, there are matters of which no jest can be made. The whole company, indeed, seemed now deeply to feel that in the costume and bearing[47] of the stranger neither wit nor propriety existed. The figure was tall and gaunt[48], and shrouded from head to foot in the habiliments[49] of the grave. The mask which concealed the visage[50] was made so nearly to resemble the countenance of a stiffened corpse that the closest scrutiny[51] must have had difficulty in detecting the cheat. And yet all this might have been endured, if not approved, by the mad revellers around. But the

闷钟声，要比在远处其他房间纵情狂欢的人听上去更加阴沉压抑。

但是，其他房间挤得密不透风，充满活力的心脏兴奋跳动。狂欢继续高潮迭起，直到最后午夜的钟声响起。于是，如我所述，音乐随即停止；跳华尔兹的人也安静了下来；所有的一切都像先前那样出现了令人不安的中断。但现在，时钟要敲响十二下；因此，也许会有更多的思想悄悄潜入狂欢者当中那些善于思考者更多时间的沉思冥想之中。也许正因为如此，在最后一下钟声的回响完全陷入寂静之前，有许多人正好有空注意到一个先前从未引人注意的戴面具人的出现。这个新来者的消息不胫而走，最后整个人群都响起了嗡嗡声或咕哝声，纷纷表示不满和吃惊——到后来，表达的都是恐怖、惊骇和厌恶。

完全可以认为，在我描绘的这个奇幻集会中，普通人的出现不可能引起如此轩然大波。其实，这天夜里的假面舞会几乎没有限制；但是，这个可疑的人比希律王更过分，而且不拘礼仪的君主也望尘莫及。那些最鲁莽的人都不可能不让情感拨动心弦。甚至对那些完全着迷、视生死为儿戏的人来说，有些事也绝不能视为儿戏。事实上，所有在场的人现在好像都深深地感到陌生人的装束和举止既无情趣，又不得体。这个人又高又瘦，从头到脚都裹着寿衣。那张遮住容貌的面具几乎完全接近僵尸的面容，就是凑上去仔细打量也难辨真伪。然而，即使四周狂欢的人不赞成这一切，却也能容忍。但是，这个戴面具的陌生人竟然扮成红死魔的模样。他

穷奢极欲的欢宴，骄奢淫逸的场面，别出心裁的房间布置，最西边那间令人惊骇的黑屋，以及伴随黑屋里黑檀木钟发出的沉闷钟声而出现的慌乱、颤抖和沉思：这一场最不寻常的化装舞会，毋宁说是一群纵情狂欢的梦中人的一次盛大庆典。

mummer[52] had gone so far as to assume the type of the Red Death. His **vesture**[53] was dabbled in blood—and his broad brow, with all the features of the face, was besprinkled with the scarlet horror.

When the eyes of Prince Prospero fell upon this **spectral**[54] image (which with a slow and solemn movement, as if more fully to sustain its role, stalked to and fro among the waltzers) he was seen to be **convulsed**[55], in the first moment with a strong shudder either of terror or distaste; but, in the next, his brow reddened with rage.

"Who dares?" he demanded hoarsely of the courtiers who stood near him—"who dares insult us with this **blasphemous**[56] mockery? Seize him and unmask him—that we may know whom we have to hang at sunrise, from the battlements!"

It was in the eastern or blue chamber in which stood the Prince Prospero as he uttered these words. They rang throughout the seven rooms loudly and clearly—for the prince was a bold and robust man, and the music had become hushed at the waving of his hand.

It was in the blue room where stood the prince, with a group of pale courtiers by his side. At first, as he spoke, there was a slight rushing movement of this group in the direction of the intruder, who, at the moment was also near at hand, and now, with deliberate and stately step, made closer approach to the speaker. But from a certain nameless awe with which the mad assumptions of the mummer had inspired the whole party, there were found none who put forth hand to seize him; so that, **unimpeded**[57], he passed within a yard of the prince's person; and, while the vast assembly, as if with one impulse, shrank from the centres of the rooms to the walls, he made his way uninterruptedly, but with the same solemn and measured step which had distinguished him from the first, through the blue chamber to the purple—through the purple to the green—through the green to the orange—through this again to the white—and

52. mummer
　　n. 哑剧演员；演员
53. vesture
　　n. 衣服；罩袍
54. spectral
　　adj. 鬼怪的
55. convulse
　　vt. 使抽搐
56. blasphemous
　　adj. 亵渎神明的
57. unimpeded
　　adj. 未受阻止的；未受阻碍的

的衣服沾着鲜血——宽阔的前额和五官都布满了猩红色的恐怖。

这个幽灵似的陌生人缓慢庄严地在跳华尔兹的人群中昂首阔步走来走去，仿佛是要更加充分地继续扮演这个角色。当普洛斯彼罗君主的目光落到这个幽灵似的身影，不知是害怕还是恶心，他浑身抽搐，猛烈颤抖，但紧接着就气得满脸通红。

"谁敢？"他声音嘶哑地问身边的朝臣——"谁敢用这种亵渎神明的嘲笑侮辱我们？抓住他，揭去他的面具——日出时，我们就会知道在城垛上吊死的是谁了！"

说这些话时，普洛斯彼罗君主正站在东面、东头或蓝屋。他的声音响亮清晰，传遍了七个房间——因为君主生性粗犷豪放，而音乐早已随着他的挥手停止了演奏。

普洛斯彼罗君主正站在蓝屋里，一群脸色苍白的朝臣站在他身边。起先，他说话时，这群朝臣朝此刻也近在咫尺的那个闯入者的方向微微逼近；不料那不速之客竟迈着从容而庄重的步伐朝君主走来。他的嚣张在所有人的心里都激起了一种莫名的恐惧，没有人敢伸手去抓住他；因此，他畅行无阻，离君主本人不到一码远了；此时那一大群狂欢的人好像在一种推力作用下，纷纷从房间中央退到了墙边；他无遮无拦继续前进，但还是迈着那样一开始就与众不同的庄严整齐的步伐，穿过蓝屋，走进紫屋——穿过紫屋，走进绿屋——穿过绿屋，走进黄屋——又穿过黄屋，走进白屋——在一个抓住他的行动开始之前，他甚至已快要进入紫罗兰色房间。但

一个先前从未引起注意的戴面具人的出现，之所以引起轩然大波，是因为他扮演的是红死魔的角色，午夜钟声似乎成了狂欢者的丧钟。

even thence to the violet, ere a decided movement had been made to arrest him. It was then, however, that the Prince Prospero, maddening with rage and the shame of his own momentary cowardice, rushed hurriedly through the six chambers, while none followed him on account of a deadly terror that had seized upon all. He bore aloft a drawn dagger, and had approached, in rapid **impetuosity**[58], to within three or four feet of the retreating figure, when the latter, having attained the extremity of the velvet apartment, turned suddenly and confronted his pursuer. There was a sharp cry—and the dagger dropped gleaming upon the sable carpet, upon which, instantly afterwards, fell **prostrate**[59] in death the Prince Prospero. Then, summoning the wild courage of despair, a throng of the revellers at once threw themselves into the black apartment, and, seizing the mummer, whose tall figure stood erect and motionless within the shadow of the ebony clock, gasped in unutterable horror at finding the grave **cerements**[60] and corpse-like mask which they handled with so violent a rudeness, untenanted by any **tangible**[61] form.

And now was acknowledged the presence of the Red Death. He had come like a thief in the night. And one by one dropped the revellers in the blood-bedewed halls of their revel, and died each in the despairing **posture**[62] of his fall. And the life of the ebony clock went out with that of the last of the gay. And the flames of the tripods **expired**[63]. And Darkness and Decay and the Red Death held **illimitable**[64] dominion over all.

58. impetuosity
   n. 冲动；性急
59. prostrate
   adj. 俯卧的
60. cerement
   n. 寿衣
61. tangible
   adj. 可触知的；有形的
62. posture
   n. （身体的）姿势
63. expire
   vi. 熄灭
64. illimitable
   adj. 无限的

就在这时，君主因自己一时胆怯而恼羞成怒，飞身冲过六个房间；大家都吓得要死，没有一个人跟随他。他高举一把出鞘的短剑，心急火燎逼向那个撤退的人，两人相距三四英尺，此时后者已到了黑屋尽头。他突然转身，面对追上他的君主。这时传来一声刺耳的惨叫——那把短剑寒光一闪，掉落在黑地毯上。随后，普洛斯彼罗君主的尸体扑倒在地。这时，一群狂欢的人才鼓起拼命的勇气，一哄而上冲进了黑屋，一把抓住那个假面人。只见他高大的身躯一动不动直立在黑檀木钟的阴影里，他们一把抓住他，用力过猛，抓在手里的竟是寿衣和僵尸面具，里面没有肉身；见此情景，他们都瞠目结舌、恐惧万分。

七个房间的意象生动形象，独特神奇，让我们体会到一种恐怖而真实的刀光剑影。

　　此时，大家才公认"红死魔"来到了面前。他像贼一样在夜间到来。狂欢的人一个接一个倒在他们狂欢过的鲜血满地的舞厅里，每个人死去时都是一副倒下时的绝望姿势。黑檀木钟也随着最后一个狂欢者生命的终结而寿终正寝。三脚支架火盆里的火焰也熄灭了。黑暗、腐朽和红死魔开始了对一切漫漫无期的统治。

名篇赏析

　　持续的恐怖、惊骇，令人窒息，让人绝望："红死魔"来到了人们面前，修道院四周围着的那道坚固的高墙没有挡住它，快乐、大胆而精明的普洛斯彼罗君主和他的朝臣没有战胜它！从某种意义上说，人类的历史就是一部人类与病魔的斗争史。《红死魔的假面舞会》为我们讲述了一个君主带领他的朝臣与病魔斗争的故事，发人深省。

Edgar Allan Poe

椭圆形画像

姓名	埃德加·爱伦·坡
出生日期	1809年1月19日
出生地	美国波士顿
性别	男

成就和特色

　　美国著名作家、文艺评论家、侦探小说鼻祖、恐怖小说大师、科幻小说先驱之一。他的小说风格怪异离奇，充满恐怖气氛，语言和形式精致优美、内容多样。1841年，他发表的《莫格街谋杀案》被公认为最早的侦探小说。他把神秘和恐怖的文学发展到了前所未有的程度，他的神秘故事、侦探小说以及恐怖故事中的冥界气氛，在美国文学中无与伦比，在任何时代都独一无二。受到他影响的主要作家有柯南·道尔、儒勒·凡尔纳、罗伯特·路易斯·斯蒂文森、希区柯克等。

写作背景

　　男人为爱妻画肖像，妻子为了爱情，努力绽放娇颜，但逐渐完成的肖像画正一点点榨取妻子的生命。当画完成时，妻子当场身亡，只留下富有生命力色彩的妻子的肖像画在风中狞笑。

02

The Oval Portrait

The **chateau**[1] into which my **valet**[2] had ventured to make forcible entrance, rather than permit me, in my desperately wounded condition, to pass a night in the open air, was one of those piles of commingled gloom and grandeur which have so long **frowned**[3] among the **Appennines**[4], not less in fact than in the fancy of **Mrs. Radcliffe**[5]. To all appearance it had been temporarily and very lately abandoned. We established ourselves in one of the smallest and least **sumptuously**[6] furnished apartments. It lay in a remote **turret**[7] of the building. Its decorations were rich, yet tattered and antique. Its walls were hung with **tapestry**[8] and bedecked with manifold and multiform armorial trophies, together with an unusually great number of very spirited modern paintings in frames of rich golden **arabesque**[9]. In these paintings, which depended from the walls not only in their main surfaces, but in very many nooks which the bizarre architecture of the chateau rendered necessary—in these paintings my incipient delirium, perhaps, had caused me to take deep interest; so that I bade Pedro to close the heavy shutters of the room —since it was already night—to light the tongues of a tall **candelabrum**[10] which stood by the head of my bed— and to throw open far and wide the fringed curtains of black velvet which enveloped the bed itself. I wished all this done that I might resign myself, if not to sleep, at least alternately

椭圆形画像

为了不让我在身负重伤的情况下露天过夜，贴身男仆冒险闯进了一座城堡。这是长久耸立在亚平宁山脉众多城堡中的一座，这些城堡既阴郁又庄严，事实上不亚于拉德克利夫太太想象中的城堡。显然，是最近才暂时没人住的。我们在一套面积最小、装饰最不豪华的房间安顿下来。房间位于城堡偏僻的塔楼里。室内装饰堂皇，但破旧过时。墙上挂着壁毯，挂满了形形色色的徽章战利品，还有琳琅满目装在华美金色蔓藤花纹画框里的充满灵性的现代画。这些画不仅挂在主要的几面墙上，而且也挂在城堡这个奇异建筑所特有的凹陷的隐蔽墙面——也许是起初的精神狂乱，使我对这些画产生了强烈的兴趣；因此，我让佩德罗关了屋里那些厚重的百叶窗——因为夜幕已经降临——点燃立在我床头高烛架上的那些蜡烛——然后完全拉开罩在床上的带流苏的黑天鹅绒帷幔。我希望，做过这一切后，即使无法入睡，至少可以交替着端详这些画，细读在枕边找到的一本旨在评述这些作品的小册子。

身负重伤的故事叙述者，首先给我们描绘了故事发生的环境和氛围。立在床头的烛台是这出戏中戏里不可或缺的一个道具，而那本旨在论述那些绘画及其来历的小册子将有助于解开故事的悬念。

The Oval Portrait 椭圆形画像　123

to the **contemplation**[11] of these pictures, and the **perusal**[12] of a small volume which had been found upon the pillow, and which **purported**[13] to criticise and describe them.

Long—long I read—and **devoutly**[14], devotedly I gazed. Rapidly and gloriously the hours flew by and the deep midnight came. The position of the candelabrum displeased me, and outreaching my hand with difficulty, rather than disturb my slumbering valet, I placed it so as to throw its rays more fully upon the book.

But the action produced an effect altogether unanticipated. The rays of the numerous candles (for there were many) now fell within a **niche**[15] of the room which had hitherto been thrown into deep shade by one of the bed-posts. I thus saw in vivid light a picture all unnoticed before. It was the portrait of a young girl just ripening into womanhood. I glanced at the painting hurriedly, and then closed my eyes. Why I did this was not at first apparent even to my own perception. But while my lids remained thus shut, I ran over in my mind my reason for so shutting them. It was an impulsive movement to gain time for thought—to make sure that my vision had not deceived me—to calm and subdue my fancy for a more sober and more certain gaze. In a very few moments I again looked fixedly at the painting.

That I now saw aright I could not and would not doubt; for the first flashing of the candles upon that canvas had seemed to **dissipate**[16] the dreamy stupor which was stealing over my senses, and to startle me at once into waking life.

The portrait, I have already said, was that of a young girl. It was a mere head and shoulders, done in what is technically termed a **vignette**[17] manner; much in the style of the favorite heads of **Sully**[18]. The arms, the bosom, and even the ends of the radiant hair, melted **imperceptibly**[19] into the vague yet deep

11. contemplation
    n. 注视
12. perusal
    n. 熟读；精读
13. purport
    vt. 声称；意指
14. devoutly
    adv. 虔诚地
15. niche
    n. 壁龛
16. dissipate
    v. 驱散
17. vignette
    n. 虚光画
18. Sully
    n.（南方英格兰人姓氏）萨利
19. imperceptibly
    adv. 察觉不到地；微细地

我久久地读着那本小书——虔诚专心地凝望那些画。几个小时在愉悦中飞逝而过，不知不觉午夜来临。烛台的位置让我不快，我不愿打扰正在睡觉的仆人，就吃力地伸出一只手挪动烛台，以便让光线更加充分地照在书上。

但是，这个动作产生了一种完全不曾预料的效果。因为有许多蜡烛，所以无数的烛光现在照进了屋里的一个壁龛，先前它被一根床柱遮挡在深深的阴影中。因此，在明亮的烛光中，我看到了一幅先前完全没有注意到的画。那是一个刚成熟为女人的年轻姑娘的画像。我匆匆瞥了一眼那幅肖像，就闭上了眼睛。起初，我也不明白自己为什么这样做。但是，我在眼帘还那样合着时，就在脑海里飞快地想了一下自己闭眼的原因。那是一种冲动，是为了赢得思考的时间——以确定视觉并没有骗我——平息我的想象力，看得更冷静、更可靠。过了一会儿，我又定定地看着那幅画。

我现在看清了。我不能也不会怀疑这一点，因为当初照到画布上的烛光似乎已经驱散了正渐渐弥漫在意识上的梦一般的恍惚，马上把我惊醒。

我曾经说过，那是一个年轻姑娘的肖像。只有头部和肩膀，是用所谓的虚光画技法画成，颇似萨利最得意的头像画风格。双臂、胸部、甚至闪亮的发梢，都不易察觉地融入了构成整幅画背景的朦胧而深沉的阴影。画框呈椭圆形，镀着一层金，以摩尔式风格饰有金银丝，

为了让光线更加充分地照在书上，故事叙述者伸手挪动烛台，意想不到地发现了挂在壁龛里的一幅令他深感不安、错把头像当活人的肖像。

shadow which formed the back-ground of the whole. The frame was oval, richly gilded and **filigreed**[20] in Moresque. As a thing of art nothing could be more admirable than the painting itself. But it could have been neither the execution of the work, nor the immortal beauty of the countenance, which had so suddenly and so vehemently moved me. **Least of all**[21], could it have been that my fancy, shaken from its half slumber, had mistaken the head for that of a living person. I saw at once that the peculiarities of the design, of the vignetting, and of the frame, must have instantly **dispelled**[22] such idea—must have prevented even its momentary entertainment. Thinking earnestly upon these points, I remained, for an hour perhaps, half sitting, half reclining, with my vision **riveted upon**[23] the portrait. At length, satisfied with the true secret of its effect, I fell back within the bed. I had found the spell of the picture in an absolute life-likeliness of expression, which, at first startling, finally confounded, subdued, and **appalled**[24] me. With deep and **reverent**[25] awe I replaced the candelabrum in its former position. The cause of my deep **agitation**[26] being thus shut from view, I sought eagerly the volume which discussed the paintings and their histories. Turning to the number which designated the oval portrait, I there read the vague and quaint words which follow:

"She was a maiden of rarest beauty, and not more lovely than full of glee. And evil was the hour when she saw, and loved, and wedded the painter. He, passionate, studious, austere[27], and having already a bride in his Art; she a maiden of rarest beauty, and not more lovely than full of glee; all light and smiles, and frolicsome[28] as the young fawn; loving and cherishing all things; hating only the Art which was her rival; dreading only the pallet[29] and brushes and other untoward instruments which deprived her of the countenance[30] of her lover. It was thus a terrible thing

20. filigreed
    adj. 饰有金银丝细工的
21. least of all
    adv. 最不；尤其
22. dispel
    vt. 驱散
23. rivet upon
    集中注意
24. appall
    vt. 使胆寒；使惊骇
25. reverent
    adj. 尊敬的；虔诚的
26. agitation
    n. 焦虑不安；激动
27. austere
    adj. 操行上一丝不苟的
28. frolicsome
    adj. 爱闹着玩的；嬉戏的
29. pallet
    n. 画家的调色板
30. countenance
    n. 面容；脸色

富丽堂皇。作为一件艺术品，最值得赞美的还是肖像本身。但是，刚才如此突然、如此强烈打动我的既不可能是精湛技法，也不可能是画中人的不朽美貌。尤其是我从半睡眠中惊醒的想象力错把画上的头像当成了活人。我马上就明白，构图、虚光、画框的种种特点肯定一下子驱散了我这种看法——必定不让我再生出丝毫这样的想法。我一边认真思考这些特点，一边半坐半倚凝视那幅肖像，保持了大约一个小时。最后，我终于领会那种效果的真正秘密后，才满意地钻进被窝。我已经在画中人绝对栩栩如生的表情中发现了这幅画的魔力。这种魔力起初让我震惊，最后让我困惑，把我征服，并令我胆寒。因为心中有了深深的敬畏，我把烛台挪回了原来的位置。因此，当那幅令我深感不安的画被挡住，我看不见之后，就急切寻找那本论述那些绘画及其来历的小册子，翻到介绍椭圆形画像的那部分，读到了下面这段含糊离奇的文字：

"她是一位美丽无双的姑娘，而她的欢快活泼，比她的美貌还可爱。而当她一见钟情嫁给画家之日，竟是不幸来临之时。他充满热情，工作勤勉，一丝不苟，而且已经把艺术当成了新娘；她是一位美丽无双的姑娘，而她的欢快活泼，比她的美貌还可爱；她轻松愉快，面带微笑，活泼得像一只小鹿；她热爱一切，珍爱一切，只是憎恨艺术，因为艺术是她的情敌；她害怕调色板、画笔和其他难以对付的画具，因为它们夺去了爱人的笑脸。因此，对这位女士来说，听到画家说要给年轻的新

当初照到画布上的烛光似乎驱散了正渐渐弥漫在故事叙述者意识上的梦一般的恍惚，他在画中人绝对栩栩如生的表情中发现了这幅画的魔力，领会了那种效果的真正秘密。

for this lady to hear the painter speak of his desire to portray even his young bride. But she was humble and obedient, and sat meekly for many weeks in the dark, high turret-chamber where the light dripped upon the pale canvas only from overhead. But he, the painter, took glory in his work, which went on from hour to hour, and from day to day. And he was a passionate, and wild, and moody man, who became lost in *reveries*[31]; so that he would not see that the light which fell so ghastly in that lone turret withered the health and the spirits of his bride, who pined visibly to all but him. Yet she smiled on and still on, uncomplainingly, because she saw that the painter (who had high renown) took a fervid and burning pleasure in his task, and wrought day and night to depict her who so loved him, yet who grew daily more dispirited and weak. And *in sooth*[32] some who beheld the portrait spoke of its resemblance in low words, as of a mighty marvel, and a proof not less of the power of the painter than of his deep love for her whom he depicted so surpassingly well. But at length, as the labor drew nearer to its conclusion, there were admitted none into the turret; for the painter had grown wild with the ardor of his work, and turned his eyes from canvas rarely, even to regard the countenance of his wife. And he would not see that the *tints*[33] which he *spread*[34] upon the canvas were drawn from the cheeks of her who sat beside him. And when many weeks had passed, and but little remained to do, save one brush upon the mouth and one tint upon the eye, the spirit of the lady again flickered up as the flame within the socket of the lamp. And then the brush was given, and then the tint was placed; and, for one moment, the painter stood *entranced*[35] before the work which he had wrought; but in the next, while he yet gazed, he grew tremulous and very pallid, and *aghast*[36], and crying with a loud voice, 'This is indeed Life itself!' turned suddenly to regard his beloved: —She was dead!"

31. revery
   n. 空想；幻想
32. in sooth
   事实上；确实
33. tint
   n. 色彩
34. spread
   v. 涂；抹；摊
35. entrance
   vt. 使出神
36. aghast
   adj. 惊骇的；吓呆的

娘画像，真是一件可怕的事儿。但是，她柔顺听话，所以就温顺地在高塔楼房间的黑暗中坐了好多星期，只有一道光线从头顶撒到灰白色的画布上。可是，他——那位画家——却以自己的工作为荣，他持续了一个小时又一个小时、一天又一天。他是一个充满热情、狂放不羁、喜怒无常、沉湎幻想的人，因此他不会看到如此可怕落入孤楼的光线摧残了新娘的身心；除了他，所有人都看到了她的憔悴。然而，她仍然继续面带微笑，没有怨言，因为她看到画家（他声望颇高）在工作中获得了热情似火的乐趣，他夜以继日地画着那么爱他的女人，但她却日渐沮丧虚弱。其实，一些看到肖像的人都低声说画得传神，是一个非凡的奇迹，不仅证明了画家的功力，更证明了画家对他出神入化刻画的人的深爱。但最后，当这幅画越来越接近尾声时，就不再允许任何人进入塔楼了，因为画家对工作的热情已经越来越疯狂，他很少从画布上转动眼睛，甚至是去看妻子的面容。他不会看到涂抹在画布上的色彩来自坐在身边的妻子的脸庞。好多星期过去了，除了嘴上一笔、眼上一点，差不多就完工了。画家妻子的精神就像烛孔里的火苗一样又摇曳闪烁起来。随后，嘴上的一笔画上了，眼上的一点也涂上了。一时间，画家站在自己画成的作品前出神；但接下来，当他还在凝视之时，他开始浑身颤抖，脸色煞白，目瞪口呆，之后大声叫道："这就是生命！"他突然转身去看自己的爱人：——她已经死了！"

当故事叙述者将烛台放回原来的位置，急切地从那本小书中寻找介绍椭圆形画像的那部分文字时，我们也在急切地想从这出戏中戏里寻找到答案。我们屏住呼吸读下去，故事越接近尾声，我们越加叹服小说家的巧妙构思：故事结束了，艺术活了，爱情死了！

The Oval Portrait 椭圆形画像　　129

名篇赏析

　　作品描述的发生在亚平宁山脉中城堡偏僻塔楼里的离奇故事，有着让人震惊、让人困惑、将人征服、又令人胆寒的魔力。作者通过重新设计情节链，使小说呈现嵌入式的叙述结构，达到形式与内容的相互呼应，同时通过叙述视角的转换赋予作品独特新奇的审美效果，使这个简单的故事变得耐人寻味。

Nathaniel Hawthorne

大红宝石

姓名	纳撒尼尔·霍桑
出生日期	1804年7月4日
出生地	美国马萨诸塞州塞勒姆镇
性别	男

成就和特色

　　美国十九世纪最杰出的浪漫主义小说家，代表作《红字》已成为世界文学的经典之一，是美国文学发展史上第一部象征主义小说。他的作品想象丰富、结构严谨。除了心理分析与描写，他还运用了象征主义手法。他构思精巧的意象增添了作品的浪漫色彩，加深了寓意。他的短篇小说细致深刻，风格独特，不少作品立意新颖，取材得当，富于诗意。内容与形式的和谐统一造成了完美强烈的艺术效果，对美国短篇小说这一突出文学类型的发展具有积极深远的影响。霍桑不愧为美国十九世纪后期浪漫主义作家的杰出代表，他的写作手法在美国乃至世界文学史上都独树一帜，直接影响了亨利·詹姆斯、威廉·福克纳、索尔·贝娄、艾萨克·辛格、托妮·莫里森等文坛巨擘。

写作背景

　　《大红宝石》叙述了八位寻宝者——六位来自不同地区、互不相识的人和一对新婚夫妇——追寻大红宝石的经过及结果。故事里的八个人实际是两组：新婚夫妻和另外六个人各为一组。通过对比，以及对大红宝石的意象描述，表达了人们对美好人性的追求。

01

The Great Carbuncle

At nightfall, once, in the olden time, on the rugged side of one of the Crystal Hills, a party of adventurers were refreshing themselves, after a **toilsome**[1] and fruitless quest for the Great Carbuncle. They had come thither, not as friends, nor partners in the enterprise, but each, save one youthful pair, impelled by his own selfish and solitary longing for this **wondrous**[2] gem. Their feeling of brotherhood, however, was strong enough to induce them to contribute a mutual aid in building a rude hut of branches, and **kindling**[3] a great fire of shattered pines, that had drifted down the headlong current of the Amonoosuck, on the lower bank of which they were to pass the night. There was but one of their number, perhaps, who had become so **estranged from**[4] natural sympathies, by the absorbing spell of the pursuit, as to acknowledge no satisfaction at the sight of human faces, in the remote and solitary region whither they had ascended. A vast extent of wilderness lay between them and the nearest settlement, while a scant mile above their heads, was that bleak verge, where the hills throw off their **shaggy**[5] mantle of forest trees, and either robe themselves in clouds, or tower naked into the sky. The roar of the Amonoosuck would have been too awful for endurance, if only a solitary man had listened, while the mountain stream talked with the wind.

The adventurers, therefore, exchanged **hospitable**[6] greetings, and welcomed one another to the hut, where each

1. toilsome
   adj. 辛苦的；劳苦的；费力的

2. wondrous
   adj. 令人惊奇的；非常的

3. kindle
   vt. 燃烧；使……着火；引起

4. estrange from
   与……疏远

5. shaggy
   adj. 蓬松的；表面粗糙的；毛发粗浓杂乱的

6. hospitable
   adj. 好客的；热情友好的

大红宝石

很久以前的一天，夜幕降临时，在水晶山崎岖的山坡上，一群寻找大红宝石的冒险家劳而无获后，正在休息，恢复体力。他们来到这里冒险，既不是朋友也不是伙伴。除了一对年轻夫妻，各自都对这块奇妙宝石怀有自私的渴望。然而，兄弟般的情谊却又很强，足以促使他们一块动手用树枝搭起一座粗陋小屋，并用顺着阿莫诺沙克河急流飞漂而下的散碎松枝燃起一堆大火，他们要在这条河下游的岸上过夜。他们当中可能只有一个人对寻找红宝石着迷，和大家自然产生的共鸣格格不入，连攀登到这样偏僻荒凉的地区能看到人的脸都不知足。一大片荒野横在他们与距离最近的村落之间，他们头顶不足一英里处就是荒野的那个边缘，那里的山峦甩掉了林木蓬松的斗篷，要么把自己裹进云里，要么赤裸裸直耸云霄。阿莫诺沙克河的咆哮，只要孤独者听到，都会心惊胆战，难以忍受，而淙淙山溪则和风娓娓交谈。

语言清新优美，拟人手法得当，顺手拈来。

因此，那些探险者相互殷勤致意，并欢迎对方到小屋里来。人人都是主人，又都是全体同伴的客人。他们在一块岩石的平面上铺开各自带来的干粮，一块分享

man was the host, and all were the guests of the whole company. They spread their individual supplies of food on the flat surface of a rock, and partook of a general repast; at the close of which, a sentiment of good-fellowship was **perceptible**[7] among the party, though repressed by the idea, that the renewed search for the Great Carbuncle must make them strangers again, in the morning. Seven men and one young woman, they warmed themselves together at the fire, which extended its bright wall along the whole front of their wigwam.

The eldest of the group, a tall, lean, weather-beaten man, some sixty years of age, was clad in the skins of wild animals, whose fashion of dress he did well to imitate, since the deer, the wolf, and the bear, had long been his most intimate companions. He was one of those ill-fated mortals, such as the Indians told of, whom in their early youth, the Great Carbuncle smote with a peculiar madness, and became the passionate dream of their existence. All, who visited that region, knew him as the Seeker, and by no other name. As none could remember when he first took up the search, there went a fable in the valley of the Saco, that for his **inordinate**[8] lust after the Great Carbuncle, he had been condemned to wander among the mountains till the end of time, still with the same feverish hopes at sunrise—the same despair at eve. Near this miserable Seeker sat a little elderly personage, wearing a high-crowned hat, shaped somewhat like a **crucible**[9]. He was from beyond the sea, a Doctor Cacaphodel, who had wilted and dried himself into a mummy, by continually stooping over charcoal furnaces, and inhaling **unwholesome**[10] fumes, during his researches in chemistry and **alchemy**[11]. It was told of him, whether truly or not, that, at the commencement of his studies, he had drained his body of all its richest blood, and wasted it, with other inestimable **ingredients**[12], in an unsuccessful experiment—and had never been a well man since. Another

7. perceptible
   adj. 可察觉的；可感知的；看得见的
8. inordinate
   adj. 过度的；无节制的；紊乱的
9. crucible
   n. 坩埚；熔罐
10. unwholesome
    adj. 不健康的；有害身体的；腐败的
11. alchemy
    n. 炼金术；炼丹术
12. ingredient
    n. 原料；（混合物的）组成部分

一顿美餐；吃完饭后，大家都露出了友好亲密的情绪，但他们对明天早上再次出发寻找大红宝石的主意有所克制，因为大家又会形同陌路。七个男人和一个年轻女人，他们围在火边取暖，火光照亮了棚屋的正面。

这群人中年纪最大的是一个高大消瘦、饱经风霜的男人，六十来岁，身穿兽皮，衣服式样模仿野兽惟妙惟肖，因为鹿、狼和熊长期以来都是他最亲密的伙伴。他正是印第安人所说的那种倒霉蛋，年纪轻轻就被大红宝石折磨得疯疯癫癫，寻找红宝石成了他们热烈追求的梦想。到过那个地区的人都知道他叫"寻宝者"，而不知道别的名字。没有人能记得他什么时候开始了寻宝，萨柯山谷里都传说他对大红宝石贪欲过度，注定要在山里流浪，直到临终时刻，日出时仍然满怀狂热的希望——日落时同样绝望。这个不幸的寻宝者身边坐着一位个子矮小的老者，这位老者头戴一顶状如坩埚的高顶帽。他来自海外，是卡卡福代尔博士，从事化学和炼金术研究，总是弯腰面对木炭炉，吸入有害烟气，使自己萎缩干瘪得像木乃伊似的。不知是真是假，据说他开始研究时，就已经抽干了自己身上最富有营养的血液，把它和其他一些极其贵重的配料混在一起，在一次失败的实验中消耗殆尽——从此身体就再也没有好转过。另一位冒险家是伊卡博德·皮戈斯诺特先生，一位重要商人兼波士顿行政委员，也是著名的诺顿先生教堂的一位长老。他的仇敌中有一个荒唐传说，皮戈斯诺特先生每天

开篇是环境描写。六个来自不同地区的探险者和一对新婚夫妇，为寻找大红宝石在水晶山崎岖的山坡不期而遇。

of the adventurers was Master Ichabod Pigsnort, a weighty merchant and selectman of Boston, and an elder of the famous Mr. Norton's church. His enemies had a ridiculous story, that Master Pigsnort was accustomed to spend a whole hour, after prayer time, every morning and evening, in wallowing naked among an **immense**[13] quantity of pine-tree shillings, which were the earliest silver coinage of Massachusetts. The fourth, whom we shall notice, had no name, that his companions knew of, and was chiefly distinguished by a sneer that always **contorted**[14] his thin visage, and by a **prodigious**[15] pair of spectacles, which were supposed to **deform**[16] and discolor the whole face of nature, to this gentleman's perception. The fifth adventurer likewise lacked a name, which was the greater pity, as he appeared to be a poet. He was a bright-eyed man, but **woefully**[17] pined away, which was no more than natural, if, as some people affirmed, his ordinary diet was fog, morning mist, and a slice of the densest cloud within his reach, sauced with moonshine, whenever he could get it. Certain it is, that the poetry, which flowed from him, **had a smack of**[18] all these dainties. The sixth of the party was a young man of haughty **mien**[19], and sat somewhat apart from the rest, wearing his plumed hat loftily among his elders, while the fire glittered on the rich embroidery of his dress, and gleamed intensely on the jewelled **pommel**[20] of his sword. This was the Lord de Vere, who, when at home, was said to spend much of his time in the burial vault of his dead progenitors, **rummaging**[21] their mouldy coffins in search of all the earthly pride and vain glory, that was hidden among bones and dust; so that, besides his own share, he had the collected haughtiness of his whole line of ancestry.

Lastly, there was a handsome youth in rustic garb, and by his side, a blooming little person, in whom a delicate shade of maiden reserve was just melting into the rich glow of a young wife's affection. Her name was Hannah, and her husband's Matthew; two

13. immense
    adj. 巨大的；广大的
14. contort
    vt. 扭曲；扭弯；弄歪
15. prodigious
    adj. 巨大的；奇异的
16. deform
    vt. 使变形；使成畸形
17. woefully
    adv. 悲伤地；不幸地
18. have a smack of
    有种……的味道
19. mien
    n. 风采；态度
20. pommel
    n.（刀剑柄）圆头；
    马鞍的鞍桥
21. rummage
    vt. 到处翻寻；搜出

早晚祷告后都习惯一丝不挂地在一大堆松树先令——马萨诸塞州最早期的一种银币——中打滚，度过整整一小时。我们要注意到的第四个人，同伴们谁也不知道他叫什么名字，只要一看他那张瘦脸和那副大眼镜，就会辨认出来。这张脸总是被一丝冷笑扭曲，那副大眼镜则会使他看到的整个大自然变形失色。第五位冒险家同样缺名少姓，这非常遗憾，因为他似乎是一名诗人。他眼睛明亮，但不幸的是面容憔悴。如果像有些人断言的那样，他的日常饮食是晨光暮霭和伸手可得的一片最厚云彩，并用无论何时都能搞到的月光调味，他这样子也就再自然不过了。当然，从他心里涌出的诗句具有这一切佳肴的风味。这群人中的第六位是一个举止傲慢的年轻人，坐得离其他人有点远，在长者们中高高地戴着一顶羽毛帽，火光照在他华美的绣花衣服上闪闪发亮，照在他镶着宝石的圆头剑柄上更是闪闪发光，这就是德维尔勋爵，据说他在家时，总是花许多时间去自家祖先的墓地，在发霉的棺材里翻寻，寻找隐藏在骨粉中的一切世俗的自尊和虚荣，结果，除了他自己那份自尊和虚荣之外，他还收集了列祖列宗的傲慢气质。

　　最后，还有一位乡下打扮的英俊青年，他身边是一位妙龄少女，她的纯洁矜持的娇美气色正在渐渐化为年轻妻子柔情缱绻的红晕。她的名字叫汉娜，丈夫叫马修；两个名字都非常朴实，但对一对单纯的夫妻还算合适。在这群异想天开对大红宝石热切期待的人中，他俩

对六位探险者的描写——年龄、外貌、装束、性格，为他们最后的结局做了铺垫。

homely names, yet well enough adapted to the simple pair, who seemed strangely out of place among the **whimsical**[22] fraternity whose wits had been set agog by the Great Carbuncle.

Beneath the shelter of one hut, in the bright blaze of the same fire, sat this varied group of adventurers, all so intent upon a single object, that, of whatever else they began to speak, their closing words were sure to be **illuminated**[23] with the Great Carbuncle. Several related the circumstances that brought them thither. One had listened to a traveller's tale of this marvellous stone, in his own distant country, and had immediately been seized with such a thirst for beholding it, as could only be **quenched**[24] in its intensest lustre. Another, so long ago as when the famous Captain Smith visited these coasts, had seen it blazing far at sea, and had felt no rest in all the intervening years, till now that he took up the search. A third, being encamped on a hunting expedition, full forty miles south of the White Mountains, awoke at midnight, and beheld the Great Carbuncle gleaming like a meteor, so that the shadows of the trees fell backward from it. They spoke of the innumerable attempts, which had been made to reach the spot, and of the singular fatality which had **hitherto**[25] withheld success from all adventurers, though it might seem so easy to follow to its source a light that overpowered the moon, and almost matched the sun. It was observable that each smiled scornfully at the madness of every other, in anticipating better fortune than the past, yet nourished a scarcely hidden **conviction**[26], that he would himself be the favoured one. As if to allay their too **sanguine**[27] hopes, they recurred to the Indian traditions, that a spirit kept watch about the gem, and bewildered those who sought it, either by removing it from peak to peak of the higher hills, or by calling up a mist from the enchanted lake over which it hung. But these tales were deemed unworthy of credit; all professing to believe, that the search had been **baffled**[28] by want of **sagacity**[29] or

22. whimsical
adj. 心情浮动的；反复无常的；古怪的
23. illuminate
vt. 阐明；说明；照亮
24. quench
vt. 熄灭；压倒；满足
25. hitherto
adv. 迄今；至今
26. conviction
n. 深信；坚强信念
27. sanguine
adj. 乐观的；自信的
28. baffle
vt. 难住；使受挫折；阻碍
29. sagacity
n. 精明；敏锐；有远见

好像格格不入。

　　在同一座棚屋下面，在同一堆火光映照中，这群形形色色的冒险者坐在那里，全都专注于一个目标，无论是先开口说什么，最后肯定会说到大红宝石。有好几位讲到了把他们带到这里的详情。一位在自己遥远的国家听一个旅行者谈起这颗奇妙宝石，马上产生了一睹为快的渴望，只有红宝石最耀眼的光芒才能满足这种渴望。另一位早在大名鼎鼎的史密斯船长航行到这一带海域时，就在遥远的海上领略过它耀眼的光芒，所以这些年都心神不安，到现在才开始搜寻。第三位说，有一次，他出去打猎，在白山以南整整四十英里的地方扎营，半夜醒来，看到大红宝石像流星一样光芒四射，连树影都直往后退。他们谈到为寻找红宝石的下落做了无数次努力，还有到目前为止让所有冒险者都纷纷败退的奇特灾祸，尽管追寻比月亮更亮、简直亮似太阳的宝石光辉可能非常容易。可以看出，每个人都嘲笑所有其他人的愚蠢行为，认为比前人运气好，几乎掩饰不住自己一定走运的信念。好像为了减少过分乐观的希望，他们重新提起了那些印第安传说，说一位神灵在看护宝石，迷惑寻宝者，要么是把宝石从一座山的峰顶移到更高一座山的峰顶，要么是在悬着红宝石的魔湖上唤起一层薄雾。但是，这些传说都不足为信；所有人都表示相信，那些冒险者之所以失败，是因为不够睿智或缺乏毅力，要么就是错综复杂的森林、山谷、大山中的其他类似原因自然

对新婚夫妇的描写——男的英俊，女的娇美，都很单纯。他们与其他人格格不入。

既比喻又夸张，修辞运用自如。

perseverance[30] in the adventurers, or such other causes as might naturally obstruct the passage to any given point, among the **intricacies**[31] of forest, valley, and mountain.

In a pause of the conversation, the wearer of the prodigious spectacles looked round upon the party, making each individual, in turn, the object of the sneer which invariably dwelt upon his **countenance**[32].

"So, fellow-pilgrims," said he, "here we are, seven wise men and one fair damsel—who, doubtless, is as wise as any gray beard of the company: here we are, I say, all bound on the same goodly enterprise. Methinks now, it were not amiss, that each of us declare what he proposes to do with the Great Carbuncle, provided he have the good hap to clutch it. What says our friend in the bear-skin? How mean you, good Sir, to enjoy the prize which you have been seeking, the Lord knows how long, among the Crystal Hills?"

"How enjoy it!" exclaimed the aged Seeker, bitterly. "I hope for no enjoyment from it—that folly has past, long ago! I keep up the search for this accursed stone, because the vain ambition of my youth has become a fate upon me, in old age. The pursuit alone is my strength—the energy of my soul—the warmth of my blood, and the pith and marrow of my bones! Were I to turn my back upon it, I should fall down dead, on the hither side of the Notch, which is the gate-way of this mountain region. Yet, not to have my wasted life time back again, would I give up my hopes of the Great Carbuncle! Having found it, I shall bear it to a certain cavern that I wot of, and there, grasping it in my arms, lie down and die, and keep it buried with me for ever."

"Oh, wretch, regardless of the interests of science!" cried Doctor Cacaphodel, with philosophic indignation. "Thou art not worthy to behold, even from afar off, the lustre of this most precious gem that ever was concocted in the laboratory

30. perseverance
    n. 坚持不懈；不屈不挠
31. intricacy
    n. 纷乱；复杂；错综
32. countenance
    n. 面容；表情

而然地阻挡了他们奔向特定地点的通道。

谈话暂停时，那个戴大眼镜的人环顾大家，脸上总是带着冷笑，把每个人都一一变成了嘲讽的对象。

"那么，朝拜宝石的同伴们，"他说，"我们来了，七个英明的男人和一位美丽少女——毫无疑问，她像我们中任何一个白胡子老头一样聪明：嗨，我们来了，为了一项共同的大事业。我想，如果没错的话，我们每个人现在倒可以都来说说，假如他交好运找到了红宝石，他会怎么做。我们这位身穿熊皮的朋友说什么？好心的先生，你打算怎么享受一直在寻找的这个宝贝，天知道在这水晶山里找了多久？"

"怎么享受啊？"这位老寻宝者苦涩地叫道。"我没有指望从中得到什么快乐——这种傻念头早已过去了！我一直在寻找这块该死的石头，因为我年轻时虚荣的野心到了老年就会命定。只有追踪它，我才有力量——我灵魂的能量——我血液的暖流——我骨中的精髓！如果我不去找它，就会一头栽倒在这诺奇山坡上死掉。这是通往这个山区的门户啊。不过，如果不浪费一生，让时光倒流，我还是不会放弃找到大红宝石的希望！找到它后，我要把它带到我知道的某个洞窟里去，到了那里，把它抱在怀里，躺下来等死，把它和我永远埋在一起。"

"噢，倒霉蛋，居然不管科学的利益！"卡卡福代尔博士带着哲学家的愤怒叫道。"你不配看到这块最珍贵宝石的光辉，就连从远处看都不配，它是在大自然这

略述其中三人是什么原因让他们来此寻宝，为下文各自详述自己寻宝的缘由做引子。

以戴大眼镜者发问引出每个人寻宝的缘由，推动故事情节的发展。

年纪最大的觅宝者寻宝只是为了满足自己追寻宝石的欲望。

The Great Carbuncle 大红宝石 **147**

of Nature. Mine is the sole purpose for which a wise man may desire the possession of the Great Carbuncle. Immediately on obtaining it—for I have a **presentiment**[33], good people, that the prize is reserved to crown my scientific reputation—I shall return to Europe, and employ my remaining years in reducing it to its first elements. A portion of the stone will I grind to **impalpable**[34] powder; other parts shall be dissolved in acids, or whatever solvents will act upon so admirable a composition; and the remainder I design to melt in the crucible, or set on fire with the blow-pipe. By these various methods, I shall gain an accurate analysis, and finally bestow the result of my labours upon the world, in a folio volume."

"Excellent!" quoth the man with the spectacles. "Nor need you hesitate, learned Sir, on account of the necessary destruction of the gem; since the perusal of your folio may teach every mother's son of us to concoct a Great Carbuncle of his own."

"But, verily," said Master Ichabod Pigsnort, "for mine own part, I object to the making of these **counterfeits**[35], as being calculated to reduce the marketable value of the true gem. I tell ye frankly, Sirs, I have an interest in keeping up the price. Here have I quitted my regular traffic, leaving my warehouse in the care of my clerks, and putting my credit to great **hazard**[36], and furthermore, have put myself in peril of death or captivity by the accursed heathen savages—and all this without daring to ask the prayers of the **congregation**[37], because the quest for the Great Carbuncle is **deemed**[38] little better than a traffic with the evil one. Now think ye that I would have done this grievous wrong to my soul, body, reputation and estate, without a reasonable chance of profit?"

"Not I, **pious**[39] Master Pigsnort," said the man with the spectacles. "I never laid such a great folly to thy charge."

33. presentiment
   n. （尤指不祥的）预感；预觉
34. impalpable
   adj. 感觉不到的；触摸不着的
35. counterfeit
   n. 赝品；伪造品
36. hazard
   n. 危险；冒险；冒险的事
37. congregation
   n. 集会；集合；圣会
38. deem
   vt. 认为；视作；相信
39. pious
   adj. 虔诚的；尽责的

个实验室里配制的。这就是我唯一的目的，不过是一个哲人可能想拥有大红宝石。诸位，一得到它——我有一种预感，这宝贝是特地留给我的，使我在科学上获得登峰造极的声誉——我要回欧洲，把自己的余生都用来把它还原成最初的元素。我还要把一部分宝石研成细微的粉末，其他部分溶解于酸或别的任何能溶解这样绝妙合成物的溶剂；剩下的，我计划把它放进坩埚熔化，或者用吹风管焚烧。通过这些不同方法，我将得到一份精确分析，最终把我的劳动成果写成一部巨著，献给世界。"

那位化学家想要分析大红宝石的结构，以出版自己的研究及成果，使自己在科学研究上的荣誉达到顶峰。

"好极了！"那个戴眼镜的人说。"博学的先生，你也不必为有没有必要破坏这颗宝石而犹豫；因为熟读你的大作，就可以教我们每个人学会配制自己的大红宝石。"

"可是，说实话，"伊卡博德·皮戈斯诺特先生说，"依我看，我反对造这些假货，因为这样做会降低真宝石的市场价值。先生们，我坦率地告诉你们，保住它的价格对我至关重要。我撇下正常的生意，把仓库交给店员们照管，拿自己的信誉冒极大的风险，而且还会冒生命危险，或者被那些该死的异教徒野蛮人俘虏——凡此种种，却不敢请求教友们祷告，因为人们都认为，寻找大红宝石就和魔鬼打交道差不多。现在想想，我会这样痛苦地委屈自己的灵魂、肉体、名誉和财产，连从中获利的一个合理机会都没有吗？"

"我不会，虔诚的皮戈斯诺特先生，"那个戴大眼镜的人说。"我绝不认为你会傻到那种地步。"

"Truly, I hope not," said the merchant. "Now, as touching this Great Carbuncle, I am free to own that I have never had a glimpse of it; but be it only the hundredth part so bright as people tell, it will surely outvalue the Great Mogul's best diamond, which he holds at an incalculable sum. Wherefore, I am minded to put the Great Carbuncle on ship board, and voyage with it to England, France, Spain, Italy, or into Heathendom, if Providence[40] should send me thither, and, in a word, dispose of[41] the gem to the best bidder[42] among the potentates[43] of the earth, that he may place it among his crown jewels. If any of ye have a wiser plan, let him expound it."

"That have I, thou sordid man!" exclaimed the poet. "Dost thou desire nothing brighter than gold, that thou wouldst transmute[44] all this ethereal[45] lustre into such dross, as thou wallowest in[46] already? For myself, hiding the jewel under my cloak, I shall hie me back to my attic chamber, in one of the darksome alleys of London. There, night and day, will I gaze upon it—my soul shall drink its radiance—it shall be diffused throughout my intellectual powers, and gleam brightly in every line of poesy that I indite[47]. Thus, long ages after I am gone, the splendor of the Great Carbuncle will blaze around my name!"

"Well said, Master Poet!" cried he of the spectacles. "Hide it under that cloak, say'st thou? Why, it will gleam through the holes, and make thee look like a Jack-o'-lantern!"

"To think!" ejaculated[48] the Lord de Vere, rather to himself, than his companions, the best of whom he held utterly unworthy of his intercourse, "to think that a fellow in a tattered[49] cloak should talk of conveying the Great Carbuncle to a garret[50] in Grub street! Have not I resolved within myself, that the whole earth contains no fitter ornament for the great hall of my ancestral castle? There

---

40. Providence
   n. 天意；天命；上帝
41. dispose of
   解决；处理；转让
   或卖掉
42. bidder
   n. 投标人；出价人
43. potentate
   n. 有权势的人；当
   权者；统治者
44. transmute
   vt. 使变形；使变质
45. ethereal
   adj. 天上的；轻
   的；虚无缥缈的
46. wallow in
   沉湎于；打滚
47. indite
   vt. 写；作（文）；
   赋（诗）
48. ejaculate
   vi. 突然激动地说
   话；喊叫
49. tattered
   adj. 破烂的；穿破烂
   衣的
50. garret
   n. 阁楼；顶楼；头

"的确，我希望不是，"商人说。"现在，我直率承认自己连一眼都没见过这颗大红宝石，但它只要有人们说的百分之一那样亮，就肯定会比莫卧儿大帝视为无价之宝的那颗最好的钻石更有价值。因此，我打算把大红宝石带上船，随它航行到英国、法国、西班牙、意大利，或者只要上帝派我去，还可以去异教徒的国家，总之，把这颗宝石卖给世界上愿出最高价的君王，他可以把它镶在自己的王冠上。如果你们谁有更明智的计划，那就阐明一下。"

"我有，你这个利欲熏心之徒！"诗人大声叫道。"难道你以为没有比黄金更亮的东西，你就要把这颗宝石非凡的光芒变成你曾经在里面打滚的渣滓吗？对我自己来说，我把宝石藏在斗篷下面，马上回到伦敦那条黑胡同里我的阁楼间去。在那里，我日日夜夜都要凝视它——我的灵魂将会汲取它的光辉——我所有的智力将会遍布其中，并在我写下的每一行诗中闪耀光芒。因此，我死去多年后，大红宝石的光彩仍会照耀我的名字！"

"说得好，大诗人！"那个戴大眼镜的人大声说道。"你是说把它藏在那个斗篷下面吗？啊，它会从斗篷的那些窟窿里透出光来，让你像一盏空心南瓜灯！"

"想想看！"德维尔勋爵突然说道，不是对同伴，而是对自己，认为他们中最出色的人也完全不配和他交谈，"想想看，一个披着破旧斗篷的家伙竟说要把大红宝石带到格拉布街的阁楼上去！我不是早就决定，整个

商人想获得它，以卖出一个好价钱而大发横财。

诗人想从宝石那里获得灵感，并最终为自己获得文学上的声誉。

shall it flame for ages, making a noonday of midnight, glittering on the suits of armour, the banners, and **escutcheons**[51], that hang around the wall, and keeping bright the memory of heroes. Wherefore have all other adventurers sought the prize in vain, but that I might win it, and make it a symbol of the glories of our lofty line? And never, on the **diadem**[52] of the White Mountains, did the Great Carbuncle hold a place half so honored, as is reserved for it in the hall of the de Veres!"

"It is a noble thought," said the Cynic, with an **obsequious**[53] sneer. "Yet, might I presume to say so, the gem would make a rare **sepulchral**[54] lamp, and would display the glories of your lordship's **progenitors**[55] more truly in the ancestral vault, than in the castle hall."

"Nay, forsooth," observed Matthew, the young rustic, who sat hand in hand with his bride, "the gentleman has bethought himself of a profitable use for this bright stone. Hannah here and I are seeking it for a like purpose."

"How, fellow!" exclaimed his lordship, in surprise. "What castle hall hast thou to hang it in?"

"No castle," replied Matthew, "but as neat a cottage as any within sight of the Crystal Hills. Ye must know, friends, that Hannah and I, being wedded the last week, have taken up the search of the Great Carbuncle, because we shall need its light in the long winter evenings; and it will be such a pretty thing to show the neighbors, when they visit us. It will shine through the house, so that we may pick up a pin in any corner, and will set all the windows a-glowing, as if there were a great fire of pine knots in the chimney. And then how pleasant, when we awake in the night, to be able to see one another's faces!"

There was a general smile among the adventurers, at

51. escutcheon
　　n. 饰有纹章的盾
52. diadem
　　n. 王权；王冠；帝王的尊严（或荣耀）
53. obsequious
　　adj. 谄媚的；奉承的；（态度上）讨好的
54. sepulchral
　　adj. 阴森森的；坟墓的；丧葬的
55. progenitor
　　n. 祖先；先辈

世界上再没有比大红宝石更适合装饰我祖传城堡大厅的吗？它将在那里永放光芒，使午夜亮如正午的阳光，照耀在挂在墙壁上的铠甲、旗帜和盾徽上，使英雄们流芳百世。因此，其他所有冒险者都是白找一场，而是让我赢得它，并把它作为我们崇高家族荣耀的象征吗？再说，白山顶上的这块大红宝石从来没有过比德维尔家大厅为它保留的位置那样荣耀的地位呐！"

"这真是一种高尚的想法。"讽刺家嘲笑说。"不过，我能否冒昧说一句，用红宝石做上一盏罕见的墓灯，照亮你的先人墓穴，这比挂在你家城堡大厅更能展示你先人的荣耀。"

"不，当然，"年轻的乡下人马修说，他和新娘手拉手坐在那里。"这位先生为这块发光的石头想到了一个好用场。我和汉娜找它的目的也一样。"

"什么，伙计！"勋爵惊叫道。"你有什么城堡配挂它吗？"

"没有什么城堡，"马修回答说，"只有一座和水晶山这一带一样干净的房子。朋友们，你们一定知道，我和汉娜上周才结婚，就开始寻找大红宝石了，因为我们在漫漫冬夜需要它照明；而且，邻居们来看我们时，也可以给他们看看这么漂亮的东西。它会把整个房子照亮，我们可以在任何角落捡起掉落的一根针。还会让所有窗户都亮堂，就像烟囱里烧有一堆松节的大火一样。那样的话，我们半夜醒来时能看清彼此的脸，会多么开心！"

那些冒险者听到这对年轻人的简单打算都露出了微

爵士寻宝是为进一步加强他家族的显赫地位。

这对新婚夫妇想用大红宝石照亮他们漫长冬夜里的小屋，为他们的邻居指路。相对于其他人的动机而言，新婚夫妇的动机要纯洁得多，所以也只有他俩才能见到宝石，同时不被宝石的光芒所伤害。

the simplicity of the young couple's project, in regard to this wondrous and invaluable stone, with which the greatest monarch on earth might have been proud to adorn his palace. Especially the man with spectacles, who had sneered at all the company in turn, now twisted his visage[56] into such an expression of ill-natured mirth, that Matthew asked him, rather peevishly[57], what he himself meant to do with the Great Carbuncle.

"The Great Carbuncle!" answered the Cynic, with ineffable[58] scorn. "Why, you blockhead, there is no such thing, in rerum natura. I have come three thousand miles, and am resolved to set my foot on every peak of these mountains, and poke my head into every chasm[59], for the sole purpose of demonstrating[60] to the satisfaction of any man, one whit less an ass than thyself, that the Great Carbuncle is all a humbug!"

Vain and foolish were the motives that had brought most of the adventurers to the Crystal Hills, but none so vain, so foolish, and so impious[61] too, as that of the scoffer with the prodigious spectacles. He was one of those wretched and evil men, whose yearnings are downward to the darkness, instead of Heavenward, and who, could they but extinguish[62] the lights which God hath kindled for us, would count the midnight gloom their chiefest glory. As the Cynic spoke, several of the party were startled by a gleam of red splendor, that showed the huge shapes of the surrounding mountains, and the rock-bestrewn bed of the turbulent river, with an illumination[63] unlike that of their fire, on the trunks and black boughs of the forest trees. They listened for the roll of thunder, but heard nothing, and were glad that the tempest came not near them. The stars, those dial-points of Heaven, now warned the adventurers to close their eyes on the blazing logs, and open them, in dreams, to the glow of the Great Carbuncle.

The young married couple had taken their lodgings in the furthest corner of the wigwam, and were separated from the rest

56. visage
n. 脸；面貌；容貌
57. peevishly
adv. 暴躁地
58. ineffable
adj. 言语难以表达、难以形容的；不可言喻的
59. chasm
n. 峡谷；深坑；裂口
60. demonstrate
vt. 证明；展示；表明
61. impious
adj. 不信教的；不虔诚的
62. extinguish
vt. 熄灭（灯等）；灭（火）；扑灭（火等）
63. illumination
n. 照明；照亮

笑，因为就是世界上最伟大的君王都可能会采用这块美妙无价的宝石装饰自己的豪宅为荣。尤其是那位戴大眼镜的人，他已经逐个嘲笑了所有的人，现在他的脸扭曲成了恶意的笑容。马修有些恼火地问他，他自己想怎么利用大红宝石。

"大红宝石！"讽刺家脸上带着难以形容的轻蔑表情回答说。"啊，你这个笨蛋，实际上根本没有这种东西。我已经走了三千英里，下定决心踏上这些山的每座峰顶，把头探进每条峡谷，就为了一个目的，要让没有你那么蠢的任何人确信，大红宝石纯粹是骗人的鬼话！"

大多数来水晶山的冒险者的动机都自负愚蠢，但谁也没有这个戴大眼镜的嘲世者更自负、更愚蠢和更邪恶。他是那种卑鄙邪恶的家伙，向往的是地狱里的黑暗而不是天堂。这种人如果能熄灭上帝为我们点燃的明灯，就会把午夜的昏暗看成他们最大的荣耀。这位嘲世者讲话时，众人中有几个人被一道灿烂的红光吓了一跳，这红光照亮了四周的崇山峻岭和汹涌澎湃、岩石遍布的河床，不像映照在树干黑枝上的火光。他们等着听轰隆隆的雷声，但什么也没有听到，他们庆幸暴风雨没有袭击他们。满天繁星——天堂的那些指针——现在警告那些冒险者闭上眼睛不看熊熊燃烧的柴火，而到梦中对着大红宝石的光芒打开眼睛。

过渡段——从梦想到现实。

那对年轻的新婚夫妇在棚屋最远的角落寄宿，凭借一道用细枝精心编织的屏障和其他人隔离开来，这道

of the party by a curtain of curiously woven twigs, such as might have hung, in deep **festoons**[64] around the bridal bower of Eve. The modest little wife had wrought this piece of **tapestry**[65], while the other guests were talking. She and her husband fell asleep with hands tenderly clasped, and awoke, from visions of unearthly radiance, to meet the more blessed light of one another's eyes. They awoke at the same instant, and with one happy smile beaming over their two faces, which grew brighter, with their consciousness of the reality of life and love. But no sooner did she recollect where they were, than the bride peeped through the **interstices**[66] of the leafy curtain, and saw that the outer room of the hut was deserted.

"Up, dear Matthew!" cried she, in haste. "The strange folk are all gone! Up, this very minute, or we shall lose the Great Carbuncle!"

In truth, so little did these poor young people deserve the mighty prize which had lured them thither, that they had slept peacefully all night, and till the summits of the hills were glittering with sunshine; while the other adventurers had tossed their limbs in feverish wakefulness, or dreamed of climbing precipices, and set off to realize their dreams with the earliest peep of dawn. But Matthew and Hannah, after their calm rest, were as light as two young deer, and merely stopped to say their prayers, and wash themselves in a cold pool of the Amonoosuck, and then to taste a morsel of food, ere they turned their faces to the mountain-side. It was a sweet emblem of **conjugal**[67] affection, as they toiled up the difficult ascent, gathering strength from the mutual aid which they afforded. After several little accidents, such as a torn robe, a lost shoe, and the **entanglement**[68] of Hannah's hair in a bough, they reached the upper verge of the forest, and were now to pursue a more adventurous course. The innumerable trunks and heavy

64. festoon
n. （如家具、建筑物上的）垂花（雕）饰
65. tapestry
n. 织锦；挂毯；绣帷
66. interstice
n. 细裂缝；空隙
67. conjugal
adj. 婚姻的；结婚的；夫妻之间的
68. entanglement
n. 纠缠；牵连

屏障就像夏娃新房悬挂的层层花彩。是那位羞怯的新娘在其他客人交谈时编织了这块挂毯。她和丈夫体贴地手拉手进入了梦乡，然后又从神秘光辉的梦境中苏醒，相互交换更愉快的目光。他们同时醒来，脸上带着同样幸福的微笑，想到鲜活的生命和爱情，他们的微笑更加亮丽。但一想到他们身在何处，新娘就透过那块树叶挂毯向外窥视，只见棚屋外间空无一人。

"起来，亲爱的马修！"她赶忙叫道。"那伙怪人全都走了！快起来，不然我们就要错过大红宝石了！"

其实，这对贫穷的年轻人完全不配得到引诱他们来这里的巨大珍品。因为他们酣睡了整整一夜，直到阳光普照山顶；其他冒险者则兴奋难眠，辗转反侧，或做梦都在攀登悬崖峭壁，天刚一透亮就出发圆自己的梦去了。但是，马修和汉娜安歇之后，像两只小鹿似的脚下生风，只停下来祷告了一会儿，并在阿莫诺沙克河的冷水潭里洗了洗脸，然后吃了点东西，就转向山腰开始爬坡。他们艰难跋涉向上攀登时，相濡以沫，汲取力量，这是夫妻情深的甜蜜象征。经过了好几次小事故——衣服挂破，鞋子跑丢，汉娜头发缠到了树枝上，他们才到达了森林上缘，眼前是一段更危险的道路。至今数不清的树干和稠密的树叶禁锢了他们的思绪，现在他们面对头顶的山风、白云、裸露的岩石、孤独的阳光，不由惊慌退缩起来。他们回头望了望穿过的那片昏暗的茫茫森林，渴望再次进入森林深处，而不要把自己交给如此辽

两位心地善良的年轻夫妻一觉醒来，发现其他的寻宝者已经先他们离去。作者隐喻八个寻宝人实际是两组。年轻夫妻为一组，其他六人为一组。接着描写两组寻宝人的寻宝的经历和结局。

The Great Carbuncle 大红宝石 **151**

foliage of the trees had hitherto shut in their thoughts, which now shrank affrighted from the region of wind, and cloud, and naked rocks, and desolate sunshine, that rose immeasurably above them. They gazed back at the obscure wilderness which they had traversed[69], and longed to be buried again in its depths, rather than trust themselves to so vast and visible a solitude.

"Shall we go on?" said Matthew, throwing his arm round Hannah's waist, both to protect her, and to comfort his heart by drawing her close to it.

But the little bride, simple as she was, had a woman's love of jewels, and could not forgo the hope of possessing the very brightest in the world, in spite of the perils with which it must be won.

"Let us climb a little higher," whispered she, yet tremulously[70], as she turned her face upward to the lonely sky.

"Come then," said Matthew, mustering his manly courage, and drawing her along with him; for she became timid again, the moment that he grew bold.

And upward, accordingly, went the pilgrims of the Great Carbuncle, now treading upon the tops and thickly interwoven branches of dwarf pines, which, by the growth of centuries, though mossy with age, had barely reached three feet in altitude. Next, they came to masses and fragments of naked rock, heaped confusedly together, like a cairn reared by giants, in memory of a giant chief. In this bleak realm of upper air, nothing breathed, nothing grew; there was no life but what was concentred in their two hearts; they had climbed so high, that Nature herself seemed no longer to keep them company. She lingered beneath them, within the verge of the forest trees, and sent a farewell glance after her children, as they strayed where her own green footprints had never been. But soon they were to be hidden from her eye. Densely and dark, the mists began to gather below, casting black spots of shadow on the vast landscape, and sailing heavily to one

69. traverse
vt. 横越；穿过；经过
70. tremulous
adv. 发抖地；胆小地；害怕地

阔如此鲜明的一片荒凉。

"我们还继续向上爬吗？" 马修说着，伸出一只手臂搂住汉娜的腰，既是保护她，也是为贴近她，好使自己得到安慰。

不过，小新娘虽然天真，却具有女人喜爱宝石的天性，无法放弃拥有世界上最灿烂宝石的希望，哪怕为此必须历尽艰难险阻。

"我们再向高处爬一点，" 她低声说道；然而，她仰望荒凉的天空时，声音颤抖。

"那就来吧，" 马修说着，鼓起阳刚之气，拉起她就走，因为他壮起胆子时，她又羞怯起来。

于是，两个红宝石朝拜者向上攀登，一路踩踏矮小却枝繁叶密盘根错节的松树枝、松树梢。这些松树生长了几百年，尽管因年久而生满苔藓，但几乎还不到三英尺高。接下来，他们又来到一片片乱七八糟堆在一起的裸露岩石间，就像是一座由巨人们堆起的纪念他们大头领的石冢。在这片荒凉的高空地带，无声无息，没有东西生长；只有在他们两颗心中的生命。他们爬得这么高，大自然都好像无法再和他们做伴了。大自然游移在他们的下面，游移在森林的边缘，并向他们投来告别的一瞥，目送她的孩子们走向她自己的绿色足迹从未到过的地方。但是，她很快就看不到他们了。浓密黑暗的雾霭开始在下面聚集，给辽阔的景色投下了一块块黑影，密密地飘往一处，好似最高的山峰召集与之亲近的云朵

一路上他们互相扶助，为了一个单纯简单的目的寻找着宝石，为他们最终看到宝石做了铺垫。

centre, as if the loftiest mountain peak had summoned a council of its **kindred**[71] clouds. Finally, the vapors welded themselves, as it were, into a mass, presenting the appearance of a pavement over which the wanderers might have trodden, but where they would vainly have sought an avenue to the blessed earth which they had lost. And the lovers yearned to behold that green earth again, more intensely, alas! than, beneath a clouded sky, they had ever desired a glimpse of Heaven. They even felt it a relief to their desolation, when the mists, creeping gradually up the mountain, concealed its lonely peak, and thus **annihilated**[72], at least for them, the whole region of visible space. But they drew closer together, with a fond and **melancholy**[73] gaze, dreading lest the universal cloud should snatch them from each other's sight.

Still, perhaps, they would have been resolute to climb as far and as high, between earth and heaven, as they could find foothold, if Hannah's strength had not begun to fail, and with that, her courage also. Her breath grew short. She refused to burthen her husband with her weight, but often **tottered**[74] against his side, and recovered herself each time by a feebler effort. At last, she sank down on one of the rocky steps of the **acclivity**[75].

"We are lost, dear Matthew," said she, mournfully. "We shall never find our way to the earth again. And, Oh, how happy we might have been in our cottage!"

"Dear heart!—we will yet be happy there," answered Matthew. "Look! In this direction, the sunshine penetrates the dismal mist. By its aid, I can direct our course to the passage of the Notch. Let us go back, love, and dream no more of the Great Carbuncle!"

"The sun cannot be yonder," said Hannah, with despondence. "By this time, it must be noon. If there could ever be any sunshine here, it would come from above our heads."

"But, look!" repeated Matthew, in a somewhat altered tone.

71. kindred
   adj. 相似的；同类的
72. annihilate
   vi. 湮没；湮灭
73. melancholy
   adj. 忧郁的；使人悲伤的；愁思的
74. totter
   vi. 摇晃；摇动；蹒跚；踉跄
75. acclivity
   n. 向上的陡坡

前来聚会。最后，层层雾霭好像化为一团，呈现出一条通天大道，仿佛两个流浪者可以走在上面，只是他们一旦离开幸福大地，就再也找不到回路。唉！这对恋人渴望再次看到绿色大地，比当初在乌云密布的天空下渴望看一眼天堂更加强烈。雾霭渐渐爬上山头，笼罩住了孤峰，于是完全湮没了他们的视野，这倒至少减轻了他们的孤独感。不过，他们挨得更紧，深情而忧郁地对望，唯恐漫天云雾夺走对方。

描写风景，如神来之笔，上天入地，纵横交错，让人留连忘返。

然而，要不是汉娜开始体力不支，勇气随之减少，他们本来会坚定不移，只要能找到立足点，就要在天地间爬得更高更远。她气喘吁吁，不愿拖累丈夫，但又常常摇摇晃晃靠在他身上，重新站稳的力气越来越弱。最后，她倒在了岩石遍地的一个山坡上。

"亲爱的马修，我们迷路了，"她伤心地说。"再也找不到回到地面的路了。还有，噢，我们在小屋里本来是多么开心啊！"

"宝贝心肝！——我们还会回到那里，"马修回答说。"看！阳光从这个方向穿透了阴霾。凭借这一点，我可以找到我们回峡谷的通道。亲爱的，我们回去吧，别再梦想大红宝石了！"

"太阳不可能在那边，"汉娜沮丧地说。"到现在，一定是中午了。如果这里可能还有阳光的话，就会从我们的头顶照下来。"

"可是，你看！"马修语调有些变化地重复道。

The Great Carbuncle 大红宝石 155

"It is brightening every moment. If not sunshine, what can it be?"

Nor could the young bride any longer deny, that a radiance was breaking through the mist, and changing its dim hue to a dusky red, which continually grew more vivid, as if brilliant particles were **interfused**[76] with the gloom. Now, also, the cloud began to roll away from the mountain, while, as it heavily withdrew, one object after another started out of its impenetrable obscurity into sight, with precisely the effect of a new creation, before the indistinctness of the old chaos had been completely swallowed up. As the process went on, they saw the gleaming of water close at their feet, and found themselves on the very border of a mountain lake, deep, bright, clear, and calmly beautiful, spreading from brim to brim of a basin that had been scooped out of the solid rock. A ray of glory flashed across its surface. The pilgrims looked whence it should proceed, but closed their eyes with a thrill of awful admiration, to exclude the fervid splendor that glowed from the brow of a cliff, **impending over**[77] the enchanted lake. For the simple pair had reached that lake of mystery, and found the long sought shrine of the Great Carbuncle!

They threw their arms around each other, and trembled at their own success; for, as the legends of this wondrous gem rushed thick upon their memory, they felt themselves marked out by fate—and the consciousness was fearful. Often, from childhood upward, they had seen it shining like a distant star. And now that star was throwing its intensest lustre on their hearts. They seemed changed to one another's eyes, in the red brilliancy that flamed upon their cheeks, while it lent the same fire to the lake, the rocks, and sky, and to the mists which had rolled back before its power. But, with their next glance, they beheld an object that drew their attention even from the mighty stone. At the base of the cliff, directly beneath the Great Carbuncle, appeared the figure of a man, with his arms extended

76. interfuse
    vt. 使融合；使混合
77. impend over
    逼近

"这光越来越亮。要不是阳光，这还能是什么？"

年轻的新娘也无法否认，一道光亮正穿破雾霭，把昏暗的色调变成了暗红色，暗红色变得越来越鲜艳，好像阴暗中渗入了灿烂的微粒。这时，山顶的云也开始远离大山，随着浓云退去，山上的景物一个接一个地从无法穿透的昏暗中显现出来。这就像旧的混沌被完全吞没之前，新的生命正好诞生的效果一样。随着眼前的变化，他们看到脚边有一片水光，原来是到了一个山湖岸边。山湖从坚固的岩石中凹出一个水潭，湖水幽深明亮，澄澈宁静，美不目瑕。一道灿烂光芒闪过湖面。两位寻宝者想看看这光从何而来，但因极度兴奋和赞叹而闭上了眼睛，避开魔湖上方悬崖上射出的炽热光芒。原来这对朴实的夫妻已经来到那个神秘湖畔，找到了人们苦苦寻觅的大红宝石圣地！

他们彼此拥抱，为自己的成功而颤抖，因为这个奇妙宝石的种种传说潮水般涌上他们的记忆，他们感到自己竟被命运挑中，反而胆怯起来。从孩提时代起，他们就常常看到它像一颗遥远的星星闪闪发亮。现在，那颗星星正把最强烈的光芒照在他们的心上。他们在彼此的眼里好像变了模样，灿烂的红光在他们的脸颊上燃烧，同样的火光映红了湖水、岩石、天空，也映红了在它的威风面前吓得退去的雾霭。但是，他们又看了一眼，只见一件东西把他们的注意力从那颗大宝石吸引开来。在悬崖底部，红宝石正下方出现一个人的身影，只见他伸

作者用大量的笔墨详述这对年轻夫妻寻找红宝石的过程，包括环境、动作、心理和语言。与下面略写其他几人寻宝过程形成对照。

两个单纯善良的年轻人终于见到了大红宝石。

in the act of climbing, and his face turned upward, as if to drink the full gush[78] of splendor. But he stirred not, no more than if changed to marble.

"It is the Seeker," whispered Hannah, convulsively[79] grasping her husband's arm. "Matthew, he is dead!"

"The joy of success has killed him," replied Matthew, trembling violently. "Or perhaps the very light of the Great Carbuncle was death!"

"The Great Carbuncle," cried a peevish voice behind them. "The Great Humbug! If you have found it, prithee point it out to me."

They turned their heads, and there was the Cynic, with his prodigious spectacles set carefully on his nose, staring now at the lake, now at the rocks, now at the distant masses of vapor, now right at the Great Carbuncle itself, yet seemingly as unconscious of its light, as if all the scattered clouds were condensed[80] about his person. Though its radiance actually threw the shadow of the unbeliever at his own feet, as he turned his back upon the glorious jewel, he would not be convinced that there was the least glimmer there.

"Where is your Great Humbug?" he repeated. "I challenge you to make me see it!"

"There," said Matthew, incensed at such perverse blindness, and turning the Cynic round towards the illuminated cliff. "Take off those abominable[81] spectacles, and you cannot help seeing it!"

Now these colored spectacles probably darkened the Cynic's sight, in at least as great a degree as the smoked glasses through which people gaze at an eclipse. With resolute bravado[82], however, he snatched them from his nose, and fixed a bold stare full upon the ruddy blaze of the Great Carbuncle. But, scarcely had he encountered it, when, with a deep, shuddering groan, he dropt his head, and pressed both hands across his miserable

78. gush
   n. 涌出；迸发
79. convulsively
   adv. 痉挛性地；惊厥地
80. condense
   vt. 使浓缩；使冷凝
81. abominable
   adj. 讨厌的；令人憎恶的
82. bravado
   n. 装作有信心的样子；虚张声势；冒险

出双臂，做出攀登的样子，仰起脸，仿佛要啜饮宝石的光芒。然而，他一动不动，就像是化成了大理石。

"那是'寻宝者'，"汉娜低声说，痉挛般抓住丈夫的胳膊，"马修，他死了！"

"成功的喜悦害死了他，"马修剧烈颤抖着回答说。"或许大红宝石的光正是死亡之光！"

"大红宝石，"他们身后传来一个怒气冲冲的声音。"大骗局！如果你们找到了它，就请指给我看。"

他们回过头，原来是那个讽刺家，鼻梁上小心翼翼地架着那副大眼镜，时而盯着湖面，时而盯着岩石，时而盯着远方的水汽，时而正对大红宝石，但他好像没有感觉到它的光芒，仿佛所有四散的云彩都聚集在他的四周。尽管大红宝石的光芒的确把这位异教徒的身影投在了他自己的脚下，但他还是不相信那里有什么闪光，因为他正背对着那块灿烂的宝石。

"你们的大骗局在哪里？"他又问道。"我要你们让我看它一眼！"

"在那里！"马修说，对他这样刚愎自用、闭眼瞎说非常生气，他让讽刺家转向那个闪亮的悬崖。"取掉那副可恶的眼镜，要看不见它才怪啦！"

现在这副有色眼镜可能模糊了讽刺家的视线，至少和人们透过烟色玻璃观看日食的程度一样。然而，他下定决心，虚张声势从鼻子上拽下眼镜，勇敢大胆地直盯着大红宝石的红光。但是，他刚遇到那光芒，就低下

略写。"寻宝者"见到了他梦寐以求的红宝石。由疯癫走向了死亡。

The Great Carbuncle 大红宝石

159

eyes. Thenceforth there was, in very truth, no light of the Great Carbuncle, nor any other light on earth, nor light of Heaven itself, for the poor Cynic. So long accustomed to view all objects through a medium that deprived them of every glimpse of brightness, a single flash of so glorious a phenomenon, striking upon his naked vision, had blinded him forever.

"Matthew," said Hannah, clinging to him, "let us go hence!"

Matthew saw that she was faint, and kneeling down, supported her in his arms, while he threw some of the thrillingly cold water of the enchanted lake upon her face and bosom. It revived her, but could not **renovate**[83] her courage.

"Yes, dearest!" cried Matthew, pressing her tremulous form to his breast, "we will go hence, and return to our humble cottage. The blessed sunshine, and the quiet moonlight, shall come through our window. We will kindle the cheerful glow of our hearth, at eventide, and be happy in its light. But never again will we desire more light than all the world may share with us."

"No," said his bride, "for how could we live by day, or sleep by night, in this awful blaze of the Great Carbuncle!"

Out of the hollow of their hands, they drank each a draught from the lake, which presented them its water **uncontaminated**[84] by an earthly lip. Then, lending their guidance to the blinded Cynic, who uttered not a word, and even stifled his groans in his own most wretched heart, they began to descend the mountain. Yet, as they left the shore, till then untrodden, of the Spirit's lake, they threw a farewell glance towards the cliff, and beheld the vapors gathering in dense volumes, through which the gem burned duskily.

As touching the other pilgrims of the Great Carbuncle, the legend goes on to tell, that the worshipful Master Ichabod

83. renovate
vt. 使恢复精力；使振作
84. uncontaminated
adj. 未被污染的；未沾染的

了头，发出一声深沉颤抖的呻吟，两手按在他那双可怜的眼睛上。从那时起，千真万确，这位可怜的讽刺家就再也看不到大红宝石的光，也看不到世界上任何其他的光，更看不到天堂的光。他早就习惯通过剥夺所有东西光亮的大眼镜来观看一切，所以红宝石只闪了一下，照到了他的肉眼上，就使他永远瞎了。

"马修，"汉娜依偎着他说，"那我们走吧！"

马修看到她晕晕乎乎，就跪下来，把她抱在怀里扶她起来，从魔湖里撩起冰冷刺骨的湖水，洒在她的脸上和胸前。这使她苏醒了过来，但无法让她重新鼓起勇气。

"是，最亲爱的！"马修把她颤抖的身体紧紧贴在自己胸前，"那咱们走，回到咱们的寒舍。神圣的阳光和恬静的月光会照进咱们家的窗户。傍晚时分，咱们会点燃欢快的炉火，在它的光照中开开心心。咱们再也犯不着渴望比世人共享的光更多的光了。"

"是啊，"新娘说，"在大红宝石可怕的光照中，咱们白天怎么生活，夜里怎么睡觉！"

他们双手从湖里掬起水喝下，这水还从来没有被任何凡人的嘴唇沾过。随后，他们领着眼睛失明的讽刺家开始下山。这个人一言不发，连他的呻吟也窒息在自己最痛苦的心里。然而，他们离开此前无人涉足的神湖岸边时，向悬崖投去告别的一瞥，看到水汽密集凝聚，宝石穿过雾霭，朦胧闪光。

至于大红宝石的其他几位朝拜者，相传可敬的伊卡

略写。戴大眼镜的愤世嫉俗者，是寻宝者中的另类，当他摘下那使大自然变形变色，把一切都变得暗淡无光的大眼镜时，宝石之光灼伤了他的眼睛，使他失明。

尽管这对新婚夫妇见到了宝石，但经过慎重考虑，他们决定放弃。他们渴望能再回到绿色大地，这种渴望远比想要看一眼天堂的那种渴望要强烈得多。于是，他们不再追求那种虚幻的超自然的光辉，而去寻求尘世间更现实的幸福。

The Great Carbuncle 大红宝石

85. speculation
   n. 一番思考；思考
   过程；思索
86. betake
   vt. 使致力于；专心
   于；使前往
87. folio
   n. 对开本
88. chandelier
   n. 枝形吊灯（烛
   台）
89. pomp
   n. 盛况；浮华；壮
   丽；夸耀

Pigsnort soon gave up the quest, as a desperate **speculation**[85], and wisely resolved to **betake**[86] himself again to his warehouse, near the town-dock, in Boston. But, as he passed through the Notch of the mountains, a war party of Indians captured our unlucky merchant, and carried him to Montreal, there holding him in bondage, till, by the payment of a heavy ransom, he had wofully subtracted from his hoard of pine-tree shillings. By his long absence, moreover, his affairs had become so disordered, that, for the rest of his life, instead of wallowing in silver, he had seldom a sixpence worth of copper. Doctor Cacaphodel, the alchemist, returned to his laboratory with a prodigious fragment of granite, which he ground to powder, dissolved in acids, melted in the crucible, and burnt with the blow-pipe, and published the result of his experiments in one of the heaviest **folios**[87] of the day. And, for all these purposes, the gem itself could not have answered better than the granite. The poet, by a somewhat similar mistake, made prize of a great piece of ice, which he found in a sunless chasm of the mountains, and swore that it corresponded, in all points, with his idea of the Great Carbuncle. The critics say, that, if his poetry lacked the splendor of the gem, it retained all the coldness of the ice. The Lord de Vere went back to his ancestral hall, where he contented himself with a wax-lighted **chandelier**[88], and filled, in due course of time, another coffin in the ancestral vault. As the funeral torches gleamed within that dark receptacle, there was no need of the Great Carbuncle to show the vanity of earthly **pomp**[89].

The Cynic, having cast aside his spectacles, wandered about the world, a miserable object, and was punished with an agonizing desire of light, for the wilful blindness of his former life. The whole night long, he would lift his splendor-blasted orbs to the

博德·皮戈斯诺特先生很快就放弃了寻找，认为这个买卖非常危险，聪明地决定撤回到自己的货栈，货栈就在波士顿市的码头附近。但他穿过山峡时，一个印第安远征队抓住了我们这个倒霉的商人，把他带到蒙特利尔关了起来，直到他从自己那堆松树先令中伤心地拿出一大笔赎金。而且，因为他这么久不在家，生意已经变得一塌糊涂，所以他后半生不仅不能在银子里打滚，连价值六便士的铜板都很少有。炼金术士卡卡福代尔博士带着一大块花岗石回到自己的实验室，把这东西研成粉末，溶解在酸液中，倒进坩埚熔化，用吹风管点火燃烧，然后把实验的结果写成了当时最重的一卷对开本的书。而且，为了所有这些目的，红宝石本身不可能比那块花岗石更好。而那位诗人，也犯了一个稍微类似的错误，把从大山阴暗处裂缝里发现的一大块冰当成了宝贝，并发誓说这东西各方面都和他想象的大红宝石一样。评论家们说，即使他的诗缺乏那块宝石的灿烂光辉，它也保留有这块冰的一切寒冷。那位德维尔勋爵呢，回到了祖居大厅，对点蜡烛的枝形吊灯心满意足；到了时间，他就会装入祖墓的另一口棺材。因为葬礼的火把在黑暗的墓道里闪光，所以无须大红宝石来炫耀世俗的浮华和虚荣。

愤世嫉俗者扔掉眼镜，满世界流浪，成了可怜虫，因为他以前有意对一切都视而不见，如今受到了惩罚，总是痛苦地渴望光明。整夜整夜，他都抬起那双被光芒

名著的力量

世界经典

名家名作赏析——传奇篇

90. idolater
   n. 崇拜者；皈依者
91. credence
   n. 信任；凭证
92. opaque
   adj. 不反光的；不
   发亮的；暗的；不
   透明的

moon and stars; he turned his face eastward, at sunrise, as duly as a Persian idolater[90]; he made a pilgrimage to Rome, to witness the magnificent illumination of Saint Peter's Church; and finally perished in the great fire of London, into the midst of which he had thrust himself, with the desperate idea of catching one feeble ray from the blaze, that was kindling earth and heaven.

Matthew and his bride spent many peaceful years, and were fond of telling the legend of the Great Carbuncle. The tale, however, towards the close of their lengthened lives, did not meet with the full credence[91] that had been accorded to it by those, who remembered the ancient lustre of the gem. For it is affirmed, that, from the hour when two mortals had shown themselves so simply wise, as to reject a jewel which would have dimmed all earthly things, its splendor waned. When other pilgrims reached the cliff, they found only an opaque[92] stone, with particles of mica glittering on its surface. There is also a tradition that, as the youthful pair departed, the gem was loosened from the forehead of the cliff, and fell into the enchanted lake, and that, at noontide, the Seeker's form may still be seen to bend over its quenchless-gleam.

Some few believe that this inestimable stone is blazing, as of old, and say that they have caught its radiance, like a flash of summer lightning, far down the valley of the Saco. And be it owned, that, many a mile from the Crystal Hills, I saw a wondrous light around their summits, and was lured, by the faith of poesy, to be the latest pilgrim of the GREAT CARBUNCLE.

刺瞎的眼睛，仰望月亮和星星；日出时，他和波斯的崇神者一样准时把脸转向东方；他还到罗马朝圣，想要目睹圣彼得大教堂的辉煌灯饰；最后，他葬身在伦敦那场大火，是他自己扑进去的，因为他在绝望中想从铺天盖地的大火里捕捉一丝微弱的光亮。

略写。交代其他五个寻宝者的结局。

马修和他的新娘度过了多年平静的日子，喜爱讲这个大红宝石的传说。然而，在他们漫长的一生快要结束时，这个故事不完全符合那些记得红宝石古老光辉的人们所讲的内容，因为有人断言，自从两个凡人非常聪明地拒绝了这块使世间万物黯然失色的宝石那个时刻起，它的光辉就渐渐消逝。其他朝拜者到达悬崖时，只发现一块没有光泽的石头，表面闪着云母的微粒。另有一种传说是，当年轻的一对离开时，宝石就从悬崖的前部脱离下来，掉进了魔湖中，而且，到了中午仍能看到"寻宝者"的身影俯在红宝石生生不息的闪光上。

讲述红宝石的结局。与主题相呼应，并再次强化主题。

只有少数人相信这无价宝石仍然光芒闪耀，还说他们曾经见过它的光辉，就像夏天的一道闪电，照到了萨科山谷深远的地方。还要承认，距离水晶山许多英里的地方，我也曾看到群山之巅有一种奇光，并以诗歌的信义发誓，我也为之着迷，愿做大红宝石的最新朝拜者。

名篇赏析

　　《大红宝石》是美国浪漫主义作家霍桑的经典短篇之一，叙述了八位探险者偶聚水晶山，他们怀有不同的目的，都想把大红宝石据为己有的故事。最终，那对新婚夫妻在愿望即将实现的瞬间，放弃了触手可得的宝石，认为它的光芒对于农舍来说过于耀眼。象征诱惑与欲望的大红宝石诠释了"知足常乐"的道德寓意。

　　宝石被认为是大自然灵性的结晶，隐喻着道德真理的光芒，它能照亮每个人的肺腑，并给每个人以公正的回报，因此只有心灵纯洁的新婚夫妻才能找到宝石，才能看到它泛出的红光，而其他人根本无缘宝石。

　　这个故事通过描写不同人物的寻宝过程和结果，表达了作者对不同人生态度的理解和对人类最珍贵品格的赞美。

Nathaniel Hawthorne

拉帕西尼的女儿

姓名	纳撒尼尔·霍桑
出生日期	1804年7月4日
出生地	美国马萨诸塞州塞勒姆镇
性别	男

成就和特色

　　美国十九世纪最杰出的浪漫主义小说家，代表作《红字》已成为世界文学的经典之一，是美国文学发展史上第一部象征主义小说。他的作品想象丰富、结构严谨。除了心理分析与描写，他还运用了象征主义手法。他构思精巧的意象增添了作品的浪漫色彩，加深了寓意。他的短篇小说细致深刻，风格独特，不少作品立意新颖，取材得当，富于诗意。内容与形式的和谐统一造成了完美强烈的艺术效果，对美国短篇小说这一突出文学类型的发展具有积极深远的影响。霍桑不愧为美国十九世纪后期浪漫主义作家的杰出代表，他的写作手法在美国乃至世界文学史上都独树一帜，直接影响了亨利·詹姆斯、威廉·福克纳、索尔·贝娄、艾萨克·辛格、托妮·莫里森等文坛巨擘。

写作背景

　　拉帕西尼医生精心培育出各种毒花毒草，以这些花草的芳香熏陶自己的亲生女儿，使其浑身充满毒素，呼口气都能令鲜花枯萎、昆虫丧命。这位把一切都当成实验对象的医生最终不但毒害了女儿的心上人，还使美艳无双的独生女也一命呜呼。

02

Rappaccini's Daughter

A young man, named Giovanni Guasconti, came, very long ago, from the more southern region of Italy, to pursue his studies at the University of Padua. Giovanni, who had but a scanty supply of gold **ducats**[1] in his pocket, took lodgings in a high and gloomy chamber of an old **edifice**[2], which looked not unworthy to have been the palace of a **Paduan**[3] noble, and which, in fact, exhibited over its entrance the armorial bearings of a family long since **extinct**[4]. The young stranger, who was not unstudied in the great poem of his country, recollected that one of the ancestors of this family, and perhaps an occupant of this very mansion, had been pictured by Dante as a partaker of the immortal agonies of his Inferno. These **reminiscences**[5] and associations, together with the tendency to heart-break natural to a young man for the first time out of his native sphere, caused Giovanni to sigh heavily, as he looked around the desolate and ill-furnished apartment.

"Holy Virgin, signor," cried old dame Lisabetta, who, won by the youth's remarkable beauty of person, was kindly endeavoring to give the chamber a habitable air, "what a sigh was that to come out of a young man's heart! Do you find this old mansion gloomy? For the love of heaven, then, put your head out of the window, and you will see as bright sunshine as you have left in Naples."

Guasconti mechanically did as the old woman advised, but could not quite agree with her that the Lombard sunshine was as

拉帕西尼的女儿

很久以前，一位名叫乔万尼·古斯康提的年轻人，从意大利遥远的南方到帕多瓦大学求学。乔万尼口袋里只有几枚达克特金币，就住进了一幢古老大厦一个又高又暗的房间。这个大厦看上去配得上做帕多瓦贵族的宅第。大厦的入口处上方确实显示有一个早已灭绝的家族的纹章。这个年轻的异乡人对自己祖国的伟大诗歌颇有研究，他想起了这个家族的一位祖先，也许正是这座大厦的主人，曾被但丁描述为地狱永恒的受难者。这些记忆和联想，加上年轻人初次离开故土自然产生的伤感，使乔万尼环顾无人居住、陈设简陋的房间，发出了重重的叹息。

"圣母啊，先生！"丽莎贝塔老太太叫道。年轻人一表人才，赢得了老人的心，她正在好心地尽力把房间收拾得适合住人，"年轻人，怎么伤心叹气啊！你觉得这座老宅阴沉吗？那么，看在上天的份上，把你的头伸到窗外，你就会看到明媚的阳光，跟你离开那不勒斯时一样。"

吉斯康提按照老太太的建议机械地把头伸出窗外，但并不完全同意她说的伦巴第的阳光像南部意大利的阳光一

故事开头有意与但丁的《神曲》相联系，预示着这个名叫乔万尼·古斯康提的年轻异乡人将像但丁一样踏上一条经历天堂与地狱考验的探寻之旅。

cheerful as that of southern Italy. Such as it was, however, it fell upon a garden beneath the window, and expended its fostering influences on a variety of plants, which seemed to have been **cultivated**[6] with exceeding care.

"Does this garden belong to the house?" asked Giovanni.

"Heaven forbid, signor! —unless it were fruitful of better pot-herbs than any that grow there now," answered old Lisabetta. "No; that garden is cultivated by the own hands of Signor Giacomo Rappaccini, the famous Doctor, who, I **warrant**[7] him, has been heard of as far as Naples. It is said he distils these plants into medicines that are as potent as a charm. Oftentimes you may see the Signor Doctor at work, and perchance the Signora his daughter, too, gathering the strange flowers that grow in the garden."

The old woman had now done what she could for the aspect of the chamber, and, commending the young man to the protection of the saints, took her departure.

Giovanni still found no better occupation than to look down into the garden beneath his window. From its appearance, he judged it to be one of those botanic gardens, which were of earlier date in Padua than elsewhere in Italy, or in the world. Or, not improbably, it might once have been the pleasure-place of an **opulent**[8] family; for there was the ruin of a marble fountain in the centre, sculptured with rare art, but so wofully shattered that it was impossible to trace the original design from the chaos of remaining fragments. The water, however, continued to gush and sparkle into the sunbeams as cheerfully as ever. A little **gurgling**[9] sound ascended to the young man's window, and made him feel as if a fountain were an immortal spirit, that sung its song unceasingly, and without heeding the **vicissitudes**[10] around it; while one century embodied it in marble, and another scattered the perishable **garniture**[11] on the soil. All about the pool into which the water subsided, grew various plants, that seemed to require a plentiful supply of moisture for the nourishment of gigantic leaves, and, in some instances, flowers

6. cultivate
   vt. 培养；陶冶；耕作
7. warrant
   vt. 保证；担保
8. opulent
   adj. 丰富的；富裕的；大量的
9. gurgle
   vi. 作汩汩声；作咯咯声
10. vicissitude
    n. 变迁；盛衰
11. garniture
    n. 装饰品；附属品；配件

样令人愉快。然而，这阳光还是落在了窗下花园里，抚育着各种各样的花草，这些花草似乎受到了精心培育。

"这花园属于这座大厦吗？"乔万尼问道。

"老天保佑绝对没这回事，先生！——除非花园里能长些比现在生在那片的东西好一点的野菜，"老丽莎贝塔答道。"不是，那个花园是著名医生贾科默·拉帕西尼先生亲手栽种的，我敢保证，那不勒斯那么远的地方都听说过他。据说，他从这些花草中提取的药像符咒一样有效。你可能会经常看到医生大人干活，也许他家小姐也在采摘花园里那些奇异的花朵。"

老太太现在力所能及收拾好了房间，然后把年轻人托付给圣徒们保佑之后，就离开了。

乔万尼百无聊赖，索性去俯视窗下的花园。他从外观判断这是帕多瓦的植物园之一，在帕多瓦的这些植物园比意大利或世界上其他地方出现得却要早。要么很可能这里曾经是一个富裕家庭的游乐场，因为园子中央有一座大理石喷泉的废墟，尽管精雕细刻，但非常不幸的是已经碎裂，在剩下的乱七八糟的碎片中不可能找到原来的图案。然而，泉水继续喷涌，仍然在阳光下闪着快乐的光芒。小小的汩汩声向上传到了年轻人的窗口，使他感到喷泉好像永恒的精灵，不断歌唱，没有留意周围的兴衰变迁；某一个世纪它被赋予大理石的形体，另一个世纪却成了容易腐烂的装饰品散碎在了地上。泉水流入的水池周围长满了各种各样的植物，它们巨大的叶子好像需要大量水分来滋养。有些植物的花朵非常娇美。尤其是有一个灌木丛，长在水池中央的一只大理石

Rappaccini's Daughter 拉帕西尼的女儿

gorgeously magnificent. There was one shrub in particular, set in a marble vase in the midst of the pool, that bore a **profusion**[12] of purple blossoms, each of which had the lustre and richness of a gem; and the whole together made a show so **resplendent**[13] that it seemed enough to illuminate the garden, even had there been no sunshine. Every portion of the soil was peopled with plants and herbs, which, if less beautiful, still bore tokens of **assiduous**[14] care; as if all had their individual virtues, known to the scientific mind that fostered them. Some were placed in urns, rich with old carving, and others in common garden-pots; some crept serpent-like along the ground, or climbed on high, using whatever means of ascent was offered them. One plant had wreathed itself round a statue of **Vertumnus**[15], which was thus quite veiled and shrouded in a drapery of hanging foliage, so happily arranged that it might have served a sculptor for a study.

While Giovanni stood at the window, he heard a rustling behind a screen of leaves, and became aware that a person was at work in the garden. His figure soon emerged into view, and showed itself to be that of no common laborer, but a tall, **emaciated**[16], **sallow**[17], and sickly looking man, dressed in a scholar's garb of black. He was beyond the middle term of life, with gray hair, a thin gray beard, and a face singularly marked with intellect and cultivation, but which could never, even in his more youthful days, have expressed much warmth of heart.

Nothing could exceed the intentness with which this scientific gardener examined every shrub which grew in his path; it seemed as if he was looking into their inmost nature, making observations in regard to their creative essence, and discovering why one leaf grew in this shape, and another in that, and wherefore such and such flowers differed among themselves in hue and perfume. Nevertheless, in spite of the deep intelligence on his part, there was no approach to intimacy between himself and these vegetable existences. On the contrary, he avoided their actual touch, or the direct inhaling of their odors, with

12. profusion
    n. 丰富；充沛；慷慨
13. resplendent
    adj. 光辉的；华丽的
14. assiduous
    adj. 刻苦的；勤勉的
15. Vertumnus
    n. 威耳廷努斯（罗马神话中的神；掌管四季变化、庭园和果树之神）
16. emaciated
    adj. 瘦弱的；憔悴的
17. sallow
    adj. 气色不好的；灰黄色的

花盆里，紫色花朵挂满枝头，每一朵花都如宝石般亮泽和华美；整个树丛光辉灿烂，即使没有任何阳光，好像也足以照亮花园。每一块土地都种满了花木药草，即使没有那么漂亮，也仍然带有辛勤护理的痕迹。好像所有花草都有各自的价值，培育它们的科学家对此很了解。有的种在雕有古花纹的瓮里，有的栽在普通花盆里，有的像蛇一样匍匐在地，要么是不管给它们提供什么攀援方式，都会爬到高处。其中一棵还把自己缠绕在一座花果之神雕像上，只见它藤叶悬垂，把雕像遮挡得严严实实，这样安排恰到好处，可供雕刻家研究一番。

乔万尼站在窗边，听到一道叶屏后面沙沙作响，才知道有人在园子里干活。这个人的身影很快就出现在了他的眼前，看样子那绝不是普通劳动者，而是一位身材高大、面黄肌瘦、病病歪歪的男子，只见他身穿学者黑色长袍，人过中年，头发花白，胡子稀疏灰白，脸上显示出异乎寻常的智慧和修养，但这张脸即使在更年轻的岁月，也绝不可能表露多少内心的热情。

这位训练有素的园丁无比专心地查看着栽种的每棵灌木，好像他要看透它们的内在本质，观察它们散发的芳香，揭示这片叶子长这个形状、那片叶子又长那个形状的原因，以及为什么花朵不同、颜色和香味也不一样。然而，尽管他对这些花草了解深刻，但他和它们之间毫不亲近。相反，他避免去实际触摸它们，也避免直接吸入它们的气味，这种谨慎给乔万尼留下了极为不快的印象，因为这个人的行为就像一个走在毒蛇猛兽的邪恶势力中的人的那样，让他们一时放纵，就会给他带来

乔万尼俯视给他留下第一印象的拉帕西尼医生的花园。拉帕西尼医生的花园既是限制和阐释主人公活动的特定语境，也是体现作品意蕴、象征尘世伊甸园善恶并存的重要意象。

a caution that impressed Giovanni most disagreeably; for the man's demeanor was that of one walking among **malignant**[18] influences, such as savage beasts, or deadly snakes, or evil spirits, which, should he allow them one moment of license, would wreak upon him some terrible fatality. It was strangely frightful to the young man's imagination, to see this air of insecurity in a person cultivating a garden, that most simple and innocent of human toils, and which had been alike the joy and labor of the unfallen parents of the race. Was this garden, then, the Eden of the present world?—and this man, with such a perception of harm in what his own hands caused to grow, was he the Adam?

The distrustful gardener, while plucking away the dead leaves or pruning the too **luxuriant**[19] growth of the shrubs, defended his hands with a pair of thick gloves. Nor were these his only armor. When, in his walk through the garden, he came to the magnificent plant that hung its purple gems beside the marble fountain, he placed a kind of mask over his mouth and nostrils, as if all this beauty did but conceal a deadlier malice. But finding his task still too dangerous, he drew back, removed the mask, and called loudly, but in the infirm voice of a person affected with inward disease:"Beatrice!—Beatrice!"

"Here am I, my father! What would you?" cried a rich and youthful voice from the window of the opposite house; a voice as rich as a tropical sunset, and which made Giovanni, though he knew not why, think of deep hues of purple or crimson, and of perfumes heavily **delectable**[20]. — "Are you in the garden?"

"Yes, Beatrice," answered the gardener, "and I need your help."

Soon there emerged from under a **sculptured**[21] portal the figure of a young girl, arrayed with as much richness of taste as the most splendid of the flowers, beautiful as the day, and with a bloom so deep and vivid that one shade more would have been too much. She looked **redundant**[22] with life, health, and energy; all of which **attributes**[23] were bound down and compressed, as it were, and **girdled**[24] tensely, in their

---

18. malignant
    adj. 恶性的；有害的；有恶意的
19. luxuriant
    adj. 繁茂的；丰富的；肥沃的
20. delectable
    adj. 美味的；令人愉快的
21. sculpture
    vt. 雕塑；雕刻
22. redundant
    adj. 多余的；冗长的；累赘的
23. attribute
    n. 属性；特质
24. girdle
    vt. 围绕；绕……而行；用带子捆扎

可怕的不幸。这种不安的气氛给年轻人的想象力带来一种异常的恐惧，这个人是在干着园艺活，这是人类最单纯、最无害的劳作，就像尚未堕落的人类始祖的乐趣和劳动一样。那么，这园子是当代的伊甸园吗？——这个人竟感到会受到自己亲手栽培的东西的伤害，难道他是亚当吗？

这个疑心重重的园丁拽掉枯叶，或修剪长得过于茂盛的灌木时，戴厚厚的手套保护自己的双手。这还不是他唯一的防护。他穿过花园，来到大理石喷泉边那棵结满紫宝石一样花朵的绚丽植物面前，戴上了一种遮住口鼻的面具，好像这一切美丽只是在掩藏一种更致命的毒害。但是，他还是觉得太危险，就退回去，摘下面具，大声叫喊："比阿特丽斯！——比阿特丽斯！"但他声音虚弱发颤，好像患有隐疾。

拉帕西尼医生不是当今的亚当，而是当今尘世伊甸园训练有素的园丁。

"我在这里，爸爸！你要什么？"对面房子的窗口传来一个年轻圆润的声音，那声音像热带的夕阳一样绚丽，这使乔万尼不知为什么想到了紫色或深红色和芬芳馥郁的香气。"您是在园子里吗？"

"是，比阿特丽斯，"园丁回答说，"我需要你帮忙。"

雕花拱门下面马上出现了一个少女的身影，只见她打扮艳丽，似最绚丽的花朵般风雅，如白昼般美丽，这朵花是那样浓烈鲜艳，多一分色调都会过分。她神采奕奕，充满活力；好像这一切丰富品质都被处女的腰带束缚压制，紧紧环绕。然而，乔万尼俯视花园时，思想里必定已是毛骨悚然，因为这位美丽陌生的姑娘使他感到这是另一朵花，是那些植物的人类姐妹，像它们一样美

luxuriance, by her virgin zone. Yet Giovanni's fancy must have grown **morbid**[25], while he looked down into the garden; for the impression which the fair stranger made upon him was as if here were another flower, the human sister of those vegetable ones, as beautiful as they—more beautiful than the richest of them—but still to be touched only with a glove, nor to be approached without a mask. As Beatrice came down the garden-path, it was observable that she handled and **inhaled**[26] the odor of several of the plants, which her father had most **sedulously**[27] avoided.

"Here, Beatrice," said the latter, — "see how many needful offices require to be done to our chief treasure. Yet, shattered as I am, my life might pay the penalty of approaching it so closely as circumstances demand. Henceforth, I fear, this plant must be **consigned to**[28] your sole charge."

"And gladly will I undertake it," cried again the rich tones of the young lady, as she bent towards the magnificent plant, and opened her arms as if to embrace it. "Yes, my sister, my splendor, it shall be Beatrice's task to nurse and serve thee; and thou shalt reward her with thy kisses and perfume breath, which to her is as the breath of life!"

Then, with all the tenderness in her manner that was so strikingly expressed in her words, she busied herself with such attentions as the plant seemed to require; and Giovanni, at his lofty window, rubbed his eyes, and almost doubted whether it were a girl tending her favorite flower, or one sister performing the duties of affection to another. The scene soon **terminated**[29]. Whether Doctor Rappaccini had finished his labors in the garden, or that his watchful eye had caught the stranger's face, he now took his daughter's arm and retired. Night was already closing in; oppressive exhalations seemed to proceed from the plants, and steal upward past the open window; and Giovanni, closing the lattice, went to his couch, and dreamed of a rich flower and beautiful girl. Flower and maiden were different and yet the same, and fraught with some strange peril in either shape.

25. morbid
   adj. 病态的；不正常的
26. inhale
   vt. 吸入
27. sedulously
   adv. 孜孜不倦地；勤勉地
28. consign to
   交付给
29. terminate
   vi. 结束；终止

丽，比它们中最艳丽的还美——但也只能戴着手套去触摸，不戴面具是不可靠近的。比阿特丽斯顺着花园小路走来，只见她抚摸花草，呼吸着一些花草的香气，而她的父亲对它们却唯恐避之不及。

"在这里，比阿特丽斯，"她的父亲说，"看看我们的主要宝贝需要多少照料。可是，我无能为力，如果按情况需要接近它，就可能会要了我的命。所以，我恐怕，这棵植物必须交给你来专门照管。"

"我乐意接受，"那年轻姑娘圆润的嗓音又一次嚷道，她向那株非常漂亮的灌木弯下腰，张开双臂，仿佛要拥抱它。"是的，我的姐妹，我的美人儿，照料你，伺候你，将是比阿特丽斯的任务；你会用亲吻和芬芳气息回报她哦，这对她就像生命的气息一样。"

随后，她言语中非常明显流露的所有柔情都表现在了动作上，这棵植物似乎正需要她这种忙前忙后的关怀；乔万尼站在高高的窗前，揉了揉眼睛，简直怀疑这是一位姑娘在照料最心爱的花朵，还是一对姐妹中的一个为另一个尽着爱的职责。这情景马上就结束了。是拉帕西尼医生干完了园里的活，还是他警惕的目光发现了陌生人的脸，他现在拉起女儿的胳膊，离开了。夜幕四合，闷人的花香好像从那些植物中散发出来，悄悄向上飘进了敞开的窗户；乔万尼关上花格窗，躺在床上，随后梦到了一朵娇艳的花朵和一位美丽的姑娘。花朵和姑娘不同，却又相同，而且各自的形态都充满了某种奇异的危险。

拉帕西尼医生的女儿是伊甸园里的另一朵花。作为花园意象的延伸，比阿特丽斯象征着作品女主人公善恶混合难分的两面性。

But there is an influence in the light of morning that tends to **rectify**[30] whatever errors of fancy, or even of judgment, we may have **incurred**[31] during the sun's decline, or among the shadows of the night, or in the less wholesome glow of moonshine. Giovanni's first movement on starting from sleep, was to throw open the window, and gaze down into the garden which his dreams had made so fertile of mysteries. He was surprised, and a little ashamed, to find how real and matter-of-fact an affair it proved to be, in the first rays of the sun, which gilded the dew-drops that hung upon leaf and blossom, and, while giving a brighter beauty to each rare flower, brought everything within the limits of ordinary experience. The young man **rejoiced**[32], that, in the heart of the barren city, he had the privilege of overlooking this spot of lovely and luxuriant vegetation. It would serve, he said to himself, as a symbolic language, to keep him in communion with Nature. Neither the sickly and thought-worn Doctor Giacomo Rappaccini, it is true, nor his brilliant daughter, were now visible; so that Giovanni could not determine how much of the **singularity**[33] which he attributed to both, was due to their own qualities, and how much to his wonder-working fancy. But he was inclined to take a most rational view of the whole matter.

In the course of the day, he paid his respects to Signor Pietro Baglioni, Professor of Medicine in the University, a physician of eminent repute, to whom Giovanni had brought a letter of introduction. The Professor was an elderly personage, apparently of **genial**[34] nature, and habits that might almost be called **jovial**[35]; he kept the young man to dinner, and made himself very agreeable by the freedom and liveliness of his conversation, especially when warmed by a flask or two of Tuscan wine. Giovanni, conceiving that men of science, inhabitants of the same city, must needs be on familiar terms with one another, took an opportunity to mention the name of Doctor Rappaccini. But the Professor did not respond with so much cordiality as he had anticipated.

"Ill would it become a teacher of the divine art of

30. rectify
    vt. 改正；精馏
31. incur
    vt. 招致；引发；蒙受
32. rejoice
    vi. 高兴；庆祝
33. singularity
    n. 奇异；突出；稀有
34. genial
    n. 亲切的；友好的
35. jovial
    adj. 天性快活的

然而，晨光中有一种力量，常常会纠正我们在夕阳西下、夜色朦胧、月光昏沉时可能产生的无论任何错误的想象或判断。乔万尼从睡梦中醒来的第一个动作就是推开窗户，注视下面的花园，他在梦里曾经在那里做了多少神秘的事情。他吃惊而又有点惭愧地发现这个园子是多么真实和平常，第一缕阳光正给绿叶和鲜花上的露珠抹上一层金色，使每朵奇葩都更加明艳，把所有的一切都限定在平凡经历的范围内。年轻人感到高兴，在这座贫瘠城市的中心，他有这个特权俯瞰这座景色秀丽、枝繁叶茂的花园。他对自己说，这园子将会成为他和大自然交流的象征性的语言。的确，现在既看不见病病歪歪、殚精竭虑的拉帕西尼医生，也看不见他光彩照人的女儿，所以乔万尼确定不了他所认为的这父女俩不同寻常，是因为他们自己的品质，还是因为他自己的想象过于丰富。不过，他想对整个事情持非常理性的看法。

乔万尼俯视给他留下第一印象的拉帕西尼医生父女。

就在那天白天，他带着介绍信去拜访了皮埃特罗·巴格里奥尼先生——他是大学里的一位医学教授，也是一位享有盛名的内科医生。教授上了年纪，和蔼可亲，显然举止行为堪称乐天派；他留乔万尼吃饭，他的谈话自由活泼，使他十分令人愉快，尤其喝下那一两瓶托斯卡纳葡萄酒之后更是如此。乔万尼心想，住在同一座城市的科学家们彼此一定都非常熟悉，趁机提起了拉帕西尼医生的名字。但是，教授的反应并没有他原来料想的那样热情。

"作为一名神圣医学的教师，"皮埃特罗·巴格里奥尼教授这样回答乔万尼的提问，"对拉帕西尼这样

medicine," said Professor Pietro Baglioni, in answer to a question of Giovanni, "to withhold due and well-considered praise of a physician so **eminently**[36] skilled as Rappaccini. But, on the other hand, I should answer it but scantily to my conscience, were I to permit a worthy youth like yourself, Signor Giovanni, the son of an ancient friend, to **imbibe**[37] erroneous ideas respecting a man who might hereafter chance to hold your life and death in his hands. The truth is, our worshipful Doctor Rappaccini has as much science as any member of the faculty —with perhaps one single exception—in Padua, or all Italy. But there are certain grave objections to his professional character."

"And what are they?" asked the young man.

"Has my friend Giovanni any disease of body or heart, that he is so **inquisitive**[38] about physicians?" said the Professor, with a smile. "But as for Rappaccini, it is said of him—and I, who know the man well, can answer for its truth—that he cares infinitely more for science than for mankind. His patients are interesting to him only as subjects for some new experiment. He would sacrifice human life, his own among the rest, or whatever else was dearest to him, for the sake of adding so much as a grain of mustard-seed to the great heap of his **accumulated**[39] knowledge."

"Methinks he is an awful man, indeed," remarked Guasconti, mentally recalling the cold and purely intellectual aspect of Rappaccini. "And yet, worshipful Professor, is it not a noble spirit? Are there many men capable of so spiritual a love of science?"

"God forbid," answered the Professor, somewhat testily— "at least, unless they take sounder views of the healing art than those adopted by Rappaccini. It is his theory, that all medicinal virtues are **comprised**[40] within those substances which we term vegetable poisons. These he cultivates with his own hands, and is said even to have produced new varieties of poison, more horribly deleterious than Nature, without the assistance of this learned person, would ever have plagued the world withal. That the Signor Doctor does less mischief than might be expected,

36. eminently
    adv. 突出地；显著地
37. imbibe
    vt. 吸收；接受
38. inquisitive
    adj. 好奇的；好问的；爱打听的
39. accumulate
    adj. 累积的；积聚的
40. comprise
    vt. 包含；由……组成

技术高超的医生不给予适当的高度赞扬是不合适的。不过，另一方面，只是我的回答不能昧良心，不能让乔万尼先生你这样值得称赞的年轻人——一位老朋友的儿子——对今后可能会把你的生死操在手里的人怀有错误的认识。事实上，我们这位可敬的拉帕西尼医生和帕多瓦或全意大利任何学校的教授——可能有一个人除外——一样有很高的科学造诣，但他的职业道德却有一些严重的缺陷。"

"是什么缺陷？"年轻人问道。

"我的朋友乔万尼的身心莫非有什么疾病吗？不然他为什么对医生这个职业这样好奇？"教授微笑着说。"不过，至于拉帕西尼，说起他——我熟悉这个人，可以保证真实性——他关心科学要远远胜过关心人类。病人只是让他感兴趣的某种新实验对象而已。为了给他的知识大山积累哪怕一粒芥子，他宁愿牺牲人的生命，其中包括他自己的或不管什么对他至为宝贵的东西。"

"我想他真是一个可怕的人，"古斯康提一边回想拉帕西尼冷漠而纯理性的面孔，一边说。"然而，尊敬的教授，这难道不是一种高尚的精神吗？有多少人有能力如此热衷科学呢？"

"苍天不容，"教授有些不耐烦地答道。"至少，除非人们对医学的见解比拉帕西尼的那些见解合理。他认为，所有医药的功能都包含在我们称为有毒植物的那些物质中。他亲手栽培有毒植物，据说甚至培育出了一些新品种，毒性比天然生长的更有害得多，如果没有这位学问家的帮助，还会给世界造成灾祸。不可否认，医生阁下手里这些危险物质造成的危害比预料的可能会

> 任何事情都具有两面性，医学也不例外。

with such dangerous substances, is undeniable. Now and then, it must be owned, he has effected—or seemed to effect—a marvellous cure. But, to tell you my private mind, Signor Giovanni, he should receive little credit for such instances of success—they being probably the work of chance—but should be held strictly accountable for his failures, which may justly be considered his own work."

The youth might have taken Baglioni's opinions with many grains of allowance, had he known that there was a professional warfare of long continuance between him and Doctor Rappaccini, in which the latter was generally thought to have gained the advantage. If the reader be inclined to judge for himself, we refer him to certain black-letter tracts on both sides, preserved in the medical department of the University of Padua.

"I know not, most learned Professor," returned Giovanni, after musing on what had been said of Rappaccini's exclusive zeal for science— "I know not how dearly this physician may love his art; but surely there is one object more dear to him. He has a daughter."

"Aha!" cried the Professor with a laugh. "So now our friend Giovanni's secret is out. You have heard of this daughter, whom all the young men in Padua are wild about, though not half a dozen have ever had the good hap to see her face. I know little of the Signora Beatrice, save that Rappaccini is said to have instructed her deeply in his science, and that, young and beautiful as fame reports her, she is already qualified to fill a professor's chair. Perchance her father destines her for mine! Other absurd rumors there be, not worth talking about, or listening to. So now, Signor Giovanni, drink off your glass of Lacryma."

Guasconti returned to his lodgings somewhat heated with the wine he had **quaffed**[41], and which caused his brain to swim with strange fantasies in reference to Doctor Rappaccini and the beautiful Beatrice. On his way, happening to pass by a florist's, he bought a fresh bouquet of flowers.

41. quaff
vt. 大口地喝；痛饮

少。必须承认，有时他的药疗效奇妙——或者看上去疗效奇妙。不过，我把私下的想法告诉你，乔万尼先生，他这些成功的例子不应该受到太多的赞扬——它们可能是碰运气——但他对失败确实应负责任，因为公平地说，那可能就是他一手造成的。"

如果年轻人知道巴格里奥尼教授和拉帕西尼医生之间长期存在学术业上的冲突，而且在这场冲突中人们常常认为后者占了上风，那他对巴格里奥尼的看法就可能会大打折扣。如果读者想自己做出判断，我们会指点他去查阅某些保存在帕多瓦大学医学系、用黑体字印的支持双方的小册子。

"最博学的教授，我不知道，"乔万尼沉思了一番刚才说到的拉帕西尼对科学专一的热情之后，又说道，"我不知道这位医生对自己的医术爱得有多么深，但他肯定还有一个更珍贵的东西。他有个女儿。"

"啊哈！"教授大声笑道。"所以现在我们的朋友乔万尼的秘密就公开了。你听说了这个女儿，帕多瓦市的所有小伙子都为她疯狂，尽管有幸见过她的芳容的人还未到五六个。我对这位比阿特丽斯小姐知道得不多，只知道拉帕西尼对她言传身教，她不仅年轻貌美名声在外，而且她已经有资格坐上教授的交椅。也许她的父亲指定要她去挖掘科学矿山呢！还有一些荒唐的谣传，不值一谈，也不值一听。好了，乔万尼先生，喝干你的杯中酒。"

吉斯康提将酒一饮而尽，返回住处途中那些灌下去的酒令他有些兴奋，这使他的大脑充满了有关拉帕西尼医生和美丽的比阿特丽斯的奇怪幻想。路上，他碰巧经过一家花店，就买了一束鲜花。

皮埃特罗·巴格里奥尼教授看穿了乔万尼的秘密，也看穿了拉帕西尼医生的秘密。

Rappaccini's Daughter 拉帕西尼的女儿

Ascending to his chamber, he seated himself near the window, but within the shadow thrown by the depth of the wall, so that he could look down into the garden with little risk of being discovered. All beneath his eye was a solitude. The strange plants were basking in the sunshine, and now and then nodding gently to one another, as if in acknowledgment of sympathy and kindred. In the midst, by the shattered fountain, grew the magnificent shrub, with its purple gems clustering all over it; they glowed in the air, and gleamed back again out of the depths of the pool, which thus seemed to overflow with colored radiance from the rich reflection that was steeped in it. At first, as we have said, the garden was a solitude. Soon, however, —as Giovanni had half hoped, half feared, would be the case, —a figure appeared beneath the antique sculptured portal, and came down between the rows of plants, inhaling their various perfumes, as if she were one of those beings of old classic fable, that lived upon sweet odors. On again beholding Beatrice, the young man was even startled to perceive how much her beauty exceeded his recollection of it; so brilliant, so vivid in its character, that she glowed amid the sunlight, and, as Giovanni whispered to himself, positively **illuminated**[42] the more shadowy intervals of the garden path. Her face being now more revealed than on the former occasion, he was struck by its expression of simplicity and sweetness; qualities that had not entered into his idea of her character, and which made him ask anew, what manner of mortal she might be. Nor did he fail again to observe, or imagine, an analogy between the beautiful girl and the gorgeous shrub that hung its gem-like flowers over the fountain; a resemblance which Beatrice seemed to have indulged a fantastic humor in heightening, both by the arrangement of her dress and the selection of its hues.

Approaching the shrub, she threw open her arms, as with a passionate ardor, and drew its branches into an intimate embrace; so intimate, that her features were hidden in its leafy bosom, and her glistening ringlets all intermingled with the flowers.

"Give me thy breath, my sister," exclaimed Beatrice; "for I am faint with common air! And give me this flower of thine,

42. illuminate
vt. 照亮；说明

他上楼回到自己的房间，坐在窗边靠墙的阴影里，这样他可以俯瞰花园，不会冒太大被人发现的风险。他目光所及全是一片落寞。奇花异草沐浴在阳光里，不时地相互轻轻点头，好像在承认意气相投，同出一族。园子中央，破败的喷泉边长着那棵华美的灌木，上面全是宝石般的紫色花朵，这些花朵在空中光彩夺目，映入池中，又从水池深处折射回来，流光溢彩，满池鲜艳。起初，像我们曾经说过的那样，园子一片落寞。然而，很快——乔万尼既希望又害怕的事情发生了——一个人影出现在了古老的雕花拱门下面，然后穿过一排排花草，一边走，一边呼吸着各种花香，就像古代传说中以芬芳为生的精灵。再次看到比阿特丽斯，年轻人吃惊地发现，她要比他记忆中的美丽得多，是那样鲜明，那样生动，在阳光下闪闪发亮，而且，当乔万尼喃喃自语时，她必定照亮了树影婆娑的园中小路。她的脸现在比上次更清楚了，脸上纯真可爱的表情让他怦然心动——他没想到她的性格中有这种品质，这使他再次产生了疑问，她可能会是什么人呢？他还又一次注意到，或者说想象到，这位美丽的姑娘和那棵繁花悬垂在喷泉上的华美灌木之间是多么相似——比阿特丽斯好像有一种奇异的性情，那就是通过精挑细选衣服及其色调提升这种相似性。

她走近那棵灌木，热情洋溢地张开双臂，亲密地拥抱它的树枝，是那样亲密，把她的脸掩藏在茂盛的树叶中，闪闪发亮的卷发和那些花朵完全融为了一体。

"把你的芬芳给我吧，我的姐妹，"比阿特丽斯叫道，"因为普通的空气会让我眩晕！把你的这朵花给我

再次看到比阿特丽斯，不免让乔万尼怦然心动。

which I separate with gentlest fingers from the stem, and place it close beside my heart."

With these words, the beautiful daughter of Rappaccini plucked one of the richest blossoms of the shrub, and was about to fasten it in her bosom. But now, unless Giovanni's draughts of wine had bewildered his senses, a singular incident occurred. A small orange-colored reptile, of the lizard or chameleon species, chanced to be creeping along the path, just at the feet of Beatrice. It appeared to Giovanni—but, at the distance from which he gazed, he could scarcely have seen anything so minute—it appeared to him, however, that a drop or two of moisture from the broken stem of the flower descended upon the lizard's head. For an instant, the reptile **contorted**[43] itself violently, and then lay motionless in the sunshine. Beatrice observed this remarkable phenomenon, and crossed herself, sadly, but without surprise; nor did she therefore hesitate to arrange the fatal flower in her bosom. There it blushed, and almost glimmered with the dazzling effect of a precious stone, adding to her dress and aspect the one appropriate charm, which nothing else in the world could have supplied. But Giovanni, out of the shadow of his window, bent forward and shrank back, and murmured and trembled.

"Am I awake? Have I my senses?" said he to himself. "What is this being?—beautiful, shall I call her?—or inexpressibly terrible?"

Beatrice now strayed carelessly through the garden, approaching closer beneath Giovanni's window, so that he was compelled to thrust his head quite out of its concealment, in order to **gratify**[44] the intense and painful curiosity which she excited. At this moment, there came a beautiful insect over the garden wall; it had perhaps wandered through the city and found no flowers nor **verdure**[45] among those antique haunts of men, until the heavy perfumes of Doctor Rappaccini's shrubs had lured it from afar. Without alighting on the flowers, this winged brightness seemed to be attracted by Beatrice, and lingered in the air and fluttered about

43. contort
    vt. 扭曲
44. gratify
    vt. 使满足；使满意
45. verdure
    n. 青翠的草木；碧绿

吧，我会用最轻柔的手指把它从茎上分离，把它放在贴心的地方。"

说着，拉帕西尼的漂亮女儿从树上摘下了一朵最鲜艳的花，正要别在胸前。但这时，发生了一件怪事，否则就是乔万尼喝酒让他产生了错觉。一条橘黄色的小爬虫、蜥蜴或变色龙之类的东西，碰巧顺着小路爬了过来，正好到达比阿特丽斯的脚边。乔万尼好像看到——不过，因为距离远，他几乎看不清这么小的东西——然而，他好像看到，折断的花枝上滴下一两滴树液，落在了蜥蜴的头上。一时间，小爬虫拼命扭来扭去，随后就躺在阳光下一动不动了。比阿特丽斯也观察到了这个奇异的现象，伤心地划着十字，但并不吃惊；她将那致命的毒花别到胸前的时候也并不因此而犹豫。鲜花在她胸前呈现红色，简直像宝石一样闪闪发亮，让人眼花缭乱，也给她的衣服和容貌增加了适当的魅力，世界上其他任何东西都无法增添这种魅力。但是，乔万尼从窗户的阴影中探出身，又缩了回去，一边喃喃自语，一边浑身颤抖。

作者洞察入微。

"我醒着吗？我神志清楚吗？"他自言自语说。"这是什么生物？——我该说她美丽，还是无法形容的可怕？"

这时，比阿特丽斯漫不经心，穿过花园，离乔万尼的窗下越来越近了，因此为了满足自己强烈而痛苦的好奇心，乔万尼不得不从藏身处伸出头。正在此时，一只漂亮的昆虫飞过了园墙，也许飞遍了全城，在那些人群经常出没的地方既没有找到鲜花，也没有找到绿树，直到拉帕西尼医生灌木的浓香把它从远处吸引过来。这个长翅膀的闪亮精灵没有落在花朵上，好像被比阿特丽斯迷住了，在空中逗留，在她头顶飞来飞去。此刻，除非乔万尼·古斯康

her head. Now here it could not be but that Giovanni Guasconti's eyes deceived him. Be that as it might, he fancied that while Beatrice was gazing at the insect with childish delight, it grew faint and fell at her feet; —its bright wings shivered; it was dead—from no cause that he could discern, unless it were the atmosphere of her breath. Again Beatrice crossed herself and sighed heavily, as she bent over the dead insect.

An impulsive movement of Giovanni drew her eyes to the window. There she beheld the beautiful head of the young man— rather a Grecian than an Italian head, with fair, regular features, and a glistening of gold among his ringlets—gazing down upon her like a being that hovered in mid-air. Scarcely knowing what he did, Giovanni threw down the bouquet which he had hitherto held in his hand.

"Signora," said he, "there are pure and healthful flowers. Wear them for the sake of Giovanni Guasconti!"

"Thanks, Signor," replied Beatrice, with her rich voice that came forth as it were like a gush of music; and with a mirthful expression half childish and half woman-like. "I accept your gift, and would fain **recompense**[46] it with this precious purple flower; but if I toss it into the air, it will not reach you. So Signor Guasconti must even content himself with my thanks."

She lifted the bouquet from the ground, and then as if inwardly ashamed at having stepped aside from her maidenly reserve to respond to a stranger's greeting, passed swiftly homeward through the garden. But, few as the moments were, it seemed to Giovanni when she was on the point of vanishing beneath the sculptured portal, that his beautiful bouquet was already beginning to wither in her grasp. It was an idle thought; there could be no possibility of distinguishing a faded flower from a fresh one, at so great a distance.

For many days after this incident, the young man avoided the window that looked into Doctor Rappaccini's garden, as if something ugly and **monstrous**[47] would have blasted his eye-

46. recompense
 vt. 赔偿；酬谢
47. monstrous
 adj. 巨大的；怪异的；畸形的

提的眼睛欺骗他，再没有别的可能了。尽管是这样，但他还是认为，在比阿特丽斯带着孩子般的欣喜凝视这只小昆虫时，它越来越衰弱，倒在她的脚边——光亮的翅膀颤抖了几下，就死了——除了她呼出的气息，他看不出是什么原因。比阿特丽斯又一次划起了十字，向那只死去的昆虫俯下身时，重重地叹了口气。

乔万尼一个冲动的动作，将她的目光吸引到了那扇窗户。她看到了那里一个年轻人的英俊脸庞——与其说是意大利人，不如说是希腊人，五官端正俊朗，金色卷发闪闪发亮——仿佛空中飞翔的精灵正在俯视着她。乔万尼不由自主把手里一直握着的那束鲜花抛了下去。

"小姐，"他说，"这是一些纯洁健康的鲜花。看在乔万尼·古斯康提的面子上，戴上吧！"

"谢谢，先生，"比阿特丽斯嗓音圆润地答道，就像流泻出来的音乐一样，脸上的表情带着一半稚气一半成熟。"我接受你的礼物，还想用这朵宝贵的紫花回报你；不过，我把它扔到空中，它到不了你那里。所以，吉斯康提先生只好甘愿接受我的口头感谢了。"

她从地上拾起那束鲜花，随后好像思想上认为她打破了少女的矜持，对陌生人的问候做出回应而感到害羞，所以她飞快地穿过花园，向家里走去。不过，尽管时间不多，但在她快要消失在雕花拱门下面时，乔万尼好像看到他那束美丽的鲜花已经开始在她的手里枯萎。这是一种无端的念头；距离这么远，绝不可能看清一朵花是新鲜还是凋谢。

这件事过去之后的许多天里，年轻人都避开可以看到拉帕西尼医生花园的那扇窗户，好像他不自觉看一

比阿特丽斯小姐是乔万尼游历毒花伊甸园的同行者，她既是爱的诱惑者，也是乔万尼的精神救赎者，代表着美与恶同在的尘世生活，是尘世生命的全部象征。

坠入爱河的乔万尼此时已经无法摆脱内心的挣扎。

48. unintelligible
    adj. 莫明其妙的；
    无法了解的
49. proximity
    n. 亲近；接近
50. temperament
    n. 气质；性情；性格
51. affinity
    n. 密切关系；吸引
    力；类同
52. baneful
    adj. 有害的；有毒
    的；使人苦恼的
53. assuage
    vt. 平息；缓和；减轻
54. accelerate
    vt. 使……加快；
    使……增速

sight, had he been betrayed into a glance. He felt conscious of having put himself, to a certain extent, within the influence of an **unintelligible**[48] power, by the communication which he had opened with Beatrice. The wisest course would have been, if his heart were in any real danger, to quit his lodgings and Padua itself, at once; the next wiser, to have accustomed himself, as far as possible, to the familiar and day-light view of Beatrice; thus bringing her rigidly and systematically within the limits of ordinary experience. Least of all, while avoiding her sight, should Giovanni have remained so near this extraordinary being, that the **proximity**[49] and possibility even of intercourse, should give a kind of substance and reality to the wild vagaries which his imagination ran riot continually in producing. Guasconti had not a deep heart—or at all events, its depths were not sounded now—but he had a quick fancy, and an ardent southern **temperament**[50], which rose every instant to a higher fever-pitch. Whether or no Beatrice possessed those terrible attributes—that fatal breath—the **affinity**[51] with those so beautiful and deadly flowers—which were indicated by what Giovanni had witnessed, she had at least instilled a fierce and subtle poison into his system. It was not love, although her rich beauty was a madness to him; nor horror, even while he fancied her spirit to be imbued with the same **baneful**[52] essence that seemed to pervade her physical frame; but a wild offspring of both love and horror that had each parent in it, and burned like one and shivered like the other. Giovanni knew not what to dread; still less did he know what to hope; yet hope and dread kept a continual warfare in his breast, alternately vanquishing one another and starting up afresh to renew the contest. Blessed are all simple emotions, be they dark or bright! It is the lurid intermixture of the two that produces the illuminating blaze of the infernal regions.

Sometimes he endeavored to **assuage**[53] the fever of his spirit by a rapid walk through the streets of Padua, or beyond its gates; his footsteps kept time with the throbbings of his brain, so that the walk was apt to **accelerate**[54] itself to a race. One

眼，什么丑陋恐怖的东西就会损害他的眼睛似的。他意识到，既然他已经开口和比阿特丽斯交谈，他自己在某种程度上就受到了一种莫名其妙的力量的影响。如果他的心灵处在任何真正的危险中，上策就是马上离开这个住处和帕多瓦；中策是尽可能使自己习惯于那熟悉的阳光下的比阿特丽斯形象——从而严格而有条不紊地将它保持在日常经验范围之内。下策就是，避免见她，即使乔万尼继续留在这个非凡女孩近旁，离得这样近，甚至会有亲近和交往的可能，即使这会给他不断产生的胡思乱想提供某种真实感。古斯康提并不是个深沉的人——或者至少现在还不知道他是不是深沉——但他具有敏捷的想象力和南方人热情洋溢的性情，这种性情随时都会达到更加狂热的顶峰。无论比阿特丽斯是否具有那些可怕的品质——那种致命的气息——与那些美丽的死亡之花的密切关系——乔万尼曾经目睹，至少她已经把一种猛烈而微妙的毒素慢慢注入进了他的体内。这不是爱情，尽管她的美艳让他疯狂；这也不是恐怖，即使在他想象那种遍及她肉体的毒素也充满了她的灵魂；仅仅是爱情和恐怖的疯狂产物，一雌一雄，彼此互补，像爱情般燃烧，又像恐怖般颤抖。乔万尼不知道该害怕什么，更不知道该希望什么；然而，希望和恐惧在他胸中不断激烈搏斗，轮番征服对方，此起彼伏没完没了。无论是黑暗还是光明，所有单纯的感情都会受到祝福！爱情和恐怖的可怕混合物才会产生地狱里耀眼的光焰。

　　有时，为了缓和狂热情绪，他疾步穿过帕多瓦大街，或者疾步走到城门外；他的脚步合着簌簌跳动的大脑的节拍，因此他越走越快，就像在赛跑一样。有一

> 爱情和恐怖彼此互补，希望和恐惧相互纠结，产生了毒花伊甸园里耀眼的光焰。

day, he found himself arrested; his arm was seized by a portly personage who had turned back on recognizing the young man, and expended much breath in overtaking him.

"Signor Giovanni!—stay, my young friend!" —cried he. "Have you forgotten me? That might well be the case, if I were as much altered as yourself."

It was Baglioni, whom Giovanni had avoided, ever since their first meeting, from a doubt that the Professor's **sagacity**[55] would look too deeply into his secrets. Endeavoring to recover himself, he stared forth wildly from his inner world into the outer one, and spoke like a man in a dream.

"Yes; I am Giovanni Guasconti. You are Professor Pietro Baglioni. Now let me pass!"

"Not yet—not yet, Signor Giovanni Guasconti," said the Professor, smiling, but at the same time **scrutinizing**[56] the youth with an earnest glance. "What, did I grow up side by side with your father, and shall his son pass me like a stranger, in these old streets of Padua? Stand still, Signor Giovanni; for we must have a word or two before we part."

"Speedily, then, most worshipful Professor, speedily!" said Giovanni, with feverish impatience. "Does not your worship see that I am in haste?"

Now, while he was speaking, there came a man in black along the street, stooping and moving feebly, like a person in inferior health. His face was all overspread with a most sickly and sallow hue, but yet so pervaded with an expression of piercing and active intellect, that an observer might easily have overlooked the merely physical attributes, and have seen only this wonderful energy. As he passed, this person exchanged a cold and distant salutation with Baglioni, but fixed his eyes upon Giovanni with an **intentness**[57] that seemed to bring out whatever was within him worthy of notice. Nevertheless, there was a peculiar quietness in the look, as if taking merely a **speculative**[58], not a human interest, in the young man.

"It is Doctor Rappaccini!" whispered the Professor, when

55. sagacity
 n. 睿智；聪敏；有远见
56. scrutinize
 vt. 细看；详细检查
57. intentness
 n. 热心；专心
58. speculative
 adj. 投机的；推测的；思索性的

天，他突然被人拦住，一个身材魁梧的人一把抓住他的胳膊：刚才这个人认出他后，就回转身追他，直追得他上气不接下气。

"乔万尼先生！——留步，年轻的朋友！"他叫道。"你把我忘了吗？如果我像你一样变化这么大，很可能也会是这样。"

原来是巴格里奥尼，自从他们第一次见面以来，乔万尼就躲着他，唯恐睿智的教授看透他内心深处的秘密。他努力恢复镇定，急切地想从内心世界回到外部世界中来，说话像做梦似的。

"是的，我是乔万尼·古斯康提。你是皮埃特罗·巴格里奥尼教授。现在让我过去吧！"

"还不行——还不行，乔万尼·古斯康提先生，"教授微笑着说，但同时认真地打量着这个年轻人。"怎么了，我不是和你的父亲并肩长大的吗？他的儿子在帕多瓦古老的大街上居然像陌生人一样跟我擦肩而过？乔万尼先生，站着别动，因为分手前我们必须说一两句话。"

"那就快点，最尊敬的教授，快点！"乔万尼急不可待地说。"阁下没见我有急事吗？"

与巴格里奥尼教授不期而遇。

他正说着，沿街走来一个黑衣人。黑衣人弯着腰，有气无力地走着，像是一个健康状态欠佳的人。他满面病容，气色发黄，但脸上充满了敏锐活跃的智慧表情，因此旁观者很容易忽视他的体质，只看到他这种惊人的活力。他路过时，这个人和巴格里奥尼冷淡疏远地相互问候，却用专注的目光盯着乔万尼，仿佛要看清他内心值得注意的一切。不过，这目光异常平静，好像对这年轻人的兴趣仅仅是探索性的，而非人性的。

"是拉帕西尼医生！"陌生人走过去后，教授低声

the stranger had passed. — "Has he ever seen your face before?"

"Not that I know," answered Giovanni, starting at the name.

"He has seen you!—he must have seen you!" said Baglioni, hastily. "For some purpose or other, this man of science is making a study of you. I know that look of his! It is the same that coldly illuminates his face, as he bends over a bird, a mouse, or a butterfly, which, in pursuance of some experiment, he has killed by the perfume of a flower; —a look as deep as Nature itself, but without Nature's warmth of love. Signor Giovanni, I will stake my life upon it, you are the subject of one of Rappaccini's experiments!"

"Will you make a fool of me?" cried Giovanni, passionately. "That, Signor Professor, were an untoward experiment."

"Patience, patience!" replied the **imperturbable**[59] Professor. "I tell thee, my poor Giovanni, that Rappaccini has a scientific interest in thee. Thou hast fallen into fearful hands! And the Signora Beatrice? What part does she act in this mystery?"

But Guasconti, finding Baglioni's **pertinacity**[60] intolerable, here broke away, and was gone before the Professor could again seize his arm. He looked after the young man intently, and shook his head.

"This must not be," said Baglioni to himself. "The youth is the son of my old friend, and shall not come to any harm from which the arcana of medical science can preserve him. Besides, it is too insufferable an impertinence in Rappaccini thus to **snatch**[61] the lad out of my own hands, as I may say, and make use of him for his infernal experiments. This daughter of his! It shall be looked to. Perchance, most learned Rappaccini, I may foil you where you little dream of it!"

Meanwhile, Giovanni had pursued a circuitous route, and at length found himself at the door of his lodgings. As he crossed the threshold, he was met by old Lisabetta, who smirked and

59. imperturbable
adj. 冷静的；泰然自若的
60. pertinacity
n. 顽固；执拗
61. snatch
vt. 夺取

说道。"他以前没有见过你吗？"

"我不知道，"乔万尼答道，同时听到这个名字吃了一惊。

"他曾经见过你！——他一定见过你！"巴格里奥尼匆匆说道。"出于某种原因，这位科学家正在对你进行研究。我知道他那个样子！就像他弯腰盯着一只小鸟、老鼠或蝴蝶时一样一脸寒光，这些小动物都是他按照某种实验用花香薰死的；——他的样子和大自然一样深奥，但没有大自然爱的温暖。乔万尼先生，我愿用生命打赌，你是拉帕西尼其中的一个实验对象！"

"你想愚弄我吗？"乔万尼情绪激昂地叫道。"教授先生，那可是一项不幸的实验。"

"沉住气，沉住气！"教授沉着冷静地答道。"可怜的乔万尼，我告诉你，拉帕西尼对你产生了科学的兴趣。你已经落入了魔掌！还有比阿特丽斯小姐？她在这出神秘剧里扮演什么角色？"

但是，乔万尼发现巴格里奥尼固执，难以忍受，就挣脱开来，还没等教授再次拉住他，就跑得无影无踪了。教授目不转睛地望着年轻人的背影，摇了摇头。

"这肯定不行，"巴格里奥尼自言自语说。"这个年轻人是我老朋友的儿子，不能让他受到任何伤害，医学的秘术能保护他。再说，拉帕西尼蛮横无理，让人无法忍受，居然想从我手里夺走这个小伙子，我可以说，用他来做那种恶魔般的实验。还有他这个女儿！这要注意。说不定，最博学的拉帕西尼，你做梦也想不到我会阻止你！"

此时，乔万尼拐弯抹角，终于回到了自己的住所门

应该说，巴格里奥尼教授是乔万尼游历毒花伊甸园的阻止者。

smiled, and was evidently desirous to attract his attention; vainly, however, as the **ebullition**[62] of his feelings had momentarily subsided into a cold and dull vacuity. He turned his eyes full upon the withered face that was **puckering**[63] itself into a smile, but seemed to behold it not. The old dame, therefore, laid her grasp upon his cloak.

"Signor!—Signor!" whispered she, still with a smile over the whole breadth of her visage, so that it looked not unlike a **grotesque**[64] carving in wood, darkened by centuries— "Listen, Signor! There is a private entrance into the garden!"

"What do you say?" exclaimed Giovanni, turning quickly about, as if an **inanimate**[65] thing should start into feverish life. —"A private entrance into Doctor Rappaccini's garden!"

"Hush! hush!—not so loud!" whispered Lisabetta, putting her hand over his mouth. "Yes; into the worshipful Doctor's garden, where you may see all his fine shrubbery. Many a young man in Padua would give gold to be admitted among those flowers."

Giovanni put a piece of gold into her hand.

"Show me the way," said he.

A surmise, probably excited by his conversation with Baglioni, crossed his mind, that this **interposition**[66] of old Lisabetta might perchance be connected with the intrigue, whatever were its nature, in which the Professor seemed to suppose that Doctor Rappaccini was involving him. But such a suspicion, though it disturbed Giovanni, was inadequate to restrain him. The instant he was aware of the possibility of approaching Beatrice, it seemed an absolute necessity of his existence to do so. It mattered not whether she were angel or demon; he was **irrevocably**[67] within her sphere, and must obey the law that whirled him onward, in ever lessening circles, towards a result which he did not attempt to **foreshadow**[68]. And yet, strange to say, there came across him a sudden doubt, whether this intense interest on his part were not **delusory**[69] —whether it were really of so deep and positive a nature as to

62. ebullition
   n. 沸腾；感情迸发
63. pucker
   vt. 使起皱；使缩拢
64. grotesque
   adj. 奇形怪状的；奇怪的
65. inanimate
   adj. 无生命的；无生气的
66. interposition
   n. 干涉；介入；放入
67. irrevocably
   adv. 不能取消地；不能撤回地
68. foreshadow
   vt. 预示；成为……的前兆
69. delusory
   adj. 迷惑的；困惑的

前。他跨过门槛时，遇到了老丽莎贝塔，只见她假惺惺地笑着，显然是想引起他的注意，但无济于事，因为年轻人迸发的情绪已经暂时平息下来，变成了冷淡呆滞的空虚。他把目光完全转向那张堆满笑容、皱纹斑斑的脸庞，却好像视而不见。因此，老太太一把抓住了他的宽大外衣。

"先生！——先生！"她低声喊道，仍然满脸堆笑，活像一只年久发黑、奇形怪状的木雕。"听着，先生！有一个秘密入口通向花园！"

比喻贴切。

"你说什么？"乔万尼飞快地转过身，大声问道，好像死气沉沉的东西突然生机勃勃。"有一道暗门通向拉帕西尼医生的花园！"

"嘘！嘘！——不要这么大声！"丽莎贝塔一只手捂住乔万尼的嘴，低声说道。"是的，能进入尊敬的医生家的花园，你在那里可以见到他所有的漂亮花草。帕多瓦城里许多年轻人为了进去看那些花，都愿意拿金子呢。"

看似调侃，实则有意。

乔万尼把一枚金币放进她的手里。

"给我带路，"他说。

可能是由和巴格里奥尼的谈话所致，他心里猜测，说不定老丽莎贝塔的介入和阴谋有关，无论这阴谋的性质是什么，教授似乎猜测到拉帕西尼医生要他卷进去。不过，尽管这种疑虑让他不安，但不足以阻止他。他知道有可能接近比阿特丽斯时，这样做好像对他的生命是绝对必要的。她是天使还是魔鬼都无关紧要；他无法挽回地进入了她的领域，必须顺其自然急转向前，进入越来越小的圈子，奔向他不想努力预测的一个结果。然而，说来奇怪，他突然产生了怀疑，他这种强烈兴趣是

Rappaccini's Daughter 拉帕西尼的女儿 **197**

justify him in now thrusting himself into an incalculable position —whether it were not merely the fantasy of a young man's brain, only slightly, or not at all, connected with his heart!

He paused—hesitated—turned half about—but again went on. His withered guide led him along several obscure passages, and finally undid a door, through which, as it was opened, there came the sight and sound of rustling leaves, with the broken sunshine glimmering among them. Giovanni stepped forth, and forcing himself through the **entanglement**[70] of a shrub that wreathed its tendrils over the hidden entrance, he stood beneath his own window, in the open area of Doctor Rappaccini's garden.

How often is it the case, that, when impossibilities have come to pass, and dreams have **condensed**[71] their misty substance into **tangible**[72] realities, we find ourselves calm, and even coldly **self-possessed**[73], amid circumstances which it would have been a **delirium**[74] of joy or agony to anticipate! Fate delights to thwart us thus. Passion will choose his own time to rush upon the scene, and lingers **sluggishly**[75] behind, when an appropriate adjustment of events would seem to summon his appearance. So was it now with Giovanni. Day after day, his pulses had throbbed with feverish blood, at the improbable idea of an interview with Beatrice, and of standing with her, face to face, in this very garden, basking in the **oriental**[76] sunshine of her beauty, and snatching from her full gaze the mystery which he deemed the riddle of his own existence. But now there was a singular and untimely **equanimity**[77] within his breast. He threw a glance around the garden to discover if Beatrice or her father were present, and perceiving that he was alone, began a critical observation of the plants.

The aspect of one and all of them dissatisfied him; their **gorgeousness**[78] seemed fierce, passionate, and even unnatural. There was hardly an individual shrub which a wanderer, straying by himself through a forest, would not have been startled to find growing wild, as if an unearthly face had glared at him out of the thicket. Several, also, would have

70. entanglement
    n. 纠缠；铁丝网；缠绕物
71. condense
    vt. 使浓缩；使压缩
72. tangible
    adj. 有形的；切实的；可触摸的
73. self-possessed
    adj. 镇静的；冷静的；有自制力的
74. delirium
    n. 精神错乱；发狂；狂热
75. sluggishly
    adv. 懒怠地；慢吞吞地
76. oriental
    adj. 东方的；东方人的
77. equanimity
    n. 平静；镇定
78. gorgeousness
    n. 豪华；华丽

否虚妄——这是否具有如此深刻明确的本性，限制足以把他自己推到无法预知的境地——是否仅仅是年轻人脑子里的幻想，和他的心灵关系极小或毫无关系！

他停下来——犹豫不决——半转过身——但又接着向前走。枯瘦的向导领着他走过好几条昏暗的过道，终于打开一扇门。穿过打开的这扇门，只见树叶飒飒作响，斑驳的阳光在树叶间隐约闪现。乔万尼走上前，奋力穿过藤蔓纠缠、卷须环绕的隐蔽入口，站在了拉帕西尼医生花园的空地上，站到了他自己的窗下。

枯瘦的向导——丽莎贝塔老太太将乔万尼引入了毒花伊甸园。

情况常常是这样，不可能的事最终会发生，当梦想凝聚起它缥缈的迷雾变成伸手可及的现实，我们发现自己那么平静，甚至冷静沉着，原来料想这种情况会让我们欣喜若狂或痛苦万分呢！命运就喜欢这样阻挠我们。激情会自行其是，冲到现场，但当时机发生变化，需要它出现时，它却行动迟缓拖在后面。乔万尼现在就是这样。日复一日，想着和比阿特丽斯会见，想着和她面对面站在一起，就在这园子里，沐浴在她东方阳光般的美丽之中，从她的整个凝视中了解他所谓的生命之谜，一想到这不可能之事，他就热血沸腾，脉搏簌簌直跳。然而，他现在的心情却奇怪而不合时宜地十分平静。他环顾花园四周，想看看比阿特丽斯或她的父亲在不在，却发现只有他独自一人，他开始挑剔地观察那些植物。

它们的面貌，他一个也不满意；它们眩目艳丽，看上去热烈刺眼，甚至不自然。就像漫游者穿过森林时迷路，发现每个灌木都长得狂乱，仿佛一张鬼脸从灌木丛中对他怒目而视，这让他大惊失色。还有好几棵的样子

shocked a delicate instinct by an appearance of **artificialness**[79], indicating that there had been such **commixture**[80], and, as it were, adultery of various vegetable species, that the production was no longer of God's making, but the monstrous offspring of man's **depraved**[81] fancy, glowing with only an evil mockery of beauty. They were probably the result of experiment, which, in one or two cases, had succeeded in mingling plants individually lovely into a compound possessing the questionable and **ominous**[82] character that distinguished the whole growth of the garden. In fine, Giovanni recognized but two or three plants in the collection, and those of a kind that he well knew to be poisonous. While busy with these contemplations, he heard the rustling of a silken garment, and turning, beheld Beatrice emerging from beneath the sculptured portal.

Giovanni had not considered with himself what should be his **deportment**[83]; whether he should apologize for his intrusion into the garden, or assume that he was there with the privity, at least, if not by the desire, of Doctor Rappaccini or his daughter. But Beatrice's manner placed him at his ease, though leaving him still in doubt by what agency he had gained admittance. She came lightly along the path, and met him near the broken fountain. There was surprise in her face, but brightened by a simple and kind expression of pleasure.

"You are a **connoisseur**[84] in flowers, Signor," said Beatrice with a smile, alluding to the bouquet which he had flung her from the window. "It is no marvel, therefore, if the sight of my father's rare collection has tempted you to take a nearer view. If he were here, he could tell you many strange and interesting facts as to the nature and habits of these shrubs, for he has spent a life-time in such studies, and this garden is his world."

"And yourself, lady"—observed Giovanni— "if fame says true—you, likewise, are deeply skilled in the virtues indicated by these rich blossoms, and these spicy perfumes. Would you deign to be my instructress, I should prove an apter scholar than under

79. artificialness
    n. 人为之事；装作；不自然
80. commixture
    n. 混合；混合物
81. depraved
    adj. 堕落的；腐化的；卑鄙的
82. ominous
    adj. 预兆的；不吉利的
83. deportment
    n. 举止；行为；态度
84. connoisseur
    n. 鉴赏家；内行

矫揉造作，一定会让脆弱的人大吃一惊，表明是好几种植物混合，可以说是杂交的结果，不再是上帝的造物，而是人类堕落幻想的畸形产物，只是因为对美的恶意嘲笑而光彩夺目。它们可能是园丁实验的结果，也有一两个是从非常可爱的植物混合而成的可疑不祥的物种，这使它们在整个园子的植物中都引人注目。总之，乔万尼在所有植物中只认出了两三种植物，那都是他熟知的一些有毒的植物。他正沉思冥想，这时听到丝绸衣服的飒飒声，就转过头，只见比阿特丽斯从雕花拱门下面走了出来。

乔万尼没有考虑过他应该有什么举动，是为闯进花园道歉，还是设想自己到这里至少得到了拉帕西尼医生或他女儿的默许，即使这并不是他们的心愿。但是，比阿特丽斯的举止让他放下心来，尽管他得到了什么人允许让他进入花园仍是一个疑问。她脚步轻盈地沿着小路走来，在破败的喷泉边和他迎面相遇。她露出了吃惊的神色，但又露出了天真善良的喜悦之情。

在毒花伊甸园中，与比阿特丽斯小姐第一次迎面相遇。

"您对鲜花是个内行啊，先生，"比阿特丽斯微笑着说，她是暗指他从窗口给她抛下的花束。"所以，如果是父亲的奇花异草吸引你就近观看，这并不奇怪。如果他在这里，就会告诉您这些花草习性方面的许多新鲜有趣的事儿，因为他毕生都从事这种研究，这个园子就是他的世界。"

"还有您自己，小姐，"乔万尼说。"如果名不虚传——您同样深知这些鲜花和浓厚的香气。如果您愿屈尊指导，我一定会比在拉帕西尼先生手下学得更快。"

"有这种无稽之谈吗？"比阿特丽斯银铃般欢笑

Signor Rappaccini himself."

"Are there such idle rumors?" asked Beatrice, with the music of a pleasant laugh. "Do people say that I am skilled in my father's science of plants? What a jest is there! No; though I have grown up among these flowers, I know no more of them than their hues and perfume; and sometimes, methinks I would fain rid myself of even that small knowledge. There are many flowers here, and those not the least brilliant, that shock and offend me, when they meet my eye. But, pray, Signor, do not believe these stories about my science. Believe nothing of me save what you see with your own eyes."

"And must I believe all that I have seen with my own eyes?" asked Giovanni pointedly, while the recollection of former scenes made him shrink. "No, Signora, you demand too little of me. Bid me believe nothing, save what comes from your own lips."

It would appear that Beatrice understood him. There came a deep flush to her cheek; but she looked full into Giovanni's eyes, and responded to his gaze of uneasy suspicion with a queen-like haughtiness.

"I do so bid you, Signor!" she replied. "Forget whatever you may have fancied in regard to me. If true to the outward senses, still it may be false in its essence. But the words of Beatrice Rappaccini's lips are true from the heart outward. Those you may believe!"

A fervor glowed in her whole aspect, and beamed upon Giovanni's consciousness like the light of truth itself. But while she spoke, there was a fragrance in the atmosphere around her rich and delightful, though evanescent[85], yet which the young man, from an indefinable[86] reluctance, scarcely dared to draw into his lungs. It might be the odor of the flowers. Could it be Beatrice's breath, which thus embalmed[87] her words with a strange richness, as if by steeping them in her heart? A faintness passed like a shadow over Giovanni, and flitted away; he seemed to gaze through the beautiful girl's eyes into her transparent[88]

85. evanescent
    adj. 容易消散的；
    逐渐消失的；会凋
    零的
86. indefinable
    adj. 难下定义的；
    模糊不清的
87. embalm
    vt. 铭记于心；使不朽
88. transparent
    adj. 透明的；坦率的

道。"有人说我精通父亲的植物学？这真是笑话！不，尽管我在这些鲜花中长大，但仅仅知道它们的颜色和香味；有时，我想我连这小小的知识也想摆脱。这里有许多鲜花，它们一呈现在我眼前，就让我震惊和不快，那些鲜花并不是不鲜艳。不过，先生，请不要相信这些有关我学识的传闻。对于我，除了您亲眼所见，什么也不要相信。"

"那我必须相信我的亲眼所见吗？"想起先前让乔万尼害怕的那些情景，他直截了当地问道。"不，小姐，您对我的要求太少了。吩咐我只相信您亲口所说的东西。"

看来比阿特丽斯明白他的意思，脸上泛起了深深的红晕，但她正视着乔万尼的眼睛，然后以女王般的傲慢回应他不安怀疑的目光。

"那我就吩咐您，先生！"她答道。"忘掉您可能对我的任何猜想。即使外表感觉真实，其本质仍可能是虚假。不过，比阿特丽斯说的这些话都是肺腑之言。那些您可以相信！"

她的整个脸庞热情洋溢，就像真理之光照耀在乔万尼的意识之上。然而，她说话时，她四周的空气中散发出一种芳香，馥郁宜人，尽管转瞬即逝，但因为勉强，难以描述，所以年轻人几乎不敢吸入肺部。也许是花香。可能是比阿特丽斯的呼吸使她的话语充满奇异的芬芳，就像这些话语在她的心灵中浸泡过一样？一阵晕眩像幽灵一样袭向乔万尼，但又飞掠而去；他好像从这个美丽姑娘的眼中看到了她透明的灵魂，于是他不再感到怀疑和害怕。

动静结合，相得益彰。起承转合，顺理成章。

Rappaccini's Daughter 拉帕西尼的女儿

89. diffuse
vt. 扩散；传播

soul, and felt no more doubt or fear.

The tinge of passion that had colored Beatrice's manner vanished; she became gay, and appeared to derive a pure delight from her communion with the youth, not unlike what the maiden of a lonely island might have felt, conversing with a voyager from the civilized world. Evidently her experience of life had been confined within the limits of that garden. She talked now about matters as simple as the day-light or summer-clouds, and now asked questions in reference to the city, or Giovanni's distant home, his friends, his mother, and his sisters; questions indicating such seclusion, and such lack of familiarity with modes and forms, that Giovanni responded as if to an infant. Her spirit gushed out before him like a fresh rill, that was just catching its first glimpse of the sunlight, and wondering, at the reflections of earth and sky which were flung into its bosom. There came thoughts, too, from a deep source, and fantasies of a gem-like brilliancy, as if diamonds and rubies sparkled upward among the bubbles of the fountain. Ever and anon, there gleamed across the young man's mind a sense of wonder, that he should be walking side by side with the being who had so wrought upon his imagination—whom he had idealized in such hues of terror—in whom he had positively witnessed such manifestations of dreadful attributes—that he should be conversing with Beatrice like a brother, and should find her so human and so maiden-like. But such reflections were only momentary; the effect of her character was too real, not to make itself familiar at once.

In this free intercourse, they had strayed through the garden, and now, after many turns among its avenues, were come to the shattered fountain, beside which grew the magnificent shrub with its treasury of glowing blossoms. A fragrance was **diffused**[89] from it, which Giovanni recognized as identical with that which he had attributed to Beatrice's breath, but incomparably more powerful. As her eyes fell upon it, Giovanni beheld her press her hand to her bosom, as if her heart were throbbing suddenly and painfully.

曾经让比阿特丽斯脸红的那种激情迅速消失了；她变得快乐起来，就像孤岛上的一位寂寞少女跟来自文明世界的航行者交谈时感受的那样，她似乎从跟年轻人交谈中得到了由衷的快乐。显然，她的人生体验已经限制在了这座花园的范围内。她时而谈论日光或夏云这种简单事，时而问起城里、乔万尼远方的家、他的朋友们、他的母亲和姐妹这些问题，这些问题显示她是那样与世隔绝，对一些时尚和生活方式如此缺乏了解，所以乔万尼就像回答婴儿一样。她的灵魂就像见到第一眼阳光的鲜活小溪一样在他面前喷涌而出，并对映照在怀中的天地倒影感到惊奇。深深的源泉喷涌出的思想和宝石般灿烂的幻想，就像钻石和红宝石在汩汩喷涌的泉水中向上闪闪发亮。惊奇的念头不时闪过年轻人的脑海，他将要和这个令他魂牵梦绕的人并肩而行——他曾经那么恐惧地想象过她——他确实曾经亲眼见过她露出那些可怕的特征——现在他要像兄弟一样和她交谈，还会发现她这样通情达理，这样娇羞。但是，这些想法只是转瞬即逝；她的个性力量太真实了，马上就让他感到亲切。

这样的语言简直像是从心底流出来似的，色香形声俱全，惊为天语。

他们就这样无拘无束地交谈着，漫步穿过花园，沿着林荫道拐了许多弯之后，现在最终来到了毁坏的喷泉边。喷泉边长着那株华丽的灌木，鲜花朵朵，生机勃勃，散发出阵阵芳香，乔万尼闻出这和比阿特丽斯的气息完全一样，但更强烈无比。乔万尼看到她的目光落在那棵树上时，她一只手按住胸口，好像她的心突然痛苦地怦怦直跳起来。

"有生以来第一次，"她对那棵树喃喃说道，"我

"For the first time in my life," murmured she, addressing the shrub, "I had forgotten thee!"

"I remember, Signora," said Giovanni, "that you once promised to reward me with one of these living gems for the bouquet, which I had the happy boldness to fling to your feet. Permit me now to pluck it as a memorial of this interview."

He made a step towards the shrub, with extended hand. But Beatrice darted forward, uttering a shriek that went through his heart like a dagger. She caught his hand, and drew it back with the whole force of her slender figure. Giovanni felt her touch thrilling through his fibres.

"Touch it not!" exclaimed she, in a voice of agony. "Not for thy life! It is fatal!"

Then, hiding her face, she fled from him, and vanished beneath the sculptured portal. As Giovanni followed her with his eyes, he beheld the emaciated figure and pale intelligence of Doctor Rappaccini, who had been watching the scene, he knew not how long, within the shadow of the entrance.

No sooner was Guasconti alone in his chamber, than the image of Beatrice came back to his passionate musings, invested with all the witchery that had been gathering around it ever since his first glimpse of her, and now likewise imbued with a tender warmth of girlish womanhood. She was human: her nature was **endowed with**[90] all gentle and feminine qualities; she was worthiest to be worshipped; she was capable, surely, on her part, of the height and heroism of love. Those tokens, which he had hitherto considered as proofs of a frightful peculiarity in her physical and moral system, were now either forgotten, or, by the subtle sophistry of passion, **transmuted**[91] into a golden crown of enchantment, rendering Beatrice the more admirable, by so much as she was the more unique. Whatever had looked ugly, was now beautiful; or, if incapable of such a change, it stole away and hid itself among those shapeless half-ideas, which throng the dim region beyond the daylight of our perfect consciousness.

90. endow with
   赋予；天生具有
91. transmute
   vt. 使变形；使变质

忘记了你！"

"我想起来了，小姐，"乔万尼说，"您曾经答应要赏给我一朵这样活宝石一样的鲜花，因为我冒昧把一束花抛到了您的脚下。现在允许我摘下一朵，作为这次会面的纪念。"

他伸出手，向那棵树走了一步。但是，比阿特丽斯飞奔向前，发出一声尖叫，尖叫声像一把匕首穿透了他的心。她抓住他的手，用尽苗条身体的全部力气把它拽了回来。乔万尼感觉她的触摸让他浑身震颤。

"别碰它！"她痛苦地大声叫道。"千万别碰它！那会致命的！"

说完，她掩面从他身边跑开，消失在了雕花拱门下面。乔万尼望着她的背影，这时看到了拉帕西尼医生瘦弱的身影和苍白智慧的脸庞。这个人一直站在入口的阴影里望着这一幕，不知有多久了。

乔万尼单独呆在自己的房间时，便又充满热情地沉思起比阿特丽斯的形象。他从看到她的第一眼起，她的形象就一直笼罩着种种魔力，现在又浸透了温柔少女的款款柔情。她富有人情，她的天性被赋予女性所有的温柔气质；她完全值得崇拜。她肯定能够崇高地去爱，无畏地去爱。他至今看作她肉体和精神可怕畸形的证据，现在要么是被忘记，要么是因为激情的微妙作用，化为一项魅力金冠，使比阿特丽斯更独一无二，更令人钦佩。所有看上去丑陋的东西现在都非常漂亮；要么，即使不能这样变化，也会偷偷溜走躲藏在那些未成形的朦胧念头里，聚集到我们的完美意识之光照不到的昏暗地方。因此，乔万尼就这样过了一夜，直到黎明开始唤醒拉帕西尼医生园子里沉睡的花

乔万尼和比阿特丽斯小姐在毒花伊甸园里的第一次会面。

Thus did Giovanni spend the night, nor fell asleep, until the dawn had begun to awake the slumbering flowers in Doctor Rappaccini's garden, whither his dreams doubtless led him. Up rose the sun in his due season, and flinging his beams upon the young man's eyelids, awoke him to a sense of pain. When thoroughly aroused, he became sensible of a burning and tingling agony in his hand—in his right hand—the very hand which Beatrice had grasped in her own, when he was on the point of plucking one of the gem-like flowers. On the back of that hand there was now a purple print, like that of four small fingers, and the likeness of a slender thumb upon his wrist.

Oh, how stubbornly does love—or even that cunning semblance of love which flourishes in the imagination, but strikes no depth of root into the heart—how stubbornly does it hold its faith, until the moment comes, when it is doomed to vanish into thin mist! Giovanni wrapt a handkerchief about his hand, and wondered what evil thing had stung him, and soon forgot his pain in a reverie[92] of Beatrice.

After the first interview, a second was in the inevitable[93] course of what we call fate. A third; a fourth; and a meeting with Beatrice in the garden was no longer an incident in Giovanni's daily life, but the whole space in which he might be said to live; for the anticipation and memory of that ecstatic[94] hour made up the remainder. Nor was it otherwise with the daughter of Rappaccini. She watched for the youth's appearance, and flew to his side with confidence as unreserved[95] as if they had been playmates from early infancy—as if they were such playmates still. If, by any unwonted[96] chance, he failed to come at the appointed moment, she stood beneath the window, and sent up the rich sweetness of her tones to float around him in his chamber, and echo and reverberate[97] throughout his heart— "Giovanni! Giovanni! Why tarriest thou? Come down!" And down he hastened into that Eden of poisonous flowers.

But, with all this intimate familiarity, there was still a

92. reverie
n. 幻想；沉思；幻想曲
93. inevitable
adj. 不可避免的；必然（发生）的
94. ecstatic
adj. 狂喜的；入迷的
95. unreserved
adj. 不隐瞒的；坦白的；无限制的
96. unwonted
adj. 不习惯的；不寻常的；少有的
97. reverberate
vi. 回响；反响

朵他才睡去。而他的梦肯定又把他领回了花园。太阳按时升起，把光芒照在年轻人的眼皮上，他感到一阵疼痛，醒了过来。等完全清醒后，他才感到手上火辣辣的刺痛——是他的右手——就是比阿特丽斯曾经抓过的那只手，当时他正要去摘一朵宝石般的鲜花。现在那只手背上有一个紫印，就像四只小手指印，而他的手腕上则是一个细长的大拇指印。

梦幻与现实的有机结合。

噢，爱情——即使是那种活跃在想象中，但还没有在心里生根的巧妙爱情伪装——是多么执着，多么顽固地坚守信念，直到那个时刻——它注定会烟消云散的时刻到来！乔万尼用一块手帕包住右手，不知道是什么恶毒的东西蜇了他，随后就陷入了对比阿特丽斯的幻想，很快忘记了疼痛。

第一次会面之后不可避免就有第二次，这就是我们所说的命运。第三次，第四次；和比阿特丽斯在园子里会面不再是乔万尼日常生活中的突发事件，可以说是他生活的全部内容，因为对那个心醉神迷时刻的期待和回忆占据了剩下的所有时间。拉帕西尼的女儿也是这样。她守候年轻人出现，一见他出现，她就飞跑到他身边，充满自信，毫不拘谨，好像他们从小就形影不离——好像他们现在还是形影不离。如果在某种罕见的情况下他没有按时赴约，她就会站到他的窗下，把圆润甜美的声音送上他的房间，飘浮在他四周，在他的心里久久回荡："乔万尼！乔万尼！你为什么耽搁呀？下来吧！"于是，他匆匆下楼，跑进毒花伊甸园。

不过，尽管他们亲密熟悉，但比阿特丽斯的行为

reserve in Beatrice's **demeanor**[98], so rigidly and invariably sustained, that the idea of **infringing**[99] it scarcely occurred to his imagination. By all appreciable signs, they loved; they had looked love, with eyes that conveyed the holy secret from the depths of one soul into the depths of the other, as if it were too sacred to be whispered by the way; they had even spoken love, in those gushes of passion when their spirits darted forth in **articulated**[100] breath, like tongues of long-hidden flame; and yet there had been no seal of lips, no clasp of hands, nor any slightest caress, such as love claims and hallows. He had never touched one of the gleaming ringlets of her hair; her garment— so marked was the physical barrier between them—had never been waved against him by a breeze. On the few occasions when Giovanni had seemed tempted to overstep the limit, Beatrice grew so sad, so stern, and withal wore such a look of desolate separation, shuddering at itself, that not a spoken word was requisite to repel him. At such times, he was startled at the horrible suspicions that rose, monster-like, out of the caverns of his heart, and stared him in the face; his love grew thin and faint as the morning-mist; his doubts alone had substance. But when Beatrice's face brightened again, after the momentary shadow, she was transformed at once from the mysterious, questionable being, whom he had watched with so much awe and horror; she was now the beautiful and **unsophisticated**[101] girl, whom he felt that his spirit knew with a certainty beyond all other knowledge.

A considerable time had now passed since Giovanni's last meeting with Baglioni. One morning, however, he was disagreeably surprised by a visit from the Professor, whom he had scarcely thought of for whole weeks, and would willingly have forgotten still longer. Given up, as he had long been, to a pervading excitement, he could tolerate no companions, except upon condition of their perfect sympathy with his present state of feeling. Such sympathy was not to be expected from Professor Baglioni.

98. demeanor
   n. 风度；举止；行为
99. infringe
   vt. 侵犯；违反；破坏
100. articulated
   adj. 清晰的
101. unsophisticated
   adj. 质朴无华的；天真无邪的

还是有所保留，意志坚定，持续不变，乔万尼几乎没有想过要去违反。通过所有可以感知的迹象，他们相爱；他们含情脉脉，用眼睛把灵魂深处神圣的秘密送入对方的灵魂深处，好像太神圣，不能窃窃私语；他们甚至说到了爱，激情澎湃时，他们的情绪突然从清晰的呼吸中飞出，就像久藏的火舌一样。然而，他们没有亲吻，没有握手，连那爱情所要求并视为神圣的最轻微的拥抱也不曾有过。他从来没有触摸过她光亮的鬈发；她的衣服——他们之间的身体障碍非常显著——从来没有被微风吹起贴过他的身体。有几次，乔万尼好像试图越界时，比阿特丽斯变得非常伤心，毫不宽容，此外还带着忧郁隔膜的表情，不用说一句话，这表情本身就击退了他，让他不寒而栗。每当这种时刻，可怕的猜疑就像恶魔一样从他心灵的洞穴站起，直盯盯地看着他，吓他一跳。他的爱像晨雾一样渐渐稀薄暗淡，只剩下了怀疑。但是，当短暂的阴影过后，比阿特丽斯又面露喜色，马上转变，不再是他诚惶诚恐、心惊胆战望着的那个神秘可疑的人；她现在又成了那个美丽纯洁的女孩，他感到他的灵魂对她的信任肯定超过其他所有的一切。

毒花伊甸园是乔万尼内心挣扎的情感投射，毒花伊甸园会面因此成为其生活的全部内容。

自从乔万尼上次与巴格里奥尼见面以来，现在已经过去了很久。然而，一天上午，教授突然来访，这让他既吃惊又不快。他连续几周几乎都没有想起过教授，而且愿意把他忘得更久。他长久沉湎在兴奋之中，除了完全赞同他目前感情状态的人，其他同伴他都无法忍受。而从巴格里奥尼教授那里，是指望不了这种赞同的。

来访者漫不经心地聊了一会儿有关城里和大学里的闲话，就谈起了另一个话题。

Rappaccini's Daughter 拉帕西尼的女儿　　**211**

The visitor chatted carelessly, for a few moments, about the gossip of the city and the University, and then took up another topic.

"I have been reading an old classic author lately," said he, "and met with a story that strangely interested me. Possibly you may remember it. It is of an Indian prince, who sent a beautiful woman as a present to Alexander the Great. She was as lovely as the dawn, and gorgeous as the sunset; but what especially distinguished her was a certain rich perfume in her breath—richer than a garden of Persian roses. Alexander, as was natural to a youthful conqueror, fell in love at first sight with this magnificent stranger. But a certain sage physician, happening to be present, discovered a terrible secret in regard to her."

"And what was that?" asked Giovanni, turning his eyes downward to avoid those of the Professor.

"That this lovely woman," continued Baglioni, with emphasis, "had been nourished with poisons from her birth upward, until her whole nature was so imbued with them, that she herself had become the deadliest poison in existence. Poison was her element of life. With that rich perfume of her breath, she blasted the very air. Her love would have been poison!—her embrace death! Is not this a marvellous tale?"

"A childish fable," answered Giovanni, nervously starting from his chair. "I marvel how your worship finds time to read such nonsense, among your graver studies."

"By the bye," said the Professor, looking uneasily about him, "what singular fragrance is this in your apartment? Is it the perfume of your gloves? It is faint, but delicious, and yet, after all, by no means agreeable. Were I to breathe it long, methinks it would make me ill. It is like the breath of a flower—but I see no flowers in the chamber."

"Nor are there any," replied Giovanni, who had turned pale as the Professor spoke; "nor, I think, is there any fragrance, except in your worship's imagination. Odors, being a sort of element combined of the sensual and the spiritual, are apt to

"我最近一直在看一位古代经典作家的作品，"他说，"读到一个故事，很奇怪，它使我非常感兴趣。。也许你还记得。讲的是一位印度王子，他把一名美女作为礼物送给亚历山大大帝。她像朝霞般可爱，如夕阳般灿烂，但她尤其突出的是，她呼出的气息有一种芳香——比满园的波斯玫瑰还要浓烈。亚历山大对这位陌生的美人一见钟情，这对年轻的征服者来说是自然的事儿。但是，一位睿智的医生正好在场，发现了一个有关她的可怕秘密。"

　　"什么秘密？"乔万尼垂下目光，避开教授的眼睛，问道。

　　"这个美人，"巴格里奥尼加重语气继续说道，"从出生起就用毒药喂养，直到她的全身都充满了毒药，她自己已经成为世上最致命的毒药。毒药就是她的生命元素。她呼出的浓香就能毒害空气。她的爱一定会是毒药！——她的拥抱就是死亡。难道这不是奇妙的故事吗？"

揭露真相，昭示主题。

　　"幼稚的传说，"乔万尼神经质地从椅子上跳起来抗辩道。"我感到奇怪，阁下从事那么严肃的研究，还有时间看这种无聊的东西。"

　　"顺便说一下，"教授神情不安地打量着他说，"你的房间里是什么东西这么香？是你手套上的香水吗？尽管香气微弱，但很好闻，但说到底，一点也不令人愉快。如果我呼吸久了，我想它一定会让我生病。它像是花香——但我在你的房间里没有看到任何鲜花。"

　　"这里就没有任何鲜花，"听了教授说的话，乔万尼脸色煞白，回答道。"我想，除了阁下的想象，也没有什么香气。气味是一种感官和精神结合的东西，容易这样欺骗我们。对香味的回忆，或仅仅是这种想法本

deceive us in this manner. The recollection of a perfume—the bare idea of it—may easily be mistaken for a present reality."

"Aye; but my sober imagination does not often play such tricks," said Baglioni; "and were I to fancy any kind of odor, it would be that of some vile apothecary drug, wherewith my fingers are likely enough to be imbued. Our worshipful friend Rappaccini, as I have heard, tinctures his **medicaments**[102] with odors richer than those of Araby. Doubtless, likewise, the fair and learned Signora Beatrice would minister to her patients with draughts as sweet as a maiden's breath. But woe to him that sips them!"

Giovanni's face evinced many contending emotions. The tone in which the Professor alluded to the pure and lovely daughter of Rappaccini was a torture to his soul; and yet, the **intimation**[103] of a view of her character, opposite to his own, gave **instantaneous**[104] distinctness to a thousand dim suspicions, which now grinned at him like so many demons. But he strove hard to quell them, and to respond to Baglioni with a true lover's perfect faith.

"Signor Professor," said he, "you were my father's friend—perchance, too, it is your purpose to act a friendly part towards his son. I would fain feel nothing towards you save respect and deference. But I pray you to observe, Signor, that there is one subject on which we must not speak. You know not the Signora Beatrice. You cannot, therefore, estimate the wrong—the **blasphemy**[105], I may even say—that is offered to her character by a light or injurious word."

"Giovanni!—my poor Giovanni!" answered the Professor, with a calm expression of pity, "I know this wretched girl far better than yourself. You shall hear the truth in respect to the poisoner Rappaccini, and his poisonous daughter. Yes; poisonous as she is beautiful! Listen; for even should you do violence to my gray hairs, it shall not silence me. That old fable of the Indian woman has become a truth, by the deep and deadly science of Rappaccini, and in the person of the lovely Beatrice!"

102. medicament
　　n. 药剂；医药
103. intimation
　　n. 暗示；讽示；通知
104. instantaneous
　　adj. 瞬间的；即刻的
105. blasphemy
　　n. 亵渎神明；轻视上帝或神祇

214

身，就容易让人误以为是实际存在的香味。"

"是，但我清醒的想象力不常开这种玩笑，"巴格里奥尼说。"如果我要想象什么气味，也一定是某种讨厌的药房里的药味，因为我的手指可能沾满了这种味。我听说，我们可敬的朋友拉帕西尼把他的药物熏得比阿拉伯香料的气味还浓烈。毫无疑问，美丽博学的比阿特丽斯小姐同样会用像少女气息一样甜美的药物照顾她的病人。但是，喝这种药物的人却会倒霉！"

巴格里奥尼教授以充满寓意的传说劝阻乔万尼。

乔万尼的脸上露出了矛盾重重的情绪。教授提到拉帕西尼的纯洁可爱的女儿时那种腔调对他的心灵是一种折磨；然而，提到和他的观点相反的对她人品的看法，无数模糊的疑点马上清晰起来，此刻它们像许多魔鬼一样向他狞笑。不过，他还是竭力压住那些看法，以真正情人的完全忠诚回应巴格里奥尼。

"教授先生，"他说，"您是我父亲的朋友——恐怕您的目的也是要善待他的儿子。我对您只有尊重和遵从。不过，先生，我请您注意，有个话题我们不能谈。您不了解比阿特丽斯小姐。所以，您不能用这样轻浮中伤的话语错误评价她的人品——我甚至可以说这是对她的亵渎。"

"乔万尼！——我可怜的乔万尼！"教授带着同情镇定的表情答道，"我对这个可怜姑娘的了解远比你本人多。你应该听听关于下毒的拉帕西尼和他中毒女儿的真相了。是的，她有多美，就有多毒！听着，即使你伤害我这个白发人，也不能让我沉默。那个印度女人的古老传说已被拉帕西尼深奥致命的科学变为了现实，而且是在漂亮的比阿特丽斯身上！"

乔万尼呻吟着，捂住了脸。

Giovanni groaned and hid his face.

"Her father," continued Baglioni, "was not restrained by natural affection from offering up his child, in this horrible manner, as the victim of his insane zeal for science. For—let us do him justice—he is as true a man of science as ever distilled his own heart in an alembic. What, then, will be your fate? Beyond a doubt, you are selected as the material of some new experiment. Perhaps the result is to be death—perhaps a fate more awful still! Rappaccini, with what he calls the interest of science before his eyes, will hesitate at nothing."

"It is a dream!" muttered Giovanni to himself, "surely it is a dream!"

"But," resumed the Professor, "be of good cheer, son of my friend! It is not yet too late for the rescue. Possibly, we may even succeed in bringing back this miserable child within the limits of ordinary nature, from which her father's madness has estranged her. Behold this little silver vase! It was wrought by the hands of the renowned Benvenuto Cellini, and is well worthy to be a love-gift to the fairest dame in Italy. But its contents are invaluable. One little sip of this antidote would have rendered the most virulent poisons of the Borgias innocuous. Doubt not that it will be as **efficacious**[106] against those of Rappaccini. Bestow the vase, and the precious liquid within it, on your Beatrice, and hopefully await the result."

Baglioni laid a small, **exquisitely**[107] wrought silver phial on the table, and withdrew, leaving what he had said to produce its effect upon the young man's mind.

"We will thwart Rappaccini yet!" thought he, chuckling to himself, as he descended the stairs. "But, let us confess the truth of him, he is a wonderful man!—a wonderful man indeed! A vile **empiric**[108], however, in his practice, and therefore not to be tolerated by those who respect the good old rules of the medical profession!"

Throughout Giovanni's whole acquaintance with Beatrice,

106. efficacious
   adj. 有效的；灵验的
107. exquisitely
   adv. 精致地；精巧地
108. empiric
   n. 江湖医生

"她的父亲，"巴格里奥尼接着说道，"不顾亲生骨肉之情用这种可怕方式把自己的孩子作为他对科学疯狂热情的牺牲品。让我们为他说句公道话，因为他是一位真正的科学家，就像他把自己的心都在蒸馏器里提炼过一样。那么，你的命运又会是什么呢？毫无疑问，你被选为某种新实验的材料。也许结局会是死亡——也许是更可怕的命运！拉帕西尼在他称为科学的利益面前，对什么都毫不犹豫。"

"真是一场梦！"乔万尼喃喃自语，"肯定是一场梦！"

"不过，"教授接着说道，"不要垂头丧气，我朋友的儿子！挽救还不太晚。说不定我们还能让这个可怜的孩子恢复到正常自然的环境里来，使她父亲的疯狂行为离开她。看到这只小银瓶了吧！它出自大名鼎鼎的本维努托·塞利尼之手，而且作为一件爱情礼物送给意大利最美丽的姑娘完全配得上。但是，瓶里的东西是无价之宝。这种解毒药只呷一小点就会使波尔吉亚最致命的毒药失去作用。对付拉帕西尼的那些毒药无疑会同样灵验。你把这只瓶子和它里面宝贵的药水都献给比阿特丽斯，然后满怀希望等待结果吧。"

巴格里奥尼把一只做工精制的小银瓶放在桌上，起身告辞，让他的那番话对年轻人的思想产生作用。

"我们一定会挫败拉帕西尼！"他一边下楼，一边暗自笑道。"不过，我们要承认有关他的事实，他是一个了不起的人——确实了不起！然而，他是一个卑鄙的江湖医生，所以那些尊重医学界良好古医道的人都受不了他！"

正如我们所说，在乔万尼和比阿特丽斯的整个相识过

巴格里奥尼教授就像他讲述的那个有关印度女人的古老传说里的那位睿智医生。

he had occasionally, as we have said, been haunted by dark surmises as to her character. Yet, so thoroughly had she made herself felt by him as a simple, natural, most affectionate and **guileless**[109] creature, that the image now held up by Professor Baglioni, looked as strange and **incredible**[110], as if it were not in accordance with his own original conception. True, there were ugly recollections connected with his first glimpses of the beautiful girl; he could not quite forget the bouquet that withered in her grasp, and the insect that perished amid the sunny air, by no **ostensible**[111] agency save the fragrance of her breath. These incidents, however, dissolving in the pure light of her character, had no longer the efficacy of facts, but were acknowledged as mistaken fantasies, by whatever **testimony**[112] of the senses they might appear to be **substantiated**[113]. There is something truer and more real, than what we can see with the eyes, and touch with the finger. On such better evidence, had Giovanni founded his confidence in Beatrice, though rather by the necessary force of her high attributes, than by any deep and generous faith on his part. But, now, his spirit was incapable of sustaining itself at the height to which the early enthusiasm of passion had **exalted**[114] it; he fell down, **grovelling**[115] among earthly doubts, and defiled therewith the pure whiteness of Beatrice's image. Not that he gave her up; he did but distrust. He resolved to institute some decisive test that should satisfy him, once for all, whether there were those dreadful peculiarities in her physical nature, which could not be supposed to exist without some corresponding **monstrosity**[116] of soul. His eyes, gazing down afar, might have deceived him as to the lizard, the insect, and the flowers. But if he could witness, at the distance of a few paces, the sudden **blight**[117] of one fresh and healthful flower in Beatrice's hand, there would be room for no further question. With this idea, he hastened to the florist's, and purchased a bouquet that was still gemmed with the morning dew-drops.

It was now the customary hour of his daily interview with

109. guileless
adj. 不狡猾的；诚实的
110. incredible
adj. 难以置信的
111. ostensible
adj. 表面的；假装的
112. testimony
n. 证言；证据
113. substantiate
vt. 证实
114. exalt
vt.（高度）赞扬；歌颂
115. grovel
vi. 趴；匍匐
116. monstrosity
n. 畸形；奇怪；怪异
117. blight
n. 枯萎病

程中，对她人品的模糊猜疑偶尔曾经萦绕在他的心头。然而，她总是让他感到她是那样纯朴自然，充满深情，天真无邪，因此巴格里奥尼教授此刻描绘的那个形象看上去既陌生又难以置信，好像和他自己最初的看法也不一致。的确，第一眼看到这位美丽少女，他有过不快的回忆；他无法完全忘记在她手里枯萎的那束花，以及那只在阳光灿烂的空气中死去的昆虫，除了她芳香的气息，没有任何其他明显的原因。然而，无论怎样用感觉去证实，这些事件都看似有根有据，但它们在她人品的纯洁光芒中渐渐融化，不再具有一些事实的功效，而是被看成错误的幻觉。有些东西比我们亲眼所见、亲手所摸的更正确、更真实。凭借这种更好的证据，乔万尼对比阿特丽斯有了信心，尽管这肯定是她的高贵品质作用，而不是他具有深沉大度的信念。但现在，他的精神无法维持当初他热情澎湃曾经达到的高度；他垮了下来，匍匐在世俗的疑虑之中，于是玷污了比阿特丽斯洁白无瑕的形象。倒不是他放弃了她，只是他不信任。他决心做一次让他满意的决定性试验，只此一次，看她身上是否有那些可怕的特性，如果没有某种相应的畸形灵魂，那些特性就不可能存在。至于蜥蜴、昆虫和鲜花，因为从远处向下看，眼睛可能会误导他。但是，如果他能在几步的距离之内目睹一朵健康的鲜花在比阿特丽斯手里突然枯萎，那就不会有任何疑问了。想到这一点，他就赶紧跑到花店，买了一束上面还闪着晶莹露珠的鲜花。

铤而走险，为爱一搏。

现在通常是他每天和比阿特丽斯相会的时刻。下楼去花园之前，乔万尼没有忘记看看镜子里自己的形象；

Beatrice. Before descending into the garden, Giovanni failed not to look at his figure in the mirror; a vanity to be expected in a beautiful young man, yet, as displaying itself at that troubled and feverish moment, the token of a certain shallowness of feeling and insincerity of character. He did gaze, however, and said to himself, that his features had never before possessed so rich a grace, nor his eyes such vivacity, nor his cheeks so warm a hue of **superabundant**[118] life.

"At least," thought he, "her poison has not yet **insinuated**[119] itself into my system. I am no flower to perish in her grasp!"

With that thought, he turned his eyes on the bouquet, which he had never once laid aside from his hand. A thrill of indefinable horror shot through his frame, on perceiving that those dewy flowers were already beginning to droop; they wore the aspect of things that had been fresh and lovely, yesterday. Giovanni grew white as marble, and stood motionless before the mirror, staring at his own reflection there, as at the likeness of something frightful. He remembered Baglioni's remark about the fragrance that seemed to pervade the chamber. It must have been the poison in his breath! Then he shuddered—shuddered at himself! Recovering from his stupor, he began to watch, with curious eye, a spider that was busily at work, hanging its web from the antique **cornice**[120] of the apartment, crossing and re-crossing the artful system of interwoven lines, as vigorous and active a spider as ever dangled from an old ceiling. Giovanni bent towards the insect, and emitted a deep, long breath. The spider suddenly ceased its toil; the web **vibrated**[121] with a tremor originating in the body of the small artisan. Again Giovanni sent forth a breath, deeper, longer, and imbued with a **venomous**[122] feeling out of his heart; he knew not whether he were wicked or only desperate. The spider made a **convulsive**[123] gripe with his limbs, and hung dead across the window.

"Accursed! Accursed!" muttered Giovanni, addressing himself. "Hast thou grown so poisonous, that this deadly insect

118. superabundant
　　adj. 过多的；大量的
119. insinuate
　　vt. 暗示；使逐渐
　　巧妙地取得；使迂
　　回地潜入
120. cornice
　　n. 飞檐；檐口
121. vibrate
　　vi. 振动；颤动
122. venomous
　　adj. 恶意的；有毒的
123. convulsive
　　adj. 起痉挛的；抽
　　搐的

可以料想英俊的年轻人都有一种虚荣心，但在这种困惑不安的时刻展示虚荣，却又表现出某种程度上他感情的浅薄和性格的虚伪。然而，他的确对镜自语，说他的相貌以前从来没有这样优雅深沉，眼睛从来没有这样活泼愉快，脸颊也从来没有这样红润，呈现出活力过盛的色调。

"至少，"他想，"她的毒素还没有渗入我的体内。我绝不是将在她手里枯萎的花朵。"

他这样想着，将目光转向了他从来没有离手的那束鲜花。当察觉到那些带有露水的花朵已经开始凋萎时，一阵莫名的恐惧袭遍了他的全身；它们新鲜美丽的模样已经成为过去。乔万尼脸色变得像大理石一样苍白，站在镜前一动不动，盯着镜子里的自己，好像盯着某个可怕东西的肖像。他想起了巴格里奥尼说过的话，说香气仿佛弥漫了这个房间。那一定是自己气息中的毒素！随后，他浑身颤抖———想到自己就浑身颤抖！他从恍惚中恢复知觉，用好奇的目光开始注视一只正在忙来忙去的蜘蛛，只见这只蜘蛛正在房间古老的檐口上结网，爬来爬去织出一个纵横交错的巧妙系统——跟永远挂在旧天花板上的蜘蛛一样敏捷活跃。乔万尼向那只蜘蛛弯下腰，深深地吐出一口长气。顿时，蜘蛛停止织网；蛛网随着小工匠身体的颤抖而振动起来。乔万尼又向它吐了一口气，这口气更深更长，充满了发自内心的恶感；他不知道他是心怀恶意，还是仅仅出于绝望。蜘蛛的肢体痉挛地紧缩了一下，挂在窗上一命呜呼。

"该死！该死！"乔万尼对自己喃喃说道。"你已经变得这么毒了吗，一口气就把这只蜘蛛吹死了吗？"

为了检验自己的猜疑，乔万尼冒险试验。

perishes by thy breath?"

At that moment, a rich, sweet voice came floating up from the garden: "Giovanni! Giovanni! It is past the hour! Why tarriest thou! Come down!"

"Yes," muttered Giovanni again. "She is the only being whom my breath may not slay! Would that it might!"

He rushed down, and in an instant, was standing before the bright and loving eyes of Beatrice. A moment ago, his wrath and despair had been so fierce that he could have desired nothing so much as to wither her by a glance. But, with her actual presence, there came influences which had too real an existence to be at once shaken off; recollections of the delicate and benign power of her feminine nature, which had so often enveloped him in a religious calm; recollections of many a holy and passionate outgush of her heart, when the pure fountain had been unsealed from its depths, and made visible in its transparency to his mental eye; recollections which, had Giovanni known how to estimate them, would have assured him that all this ugly mystery was but an earthly illusion, and that, whatever mist of evil might seem to have gathered over her, the real Beatrice was a heavenly angel. Incapable as he was of such high faith, still her presence had not utterly lost its magic. Giovanni's rage was quelled into an aspect of sullen insensibility. Beatrice, with a quick spiritual sense, immediately felt that there was a gulf of blackness between them, which neither he nor she could pass. They walked on together, sad and silent, and came thus to the marble fountain, and to its pool of water on the ground, in the midst of which grew the shrub that bore gem-like blossoms. Giovanni was **affrighted**[124] at the eager enjoyment—the appetite, as it were—with which he found himself inhaling the fragrance of the flowers.

"Beatrice," asked he abruptly, "whence came this shrub!"

"My father created it," answered she, with simplicity.

124. affright
vt. 惊吓；使……
恐怖

正在这时，一个圆润甜美的声音从花园里飘了上来："乔万尼！乔万尼！时间都过了！你为什么还等啊？下来吧！"

"是，"乔万尼又喃喃说道。"她才是我的气息不能杀死的唯一生物！但愿我能！"

他冲下楼，立马就站在了比阿特丽斯明亮而充满爱意的目光前。片刻之前，他的愤怒和绝望曾经如此强烈，以致他本想只看她一眼就让她枯萎。但是，她真在那里时，她的影响却非常实在，无法马上摆脱。他想起了她女性的体贴和善良的力量，这种力量常常把他包围在宗教般的宁静之中；想起她多次从内心涌出的圣洁激情，这时就像从深处打开的纯净泉水，在他的心目中清晰透明。如果乔万尼知道怎么评价这些回忆，就会确信这一切丑陋的秘密只是一种世俗的幻觉，而且，无论邪恶的迷雾可能会怎样笼罩在她的头顶，真正的比阿特丽斯都是一位神圣的天使。尽管他无法具有如此崇高的信念，但她的出现仍然没有完全失去魔力。乔万尼的愤怒得以平息，变成了阴郁麻木的样子。思想敏锐的比阿特丽斯马上觉得，他们之间有一道彼此谁也无法逾越的黑暗鸿沟。他们一起向前走，伤心无语，就这样来到了大理石喷泉边和地上的池水边，池中央就是那棵长满宝石般花朵的灌木。乔万尼吸入这些鲜花的香气，迫不及待，好像津津有味，他对此感到恐惧。

矛盾纠结的心态表现得淋漓尽致。

"比阿特丽斯，"他突然问道，"这棵树是从哪里来的？"

"是我的父亲创造的，"她如实答道。

"创造的！创造的！"乔万尼重复说道。"你这话什么意思，比阿特丽斯？"

Rappaccini's Daughter 拉帕西尼的女儿

223

"Created it! created it!" repeated Giovanni. "What mean you, Beatrice?"

"He is a man fearfully acquainted with the secrets of nature," replied Beatrice; "and, at the hour when I first drew breath, this plant sprang from the soil, the offspring of his science, of his intellect, while I was but his earthly child. Approach it not!" continued she, observing with terror that Giovanni was drawing nearer to the shrub. "It has qualities that you little dream of. But I, dearest Giovanni—I grew up and blossomed with the plant, and was nourished with its breath. It was my sister, and I loved it with a human affection: for—alas! hast thou not suspected it? there was an awful doom."

Here Giovanni frowned so darkly upon her that Beatrice paused and trembled. But her faith in his tenderness reassured her, and made her blush that she had doubted for an instant.

"There was an awful doom," she continued, "the effect of my father's fatal love of science—which **estranged**[125] me from all society of my kind. Until Heaven sent thee, dearest Giovanni, Oh! how lonely was thy poor Beatrice!"

"Was it a hard doom?" asked Giovanni, fixing his eyes upon her.

"Only of late have I known how hard it was," answered she tenderly. "Oh, yes; but my heart was torpid, and therefore quiet."

Giovanni's rage broke forth from his sullen gloom like a lightning-flash out of a dark cloud.

"Accursed one!" cried he, with venomous scorn and anger. "And finding thy solitude wearisome, thou hast severed me, likewise, from all the warmth of life, and enticed me into thy region of unspeakable horror!"

"Giovanni!" exclaimed Beatrice, turning her large bright eyes upon his face. The force of his words had not found its way into her mind; she was merely thunder-struck.

125. estrange
　　vt. 使疏远；离间

"他是一个可怕的知晓大自然奥秘的人，"比阿特丽斯答道，"而且，在我刚出生的那个时刻，这棵树破土而出，这是他科学的孩子、智慧的孩子，而我只是他世俗的孩子。不要靠近它！"她看到乔万尼离那棵树越来越近，就大惊失色地接着说道。"它的特性你做梦都想不到。可是，最亲爱的乔万尼，我——我跟这棵树一起成长，一起盛开，而且受到了它的香气的滋养。它就是我的姐妹，我以人间亲情爱着它，因为——唉！难道你没有怀疑过吗？命运真可怕。"

听到这里，乔万尼向她阴沉皱眉，比阿特丽斯停下来，浑身颤抖。但是，对他柔情的信任又打消了她的疑虑，并使她对自己片刻的怀疑感到脸红。

"命运真可怕，"她接着说道，"因为我的父亲对科学的致命热爱，所以隔断了我和所有同类的交往。直到上天把你派来，最亲爱的乔万尼。噢！你可怜的比阿特丽斯曾是多么寂寞！"

"这命运很可怕吗？"乔万尼眼睛盯着她问道。

"只是最近我才知道它是多么可怕，"她温和地说。"噢，是的，但我的心一度麻木，因此也一度平静。"

比阿特丽斯向乔万尼倾诉衷肠，清洗自己忧郁的伤口。

乔万尼本来闷闷不乐，现在突然发怒，就像一道闪电划过一团乌云。

"该死的人！"他带着恶毒的轻蔑和愤怒叫道。"在你发现孤独厌倦后，你同样隔断了我和生活的所有温暖，并把我诱入了你那难以言表的恐怖领域！"

"乔万尼！"比阿特丽斯大声说着，她明亮的大眼睛看着他的脸。她没有领会他的话是什么意思，只是感到震惊。

"是的，你这毒物！"乔万尼气得发狂，反复说道。

"Yes, poisonous thing!" repeated Giovanni, beside himself with passion. "Thou hast done it! Thou hast blasted me! Thou hast filled my veins with poison! Thou hast made me as hateful, as ugly, as loathsome[126] and deadly a creature as thyself—a world's wonder of hideous monstrosity! Now—if our breath be happily as fatal to ourselves as to all others—let us join our lips in one kiss of unutterable hatred, and so die!"

"What has befallen me?" murmured Beatrice, with a low moan out of her heart. "Holy Virgin pity me, a poor heartbroken child!"

"Thou! Dost thou pray?" cried Giovanni, still with the same fiendish scorn. "Thy very prayers, as they come from thy lips, taint the atmosphere with death. Yes, yes; let us pray! Let us to church, and dip our fingers in the holy water at the portal! They that come after us will perish as by a pestilence. Let us sign crosses in the air! It will be scattering curses abroad in the likeness of holy symbols!"

"Giovanni," said Beatrice calmly, for her grief was beyond passion, "Why dost thou join thyself with me thus in those terrible words? I, it is true, am the horrible thing thou namest me. But thou!—what hast thou to do, save with one other shudder at my hideous misery, to go forth out of the garden and mingle with thy race, and forget that there ever crawled on earth such a monster as poor Beatrice?"

"Dost thou pretend ignorance?" asked Giovanni, scowling upon her. "Behold! This power have I gained from the pure daughter of Rappaccini!"

There was a swarm of summer-insects flitting through the air, in search of the food promised by the flower-odors of the fatal garden. They circled round Giovanni's head, and were evidently attracted towards him by the same influence which had drawn them, for an instant, within the sphere of several of the shrubs. He sent forth a breath among them, and smiled bitterly at Beatrice, as at least a score of the insects fell dead upon the

126. loathsome

adj. 讨厌的；可恶的；令人呕吐的

"你已经做了！你已经毁了我！你已经把我的血管里灌满了毒液！你已经把我变成了一个像你本人一样可恨、丑陋、讨厌和可怕的东西——一个可怕畸形的世界奇迹！好了——如果我们的气息恰好像对所有其他人一样致命——就让我们以难以言表的仇恨接吻，这样死去吧！"

"是什么降临到了我身上？"比阿特丽斯喃喃自语，从心里发出了低沉的呻吟。"圣母可怜可怜我这个伤心的可怜孩子吧！"

"你！你祈祷吗？"乔万尼仍然带着恶毒轻蔑地叫道。"就是从你嘴里说出来的祈祷也是以死亡玷污了周围的空气。是的，是的，让我们祈祷吧！让我们到教堂去，在拱门边把我们的手指浸入圣水！尾随我们而来的人会像染上瘟疫一样死去！让我们在空中画十字吧！它会以神圣的象征把诅咒撒向四面八方！"

"乔万尼，"比阿特丽斯平静地说，因为她的悲伤超过了愤怒。"为什么你用那些可怕的话把你自己和我连在一起？我的确是你指控的那种可怕东西。可是，你——你与此有什么关系呢？你只需对我可怕的痛苦又一次瑟瑟发抖，走出园子，跟你的同类交往，忘记世界上曾经爬行过可怜的比阿特丽斯这样一个怪物。"

"你是佯装无知吧？"乔万尼对她皱着眉头问道。"看！这就是我从拉帕西尼纯洁的女儿身上获得的力量！"

一群夏虫掠过空中，受到这致命园子的花香吸引，过来觅食。它们先在几棵树四周盘旋了一会儿，然后又在乔万尼头顶盘旋，显然是受到了同样力量的吸引。他向它们吹了一口气，随后向比阿特丽斯苦笑了一下，至少有二十只昆虫落地身亡。

实践证明了一切。采用类比法，说明了眼见为实、耳听为虚的道理。

Rappaccini's Daughter 拉帕西尼的女儿 227

ground.

"I see it! I see it!" shrieked Beatrice. "It is my father's fatal science? No, no, Giovanni; it was not I! Never, never! I dreamed only to love thee, and be with thee a little time, and so to let thee pass away, leaving but thine image in mine heart. For, Giovanni—believe it—though my body be nourished with poison, my spirit is God's creature, and craves love as its daily food. But my father!—he has united us in this fearful sympathy. Yes; spurn[127] me!—tread upon me!—kill me! Oh, what is death, after such words as thine? But it was not I! Not for a world of bliss would I have done it!"

Giovanni's passion had exhausted itself in its outburst from his lips. There now came across him a sense, mournful, and not without tenderness, of the intimate and peculiar relationship between Beatrice and himself. They stood, as it were, in an utter solitude, which would be made none the less solitary by the densest throng of human life. Ought not, then, the desert of humanity around them to press this insulated[128] pair closer together? If they should be cruel to one another, who was there to be kind to them? Besides, thought Giovanni, might there not still be a hope of his returning within the limits of ordinary nature, and leading Beatrice—the redeemed[129] Beatrice—by the hand? Oh, weak, and selfish, and unworthy spirit, that could dream of an earthly union and earthly happiness as possible, after such deep love had been so bitterly wronged as was Beatrice's love by Giovanni's blighting words! No, no; there could be no such hope. She must pass heavily, with that broken heart, across the borders of Time—she must bathe her hurts in some fount of Paradise, and forget her grief in the light of immortality[130]— and there be well!

But Giovanni did not know it.

"Dear Beatrice," said he, approaching her, while she

127. spurn
   vt. 唾弃；冷落；一脚踢开
128. insulated
   adj. 绝缘的；隔热的
129. redeem
   vt. 赎回；挽回；恢复
130. immortality
   n. 不朽；永存

"我看到了！我看到了！"比阿特丽斯尖叫道。"真是我的父亲致命的科学！不，不，乔万尼，那不是我干的！绝不是，绝不是！我只梦想过爱你，和你在一起呆一小会儿，就让你走开，只把你的形象留在我的心里。乔万尼——相信这一点——尽管我的身体是用毒药滋养，我的灵魂却是上帝的造物，像渴望一日三餐一样渴望爱情。可是，我的父亲！——他已经用这种可怕的感应把我们结合在了一起。是的，唾弃我——践踏我！杀了我吧！噢，听过你这番话，死算什么？可那不是我干的！苍天在上，那绝不是我干的，我也不会干那种事！"

乔万尼一阵宣泄，怒气全消。他心里现在闪过一阵忧伤感，不无温柔地想到了比阿特丽斯和他本人之间亲密而奇特的关系。他们站在那里，可以说，处在完全的孤独之中，即使在最密集的人群中，也仍然会这样孤独。那么，周围人性的荒漠不该迫使这一对与世隔绝的人更亲密吗？如果他们彼此无情，还有谁会善待他们呢？再说，乔万尼心里想，难道他就没有希望回到正常自然的环境里去，牵手比阿特丽斯——牵手获救的比阿特丽斯吗？噢，软弱、自私、卑劣的灵魂，乔万尼出言不逊，严重玷污了比阿特丽斯的爱情之后，还能梦想尘世的结合和尘世的幸福吗？不，不，不可能有希望了。她肯定会带着那颗破碎的心沉重地跨过时光的边界——她肯定会在天堂的泉边清洗自己的伤口，在永恒之光中忘记自己的忧伤——那里一切都好！

天堂的清泉能荡涤灵魂的污浊吗？这是小说的主旨。

然而，乔万尼不知道这一点。

"亲爱的比阿特丽斯，"他走近她说，正如往常

shrank away, as always at his approach, but now with a different impulse— "dearest Beatrice, our fate is not yet so desperate. Behold! There is a medicine, potent, as a wise physician has assured me, and almost divine in its efficacy. It is composed of **ingredients**[131] the most opposite to those by which thy awful father has brought this calamity upon thee and me. It is distilled of blessed herbs. Shall we not quaff it together, and thus be purified from evil?"

"Give it me!" said Beatrice, extending her hand to receive the little silver phial which Giovanni took from his bosom. She added, with a peculiar emphasis: "I will drink—but do thou await the result."

She put Baglioni's antidote to her lips; and, at the same moment, the figure of Rappaccini emerged from the portal, and came slowly towards the marble fountain. As he drew near, the pale man of science seemed to gaze with a triumphant expression at the beautiful youth and maiden, as might an artist who should spend his life in achieving a picture or a group of statuary, and finally be satisfied with his success. He paused—his bent form grew erect with conscious power, he spread out his hands over them, in the attitude of a father imploring a blessing upon his children. But those were the same hands that had thrown poison into the stream of their lives! Giovanni trembled. Beatrice shuddered very nervously, and pressed her hand upon her heart.

"My daughter," said Rappaccini, "thou art no longer lonely in the world! Pluck one of those precious gems from thy sister shrub, and bid thy bridegroom wear it in his bosom. It will not harm him now! My science, and the sympathy between thee and him, have so wrought within his system, that he now stands apart from common men, as thou dost, daughter of my pride and triumph, from ordinary women. Pass on, then, through the world, most dear to one another, and dreadful to all besides!"

131. ingredient
n. 原料；要素

他靠近时一样，她退缩了一下，但现在却出于一种不同以往的冲动。"最亲爱的比阿特丽斯，我们的命运还没有到如此绝望的地步。看！这里有一种药，一位博学的医生向我保证说，非常有效，简直灵验非凡。它的成分和你可怕的父亲给你我带来这次灾难的那些东西截然相反。它是由神圣的药草提炼而成。我们何不一起喝下去，从此洗净罪恶呢？"

"把它给我吧！"比阿特丽斯说着，伸手接住乔万尼从胸前拿出的小银药瓶。她特别强调地补充道："我愿意喝——但你要等一下结果。"

她将巴格里奥尼的解毒药放在了唇边；正在这时，拉帕西尼的身影从拱门下走出来，慢慢地向大理石喷泉走来。他越走越近，这个脸色苍白的科学家好像面带得意的神色凝视着这对俊朗男女，就像一位画家穷其一生完成一幅画作或一组雕像，终于对自己的成功心满意足一样。他停下来——刻意用力挺直伛偻的身体，向他们伸出一双手，做出父亲祈求给孩子们祝福的姿势。但是，就是那双手把毒药扔进了他们的生命小溪！乔万尼浑身颤抖。比阿特丽斯忐忑不安哆哆嗦嗦，一只手按在心口。

"我的女儿，"拉帕西尼说，"你在世界上不会再孤独了！从你的灌木姐妹上摘一朵宝石花，吩咐你的新郎戴在他的胸前。它现在不会伤害他了！我的科学，以及你和他之间的感应已经在他的体内发挥了作用，他现在不同于普通男人，就像你——我得意和自豪的女儿——不同于普通女人一样。那你们就相亲相爱，走遍天下，让所有人害怕去吧！"

"爸爸，"比阿特丽斯有气无力地说——而且她一

Rappaccini's Daughter 拉帕西尼的女儿

"My father," said Beatrice, feebly—and still, as she spoke, she kept her hand upon her heart—"wherefore didst thou inflict this miserable doom upon thy child?"

"Miserable!" exclaimed Rappaccini. "What mean you, foolish girl? Dost thou deem it misery to be endowed with marvellous gifts, against which no power nor strength could avail an enemy? Misery, to be able to quell the mightiest with a breath? Misery, to be as terrible as thou art beautiful? Wouldst thou, then, have preferred the condition of a weak woman, exposed to all evil, and capable of none?"

"I would fain have been loved, not feared," murmured Beatrice, sinking down upon the ground. "But now it matters not; I am going, father, where the evil, which thou hast striven to mingle with my being, will pass away like a dream—like the fragrance of these poisonous flowers, which will no longer taint my breath among the flowers of Eden. Farewell, Giovanni! Thy words of hatred are like lead within my heart—but they, too, will fall away as I ascend. Oh, was there not, from the first, more poison in thy nature than in mine?"

To Beatrice—so radically had her earthly part been wrought upon by Rappaccini's skill—as poison had been life, so the powerful antidote was death. And thus the poor victim of man's ingenuity and of thwarted nature, and of the fatality that attends all such efforts of **perverted**[132] wisdom, perished there, at the feet of her father and Giovanni. Just at that moment, Professor Pietro Baglioni looked forth from the window, and called loudly, in a tone of triumph mixed with horror, to the thunder-stricken man of science: "Rappaccini! Rappaccini! And is this the **upshot**[133] of your experiment?"

132. perverted
   adj. 不正当的
133. upshot
   n. 结果；结局；结尾

边说，一边仍然继续按住心口——"为什么你用这种悲惨的命运折磨自己的孩子？"

"悲惨！"拉帕西尼大声叫道。"你这话什么意思，傻丫头？你认为自己具有威力无比、所向无敌的非凡天赋是悲惨吗？你能用一口气扑灭最强大的敌人是悲惨吗？你有多美，就有多令人生畏，是悲惨吗？那么，难道你喜欢做一个软弱女人，受到一切罪恶摆布而无能为力吗？"

"我情愿得到爱，而不是恐惧，"比阿特丽斯瘫软在地喃喃说道，"但现在，无所谓了；爸爸，我要去一个地方，在那里你千方百计混入我生命的邪恶会像梦一样消失——像这些毒花的香气一样，在伊甸园的花丛中，它们无法再玷污我的呼吸。再见，乔万尼！你仇恨的话语像铅一样压在我的心里——但随着我的腾飞，它们也会消失。噢，是不是你的天性从一开始就比我的天性里的毒素多呢？"

对比阿特丽斯来说——她尘世的躯体已被拉帕西尼的技术从根本上改变——正如毒药就是生命，所以烈性解毒药就是死亡。于是，这个人类的聪明才智和刚愎天性的可怜牺牲品，这个被邪恶智慧的种种尝试注定厄运的可怜牺牲品，死在了她父亲和乔万尼的脚下。正在这时，皮埃特罗·巴格里奥尼教授从窗户望去，冲那个目瞪口呆的科学家大声呼喊，口气既得意又恐怖："拉帕西尼！拉帕西尼！这就是你实验的结果吗？"

对比阿特丽斯来说，在毒花伊甸园里长大的她，毒药与烈性解毒药，一个是她的生命，一个则意味着死亡。她最终死在了自己的父亲和自己的恋人两个男人的脚下，这就是拉帕西尼医生亲眼看到的自己在"尘世伊甸园"实验的结果。

名篇赏析

　　如果说拉帕西尼医生的花园是当今尘世的伊甸园，那么，《拉帕西尼的女儿》则是一位年轻的异乡人在毒花伊甸园的游历记。这个名叫乔万尼·古斯康提的年轻人和拉帕西尼医生的女儿比阿特丽斯这对当今尘世伊甸园里坠入爱河的亚当和夏娃，在拉帕西尼医生称为科学的利益面前，像花园里的植物一样被选为拉帕西尼医生新的实验材料，成为"科学实验"的可怜牺牲品。作品围绕毒花伊甸园，通过反复出现的意象和精妙恰当的结构与语言，为我们构建了一个神秘的象征体系和开放的主题阐释空间。

Mark Twain

狗 的 自 述

姓名	马克·吐温
出生日期	1835年11月30日
出生地	美国密苏里州佛罗里达乡村
性别	男

成就和特色

　　美国杰出的小说家、十九世界美国批判现实主义文学的奠基人、世界著名的短篇小说大师，也是美国文学史上最重要的作家之一。马克·吐温的语言艺术超凡脱俗。他只读过小学，他的语言是从群众中学来的活的语言。他在民间语言的基础上加工锤炼，进一步创造了美国的文学语言。海明威说，美国小说是从马克·吐温开始的。福克纳说，马克·吐温是第一个建立美国意识和美国语言的美国作家。马克·吐温发表幽默短篇共七十篇，其中多数为小品类，主要特色是极度夸张、幽默、滑稽。重要长篇小说有《哈克贝利·芬历险记》、《汤姆·索亚历险记》。

写作背景

　　小说以一条狗的口吻讲述了一个悲惨的故事。故事中的狗们在一起的场景宛如人类社会的缩影，狗们之间也有聚会、有冲突、有嘲讽……作为故事主角的"我"勇敢地冲入火海，挽救了小主人的生命。而人类，尤其是以作为科学家男主人为代表的人类，却残忍无情、忘恩负义，以残忍手段害死了"我"的狗娃。

名著的力量

世界经典
名家名作赏析——传奇篇

Literary Impact of Masterpieces

A Dog's Tale

1

My father was a St. Bernard, my mother was a collie, but I am a **Presbyterian**[1]. This is what my mother told me, I do not know these nice **distinctions**[2] myself. To me they are only fine large words meaning nothing. My mother had a fondness for such; she liked to say them, and see other dogs look surprised and envious, as wondering how she got so much education. But, indeed, it was not real education; it was only show: she got the words by listening in the dining-room and drawing-room when there was company and by going with the children to Sunday-school and listening there; and whenever she heard a large word she said it over to herself many times, and so was able to keep it until there was a **dogmatic**[3] gathering in the neighborhood, then she would get it off, and surprise and distress them all, from pocket-pup to **mastiff**[4], which rewarded her for all her trouble. If there was a stranger he was nearly sure to be suspicious, and when he got his breath again he would ask her what it meant. And she always told him. He was never expecting this, but thought he would catch her; so when she told him, he was the one that looked ashamed, **whereas**[5] he had thought it was going to be she. The others were always waiting for this, and glad of it and proud of her, for they knew what was going to happen, because they had had experience. When she told the

1. Presbyterian
   n. 长老会教徒
2. distinction
   n. 区别；差别
3. dogmatic
   adj. 教条的
4. mastiff
   n. 獒；大驯犬（大型猛犬之一种）
5. whereas
   conj. 然而；反之；但是

狗的自述

一

　　我的父亲是圣伯纳犬，我的母亲是柯利牧羊犬，但我是长老会教友。这是母亲告诉我的，我自己并不知道这些细微的区别。在我看来，它们只是漂亮夸大、毫无意义的字眼。我的母亲对此情有独钟；她喜欢这样说，也喜欢看其他狗露出吃惊和嫉妒的样子，好像在纳闷她怎么受了这么多教育。但是，这其实并不是真正的教育，不过是卖弄：那些词是她在有聚会时从餐厅和客厅听来的，还有的是跟孩子们一起去主日学校时在那里听到的。每当她听到一个深奥的字眼，她就反复说上多遍，这样才能记住，直到在附近开教义会，她才会说出来，令小狗到猛犬上上下下全都吃惊和难受，这是对她所有心血的回报。如果有一条生狗，他肯定要怀疑，他喘过气来后，就会问她那是什么意思。她往往会告诉他。他对此绝没有料到，他以为他会难住她；所以，当她告诉他后，他就面露羞愧，他原以为面露羞愧的会是她。其他狗总是等着这一刻，以此为乐，为她自豪，因为他们都有经验，知道会发生什么。当她讲述一个

人有人性，狗有狗性，有时人狗相通。

meaning of a big word they were all so taken up with admiration that it never occurred to any dog to doubt if it was the right one; and that was natural, because, for one thing, she answered up so promptly[6] that it seemed like a dictionary speaking, and for another thing, where could they find out whether it was right or not? for she was the only cultivated[7] dog there was. By and by, when I was older, she brought home the word Unintellectual[8], one time, and worked it pretty hard all the week at different gatherings, making much unhappiness and despondency[9]; and it was at this time that I noticed that during that week she was asked for the meaning at eight different assemblages, and flashed out a fresh definition every time, which showed me that she had more presence of mind[10] than culture, though I said nothing, of course. She had one word which she always kept on hand, and ready, like a life-preserver[11], a kind of emergency word to strap on when she was likely to get washed overboard in a sudden way—that was the word Synonymous[12]. When she happened to fetch out a long word which had had its day weeks before and its prepared meanings gone to her dump-pile, if there was a stranger there of course it knocked him groggy[13] for a couple of minutes, then he would come to, and by that time she would be away down wind on another tack[14], and not expecting anything; so when he'd hail and ask her to cash in, I (the only dog on the inside of her game) could see her canvas flicker a moment—but only just a moment—then it would belly out taut[15] and full, and she would say, as calm as a summer's day, "It's synonymous with supererogation[16]," or some godless long reptile[17] of a word like that, and go placidly[18] about and skim away on the next tack, perfectly comfortable, you know, and leave that stranger looking profane[19] and embarrassed, and the initiated[20] slatting the floor with their tails in unison and their faces transfigured[21] with a holy joy.

6. promptly
   adv. 敏捷地；迅速地
7. cultivated
   adj. 有教养的
8. unintellectual
   adj. 缺乏智力的
9. despondency
   n. 失望；沮丧
10. presence of mind
    镇定；沉着
11. life preserver
    n. （美）救生工具
12. synonymous
    adj. 同义词的
13. groggy
    adj. 头昏眼花的
14. tack
    n. 行动方向；航向
15. taut
    adj. 拉紧的；绷紧的
16. supererogation
    n. 额外工作
17. reptile
    n. 爬虫
18. placidly
    adv. 平静地
19. profane
    adj. 世俗的
20. initiate
    adj. 启蒙的
21. transfigure
    vt. 使改观

深奥字眼的意思时，它们都非常羡慕，任何狗都不会想到去怀疑这意思是否正确；这也很自然，因为，首先，她应对如流，就像是一本字典在说话一样；另外，他们能去哪里弄清这是否正确呢？因为她是那里唯一有教养的狗，渐渐地，我长大了；有一次，她记熟了"无知"这个词，而且整整一周都在各种集会上拼命卖弄，制造了许多不快和沮丧；我就是这次才注意到，那一周她在八个不同的集会上被问到这个词的意思时，每次她脱口说出的都是一个新的定义，这使我明白她与其说是有文化，不如说是镇定沉着，当然我什么也没说。她有一个词总是挂在嘴边，随时备用救急，就像救命圈一样，当有可能突然被冲下船去的危险时，她就把它套在身上——那就是Synonymous（同义词）这个名词。当她碰巧拿出几周前用过的一个长词，她原来准备的解释忘到九霄云外去了的时候，如果有一条陌生狗在那里，她肯定让他晕头转向两分钟，他才会醒过神来，此时她会调转方向，料想不会有什么事儿；所以，当他招呼她，让她解释时，我（唯一清楚她那套把戏内情的狗）可以看到她的帆颤动了一会儿——但只有一会儿——随即便绷紧鼓满了风帆，她常常像夏日那样平静地说："那是'额外工作'的同义词，"或者说出诸如此类一长串像爬虫一样邪恶的词，接着平静地走来走去，飞快地走向下一个方向，你知道，非常惬意，把那条陌生狗丢在那里，显得世俗尴尬，那些知情狗一起用尾巴扑打着地板，脸上改变了神气，显出欢天喜地的样子。

狗同样有世俗的一面，作者显然是借狗说人。

22. matinee
n. 日场；日戏；白天举行的音乐会
23. daisy
n. 极好的东西
24. anecdote
n. 轶事；奇闻
25. nub
n.（美口）（故事的）要点；（事情、问题的）核心
26. hitch
vt. 系住；急拉
27. frivolous
adj. 轻浮妄动的；无意义的
28. resentment
n. 憎恨；不满

And it was the same with phrases. She would drag home a whole phrase, if it had a grand sound, and play it six nights and two matinees[22], and explain it a new way every time—which she had to, for all she cared for was the phrase; she wasn't interested in what it meant, and knew those dogs hadn't wit enough to catch her, anyway. Yes, she was a daisy[23]! She got so she wasn't afraid of anything, she had such confidence in the ignorance of those creatures. She even brought anecdotes[24] that she had heard the family and the dinner-guests laugh and shout over; and as a rule she got the nub[25] of one chestnut hitched[26] onto another chestnut, where, of course, it didn't fit and hadn't any point; and when she delivered the nub she fell over and rolled on the floor and laughed and barked in the most insane way, while I could see that she was wondering to herself why it didn't seem as funny as it did when she first heard it. But no harm was done; the others rolled and barked too, privately ashamed of themselves for not seeing the point, and never suspecting that the fault was not with them and there wasn't any to see.

You can see by these things that she was of a rather vain and frivolous[27] character; still, she had virtues, and enough to make up, I think. She had a kind heart and gentle ways, and never harbored resentments[28] for injuries done her, but put them easily out of her mind and forgot them; and she taught her children her kindly way, and from her we learned also to be brave and prompt in time of danger, and not to run away, but face the peril that threatened friend or stranger, and help him the best we could without stopping to think what the cost might be to us. And she taught us not by words only, but by example, and that is the best way and the surest and the most lasting. Why, the brave things she did, the splendid things! she was just a soldier;

而且短语也是这样。如果有完美的短语，她就会把整个短语带回来，表演六个晚场、两个日场，而且每次都用一种新的说法解释——她不得不这样，因为她关心的只是那个短语；她对那是什么意思不感兴趣，而且她知道那些狗反正不够聪明，难不住她。是的，她是一流的狗！她这样出色，所以她无所畏惧，她对那些狗的无知很有把握。她甚至把她听到的家人和赴宴客人大声说笑的逸闻趣事也记了下来；她通常把一个笑话里的精彩之处凑到另一个笑话上去，这当然不合适，不得要领；她说到精彩处时，就倒在地板上，大笑大叫，疯疯癫癫，滚来滚去；而我可以看出她自己也在纳闷为什么她说的好像没有她当初听到时那样有趣。但是，无伤大雅；其他狗也都打滚吠叫，都暗自为自己没有听懂而羞愧，绝不会猜到错不在他们，而是谁也看不出这里面的毛病。

你从这些事情可以看到，她是一个相当自负轻率的角色；尽管如此，但她仍有一些优点，我认为那足以弥补这个不足。她心地善良，作风温和，从来不会因受到伤害而怀恨在心，而是轻松自如地从记忆中抹去，忘到脑后；她还把自己的和善方式教给她的孩子们；我们还从她那里学会在危急时刻要勇敢敏捷，不要逃跑，而是面对威胁朋友或陌生人的危险，要尽力帮助他，不要停下来去考虑我们可能会付出什么代价。而且她对我们不仅言传，而且身教，这是最好的办法，最可靠、最持久。啊，她干的那些事是多么勇敢、多么辉煌！她真是

这里的"其他狗"即指其他人等。作者在此不失时机地给他厌恶的"盲众"以辛辣讽刺。同时，与"我"的清醒形成鲜明对照。

and so modest about it—well, you couldn't help admiring her, and you couldn't help imitating her; not even a **King Charles spaniel**[29] could remain entirely **despicable**[30] in her society. So, as you see, there was more to her than her education.

2

When I was well grown, at last, I was sold and taken away, and I never saw her again. She was broken-hearted, and so was I, and we cried; but she comforted me as well as she could, and said we were sent into this world for a wise and good purpose, and must do our duties without **repining**[31], take our life as we might find it, live it for the best good of others, and never mind about the results; they were not our affair. She said men who did like this would have a noble and beautiful reward by and by in another world, and although we animals would not go there, to do well and right without reward would give to our brief lives a worthiness and dignity which in itself would be a reward. She had gathered these things from time to time when she had gone to the Sunday-school with the children, and had laid them up in her memory more carefully than she had done with those other words and phrases; and she had studied them deeply, for her good and ours. One may see by this that she had a wise and thoughtful head, **for all**[32] there was so much lightness and vanity in it.

So we said our farewells, and looked our last upon each other through our tears; and the last thing she said—keeping it for the last to make me remember it the better, I think—was, "In memory of me, when there is a time of danger to another do not think of yourself, think of your mother, and do as she would do."

Do you think I could forget that? No.

29. King Charles spaniel
    n. 查尔斯王犬（一种具有带卷毛的、黑色和棕黄色皮和长耳的英国玩赏犬品种）
30. despicable
    adj. 可鄙的；卑劣的
31. repine
    v. 抱怨
32. for all
    尽管；虽然

一名勇士，而且非常谦虚——啊，你禁不住佩服她，你也禁不住模仿她；即使一只查尔斯王犬和她在一起，也不能完全小看她。所以，你明白，她不仅仅是有教养。

这是为给下文〝我〞冒着性命危险救主人家的小娃娃做了铺垫。

二

我终于长大后，被人买走，就再也没有见过她。她很伤心，我也一样，我们当时都哭了；但是，她尽力安慰我，说我们被派到这个世界，是为了一个明智善良的目的，必须尽职尽责，不要抱怨，要随遇而安，活着要尽量顾到别人的最大利益，不管结果怎样；那不是归我们管的事情。她说喜欢这样做的人以后在另一个世界会得到高尚漂亮的报答，尽管我们野兽不会去那里，但规矩过日子，多做些好事，不求回报，将会使我们短暂的一生高尚体面，这本身就是一种报答。这些道理是她和孩子们去主日学校时常常听到的，她很用心地通通记在心里，比她记那些词和短语更加认真；而且她深刻研究这些道理，为的是对她自己和对我们都有好处。你由此可以看出尽管她脑子里有许多轻浮和虚荣的想法，但她还是聪明和肯用心思的。

于是，我们告别，含泪彼此看了最后一眼；她说的最后一句话——我想，她留在最后说，是要我记得更清楚——是：〝作为对我的纪念，当出现危险时，不要想自己，要想到你的母亲，并像她那样去做。〞

你想我会忘记这句话吗？不会。

再次提到〝当出现危险时〞该如何如何做，作者在此重复前一段中的意思，也是为了给下文〝我〞冒着生命危险救小娃娃做铺垫。这是层层铺垫、步步设伏的写作手法。

A Dog's Tale 狗的自述 **243**

It was such a charming home!—my new one; a fine great house, with pictures, and delicate decorations, and rich furniture, and no gloom anywhere, but all the wilderness of dainty[33] colors lit up with flooding sunshine; and the spacious[34] grounds around it, and the great garden—oh, greensward[35], and noble trees, and flowers, no end! And I was the same as a member of the family; and they loved me, and petted me, and did not give me a new name, but called me by my old one that was dear to me because my mother had given it me—Aileen Mavourneen. She got it out of a song; and the Grays knew that song, and said it was a beautiful name.

Mrs. Gray was thirty, and so sweet and so lovely, you cannot imagine it; and Sadie was ten, and just like her mother, just a darling slender little copy of her, with auburn[36] tails down her back, and short frocks; and the baby was a year old, and plump and dimpled[37], and fond of me, and never could get enough of hauling on my tail, and hugging me, and laughing out its innocent happiness; and Mr. Gray was thirty-eight, and tall and slender and handsome, a little bald in front, alert, quick in his movements, business-like, prompt, decided, unsentimental[38], and with that kind of trim-chiseled[39] face that just seems to glint and sparkle with frosty intellectuality[40]! He was a renowned[41] scientist. I do not know what the word means, but my mother would know how to use it and get effects. She would know how to depress a rat-terrier with it and make a lap-dog look sorry he came. But that is not the best one; the best one was Laboratory. My mother could organize a Trust on that one that would skin the tax-collars off the whole herd. The laboratory was not a book, or a picture, or a place to wash your hands in,

33. dainty
    adj. 秀丽的；迷人的
34. spacious
    adj. 宽的；宽敞的
35. greensward
    n. 草地；草坪
36. auburn
    adj. 赤褐色的
37. dimpled
    adj. 带酒窝的
38. unsentimental
    adj. 不动感情的
39. chiseled
    adj. 轮廓分明的
40. intellectuality
    n. 智力；知性
41. renowned
    adj. 有名的

三

这真是一个迷人的家！——我的新家。漂亮的大房子，还有图画、精致的装饰品、豪华的家具，没有任何阴暗的地方，所有迷人的色彩都因充足的阳光而闪亮；周围是宽敞的空地，还有一座大花园——噢，茵茵绿地，高大树木，朵朵鲜花，说都说不完！我就像是这家的一名成员；他们都爱我，宠我，没有给我起新名字，而是叫我原来的名字，我对这个名字充满深情，因为是母亲给我起的——艾琳·麦弗宁。她取自一首歌曲，格雷夫妇也知道这首歌，说这是一个漂亮的名字。

格雷太太三十岁，甜美可爱得令你无法想象；赛迪十岁，就像她妈妈一样，活脱脱是她苗条可爱的小翻版，背上垂着赤赭色的辫子，穿着短短的上衣；而婴儿才一岁，胖墩墩的，脸上长着酒窝，他非常喜欢我，总是拉我的尾巴，抱我，欢笑起来天真无邪，简直没个够；格雷先生三十八岁，高大瘦长，英俊潇洒，脑门微秃，为人机警，动作敏捷，有条有理，干脆果断，不动声色，他那副整洁漂亮、轮廓分明的脸庞简直像是闪耀着冷冰冰的智慧之光！他是一位有名的科学家。尽管我不知道科学家这个词是什么意思，但我的母亲一定知道这个词怎么用，知道怎么去卖弄它，叫别人佩服。她一定知道怎么去用它让一只逮老鼠的小狗听了垂头丧气，使一只哈巴狗看上去后悔过来。但是，这还不是最好的词；最好的词是实验室。我的母亲能靠这个词成立一个托拉斯，把所有狗的拴着缴税片的项圈都取下来。实验室不是一本书，不是一幅画，也不像大学校长的狗说的

as the college president's dog said—no, that is the lavatory; the laboratory is quite different, and is filled with jars, and bottles, and electrics, and wires, and strange machines; and every week other scientists came there and sat in the place, and used the machines, and discussed, and made what they called experiments and discoveries; and often I came, too, and stood around and listened, and tried to learn, for the sake of my mother, and in loving memory of her, although it was a pain to me, as realizing what she was losing out of her life and I gaining nothing at all; for try as I might, I was never able to **make anything out of it**[42] at all.

Other times I lay on the floor in the mistress's work-room and slept, she gently using me for a foot-stool, knowing it pleased me, for it was a caress; other times I spent an hour in the nursery, and got well **tousled**[43] and made happy; other times I watched by the crib there, when the baby was asleep and the nurse out for a few minutes on the baby's affairs; other times I **romped**[44] and raced through the grounds and the garden with Sadie till we were tired out, then slumbered on the grass in the shade of a tree while she read her book; other times I went visiting among the neighbor dogs —for there were some most pleasant ones not far away, and one very handsome and **courteous**[45] and graceful one, a curly-haired Irish setter by the name of Robin Adair, who was a Presbyterian like me, and belonged to the Scotch **minister**[46].

The servants in our house were all kind to me and were fond of me, and so, as you see, mine was a pleasant life. There could not be a happier dog that I was, nor a gratefuller one. I will say this for myself, for it is only the truth: I tried in all ways to do well and right, and honor my mother's memory and her teachings, and earn the happiness that had come to me, as best I could.

42. make anything out of it
（常用于否定句）
了解；弄清
43. tousled
adj.（头发等）蓬乱的；混乱的
44. romp
vi. 顽皮嬉闹
45. courteous
adj. 有礼貌的
46. minister
n.（基督教新教）牧师；（某些教派的）教长

那样是洗手的地方——不，那是盥洗室；实验室截然不同，里面摆满了罐子、瓶子、电器、电线和奇怪的机器；每周都有其他科学家到那里去，坐在那个地方，使用那些机器，进行讨论，还做他们所谓的试验和发现；我也常常到那里去，站在附近听，想方设法学习，为了我的母亲，同时为了深情纪念她，而这对我是一件痛苦的事儿，因为我体会到她一生耗费了多少精神，而我却一无所获；因为尽管我努力，但我根本听不明白。

　　有时我躺在女主人工作室的地板上睡觉，她温柔地把我当作脚凳，知道这样可以使我高兴，因为这也是一种爱抚；有时我在育儿室度过一小时，被弄得毛发蓬乱，却让我非常开心；有时婴儿睡着，保姆为了婴儿的事儿出去几分钟，我就守在那里的童床边；有时我跟赛迪欢蹦乱跳穿过空地和花园，直到我们筋疲力尽，然后我在树荫下的草地上安睡，她在那里看书；有时我去看望那些邻居的狗——因为有几只非常有趣的狗离我们不远，其中有一只非常漂亮、礼貌、文雅，是一只卷毛爱尔兰猎犬，名叫罗宾·阿代尔，他和我一样也是长老会教友，他的主人是苏格兰牧师。

　　我们那个家的仆人都对我非常友善，而且喜欢我，所以你明白，我生活得非常愉快。再不可能有比我更快乐、更感恩的狗了。我之所以要给自己说这种话，是因为这不过是事实：我千方百计规矩过日子，多做些好事，纪念我的母亲，牢记她的教导，尽可能获得属于我的快乐。

描写婴儿的可爱，再次为〝我〞冒着生命危险救他做了铺垫。环环相扣。
提到实验室，为后文用我的孩子狗仔做实验设下伏笔。

用充满深情的语言渲染丰富而快乐的生活，表现〝我〞与小赛迪之间充满温情的友谊。

By and by came my little puppy, and then **my cup was full**[47], my happiness was perfect. It was the dearest little **waddling**[48] thing, and so smooth and soft and velvety, and had such cunning little awkward paws, and such affectionate eyes, and such a sweet and innocent face; and it made me so proud to see how the children and their mother **adored**[49] it, and **fondled**[50] it, and exclaimed over every little wonderful thing it did. It did seem to me that life was just too lovely to—

Then came the winter. One day I was standing a watch in the nursery. That is to say, I was asleep on the bed. The baby was asleep in the **crib**[51], which was alongside the bed, on the side next the fireplace. It was the kind of crib that has a **lofty**[52] tent over it made of **gauzy**[53] stuff that you can see through. The nurse was out, and we two sleepers were alone. A spark from the wood-fire was shot out, and it lit on the slope of the tent. I suppose a quiet interval followed, then a scream from the baby awoke me, and there was that tent flaming up toward the ceiling! Before I could think, I sprang to the floor in my fright, and in a second was half-way to the door; but in the next half-second my mother's farewell was sounding in my ears, and I was back on the bed again. I reached my head through the flames and dragged the baby out by the waist-band, and tugged it along, and we fell to the floor together in a cloud of smoke; I **snatched**[54] a new hold, and dragged the screaming little creature along and out at the door and around the bend of the hall, and was still tugging away, all excited and happy and proud, when the master's voice shouted: "**Begone**[55] you cursed beast!" and I jumped to save myself; but he was furiously quick, and chased me up, striking furiously at me with his cane, I **dodging**[56] this way and that, in terror, and at last a strong blow fell upon my left foreleg, which

47. one's cup is full
    幸福极了
48. waddle
    vi. 蹒跚地走
49. adore
    v. (口) 喜爱
50. fondle
    v. 爱抚
51. crib
    n. 婴儿床
52. lofty
    adj. 高的；高耸的
53. gauzy
    adj. 轻薄透明的；如烟雾的
54. snatch
    v. 攫取；抓住
55. begone
    int. 走开! 滚蛋!
56. dodge
    v. 避开；躲避

不久，我的宝宝出世了，我开心极了，非常幸福。它是一个最可爱的小家伙，走起路来一摇一摆，身上的毛是那样光滑柔软，像天鹅绒似的，有非常可爱笨拙的小爪、充满深情的眼睛和讨人喜欢的天真脸庞；我看到孩子们和他们的母亲是那样喜欢它，爱抚它，它每做出绝妙的小动作，他们都大声欢呼，这真使我非常得意，母爱和亲情具有相通性。在我看来，生活实在太有趣，简直无法——

随后就到了冬天。有一天，我在育儿室守护。这就是说，我在床上睡觉。婴儿在小床上睡觉，小床和大床并排放在一起，在靠近壁炉那边。这种小床上挂有一顶薄纱一样的东西做的高帐，你能一眼看透。保姆出去了，只剩下我们俩在睡觉。柴火堆飞溅出了一颗火星，落在帐子的斜面上。我猜接下来安静了一阵，后来婴儿发出的尖叫声把我惊醒，只见床帐往上冒着火，烧向了天花板！我来不及想，吓得跳到了地上，一秒钟不到就快跑到了门口；但是，接下来的半秒钟，母亲临别的教导就在我耳边响起，于是我又返回了床上。我把头伸进火焰里，叼住婴儿的腰带，把他拽了出来，拖着他朝外跑，我们俩在滚滚烟雾里跌倒在地；我马上又换个地方叼住，拖着那个尖叫的小家伙向外跑，跑到门外，拖到过道拐弯处，还在不停地拖，我越发激动、开心和得意，这时男主人的声音嚷道："滚开，你这该死的畜生！"于是，为了自救，我就跳开了；但是，他行动飞快，一下子追上我，拿起手杖狠狠地打我，我吓得东躲西藏，最后重重的一棍打在了我的左前腿上，我尖叫一

made me shriek and fall, for the moment, helpless; the cane went up for another blow, but never **descended**[57], for the nurse's voice rang wildly out, "The nursery's on fire!" and the master rushed away in that direction, and my other bones were saved.

The pain was cruel, but, no matter, I must not lose any time; he might come back at any moment; so I limped on three legs to the other end of the hall, where there was a dark little stairway leading up into a **garret**[58] where old boxes and such things were kept, as I had heard say, and where people seldom went. I managed to climb up there, then I searched my way through the dark among the piles of things, and hid in the secretest place I could find. It was foolish to be afraid there, yet still I was; so afraid that I held in and hardly even whimpered, though it would have been such a comfort to whimper, because that **eases**[59] the pain, you know. But I could lick my leg, and that did some good.

For half an hour there was a **commotion**[60] downstairs, and shoutings, and rushing footsteps, and then there was quiet again. Quiet for some minutes, and that was grateful to my spirit, for then my fears began to go down; and fears are worse than pains—oh, much worse. Then came a sound that froze me. They were calling me—calling me by name—hunting for me!

It was **muffled**[61] by distance, but that could not take the terror out of it, and it was the most dreadful sound to me that I had ever heard. It went all about, everywhere, down there: along the halls, through all the rooms, in both stories, and in the basement and the cellar; then outside, and farther and farther away—then back, and all about the house again, and I thought it would never, never stop. But at last it did, hours and hours after the **vague**[62] twilight of the garret had long ago been **blotted out**[63] by black darkness.

Then in that blessed stillness my terrors fell little by little

57. descend
   vi. 下来
58. garret
   n. 顶楼；阁楼
59. ease
   vt. 减轻
60. commotion
   n. 喧哗；混乱
61. muffle
   vt. 使变得模糊或不清楚
62. vague
   adj. 模糊不清的
63. blot out
   遮盖

声，一时无助地倒在了地上；手杖又举起来要打，但没有落下来，因为保姆的声音拼命响起："育儿室着火了！"主人朝那边飞奔而去，我这才保住了其他骨头。

尽管疼痛难忍，但我无论如何也不能耽误时间；他随时都可能回来；所以，我就三条腿一瘸一拐走到过道另一头，因为那里有一道又小又黑的楼梯，通到顶楼，我听说那里放有一些旧箱之类的东西，很少有人去那里。我设法爬上那里，然后摸黑穿过一堆堆东西，藏到我能找到的最秘密的地方，藏到了那里还害怕，真蠢，但我还是害怕；我非常害怕，屏住呼吸，就连抽泣都不敢，尽管哭出来一定非常舒坦，因为你知道，这会缓解疼痛。但是，我可以舔舔腿，而且好了些。

有半小时，楼下混乱不堪，喊叫声、跑步声响成一片，然后又静了下来。安静了几分钟，这让我心里非常感激，因为这时我的恐惧心理开始平静下来；恐惧比痛苦还糟糕——噢，糟糕得多。接着又传来一个声音，把我吓呆了。他们在喊我——喊我的名字——在找我！

这喊声因离得远而模糊不清，但这无法消除其中的恐怖，而且这是我从来没有听到过的最可怕的声音。喊声到处乱跑，经过过道，穿过所有房间、两层楼、地下室和地窖都跑到了，然后又跑到了外面，越跑越远——然后又回来，在房子里整个又跑一遍，我想它再也不会停止的。但是，最后终于停止了，顶楼模糊的光线早已被黑暗遮住，过去了好几个小时。

随后，在那种可喜的清静之中，恐惧渐渐退去，我

"我"冒着生命危险将主人家的小娃娃拖离火海，却被他误以为是发了疯。用手杖打折了腿。这段对主人打"我"进行了完整的细节描写，写出了主人的狠劲和"我"的无助。让人怎不担心狗儿的命运？

A Dog's Tale 狗的自述   251

away, and I was at peace and slept. It was a good rest I had, but I woke before the twilight had come again. I was feeling fairly comfortable, and I could think out a plan now. I made a very good one; which was, to creep down, all the way down the back stairs, and hide behind the cellar door, and slip out and escape when the iceman came at dawn, while he was inside filling the refrigerator; then I would hide all day, and start on my journey when night came; my journey to—well, anywhere where they would not know me and betray me to the master. I was feeling almost cheerful now; then suddenly I thought: Why, what would life be without my puppy!

That was despair. There was no plan for me; I saw that; I must stay where I was; stay, and wait, and take what might come —it was not my affair; that was what life is—my mother had said it. Then—well, then the calling began again! All my sorrows came back. I said to myself, the master will never forgive. I did not know what I had done to make him so bitter and so **unforgiving**[64], yet I judged it was something a dog could not understand, but which was clear to a man and dreadful.

They called and called—days and nights, it seemed to me. So long that the hunger and thirst near drove me mad, and I recognized that I was getting very weak. When you are this way you sleep a great deal, and I did. Once I woke in an awful fright —it seemed to me that the calling was right there in the garret! And so it was: it was Sadie's voice, and she was crying; my name was falling from her lips all broken, poor thing, and I could not believe my ears for the joy of it when I heard her say: "Come back to us—oh, come back to us, and forgive—it is all so sad without our—"

I broke in with SUCH a grateful little yelp, and the next

64. unforgiving
adj. 无情的

才安下心，睡去。我美美休息了一阵，但晨光还没有再现，我就醒了。我感觉相当舒服，这时我可以想出一个计划了；我的计划是，顺着后面的楼梯一路悄悄爬下去，藏在地窖门后，送冰人天亮时一来，我就趁他进来往冰箱里装冰时溜出去逃跑；随后，我要藏一整天，到了晚上再启程；启程去——任何人不认识我、不会把我出卖给我的主人的地方。这时，我几乎要高兴起来了；接着，我突然想起：啊，没有我的小宝宝，生活还有什么滋味！

这令人失望。我没有办法；我明白这一点；我必须呆在原地；呆在那里，等待，听天由命——那是不归我管的事情；生活就是这样——我的母亲早就这样说过。后来——啊，后来喊声又响了起来。我所有的忧伤又回到心头。我对自己说，主人是绝不会原谅我的。我不知道自己做了什么，使他这么痛恨，这么无情，但我判断那是狗无法理解的事儿，而在人看来一清二楚，糟糕透了。

他们喊啊喊——我好像觉得喊了几天几夜。时间太久了，饿渴难忍，快要把我逼疯了，我知道我渐渐有气无力。你到了这个地步，就会睡得很多，我也是这样。有一次，我在可怕的恐惧中惊醒过来——我好像觉得喊声就在那个顶楼里！是这样；那是赛迪的声音，她在哭；可怜的孩子，她的嘴里正在断断续续喊我的名字，我听到她说："回到我们身边吧——噢，回到我们身边吧，对不起——真让人难过啊，要是没有了我们的——"我高兴得简直不敢相信自己的耳朵。

◀ 情真意切，细致入微。

我突然感激地叫了一小声，紧接着赛迪冲了过来，

moment Sadie was plunging and stumbling through the darkness and the lumber and shouting for the family to hear, "She's found, she's found!"

The days that followed—well, they were wonderful. The mother and Sadie and the servants—why, they just seemed to worship me. They couldn't seem to make me a bed that was fine enough; and as for food, they couldn't be satisfied with anything but game[65] and delicacies[66] that were out of season; and every day the friends and neighbors flocked[67] in to hear about my heroism—that was the name they called it by, and it means agriculture. I remember my mother pulling it on a kennel[68] once, and explaining it in that way, but didn't say what agriculture[69] was, except that it was synonymous with intramural[70] incandescence[71]; and a dozen times a day Mrs. Gray and Sadie would tell the tale to new-comers, and say I risked my life to save the baby's, and both of us had burns to prove it, and then the company[72] would pass me around and pet me and exclaim about me, and you could see the pride in the eyes of Sadie and her mother; and when the people wanted to know what made me limp, they looked ashamed and changed the subject, and sometimes when people hunted them this way and that way with questions about it, it looked to me as if they were going to cry.

And this was not all the glory; no, the master's friends came, a whole twenty of the most distinguished[73] people, and had me in the laboratory, and discussed me as if I was a kind of discovery; and some of them said it was wonderful in a dumb beast, the finest exhibition of instinct they could call to mind; but the master said, with vehemence[74], "It's far above instinct; it's REASON, and many a man, privileged[75] to be saved and go with you and me to a better world by right of[76]

65. game
n. （总称）猎物；野味
66. delicacy
n. 美味；佳肴
67. flock
v. 聚结
68. kennel
n. 狗窝；狗屋
69. agriculture
n. 农业
70. intramural
adj.（器官）壁内的
71. incandescence
n. 炽热
72. company
n. 一群；客人
73. distinguished
adj. 著名的；高贵的
74. vehemence
n. 激烈；热切
75. privileged
adj. 有特权的；有特别恩典的
76. by right of
凭借

她跌跌撞撞穿过黑暗和杂物，大声嚷着让她家里的人听见："找到她了，找到她了！"

随后的那些日子——啊，真是妙不可言。赛迪、她的母亲和仆人们——啊，他们简直好像都崇拜我。他们好像给我铺再好的床都嫌不够好；至于吃的，他们非给我弄些不到时令的野味和美食，才能满意；朋友和邻居们每天都成群结队涌到这里来听我的"英雄壮举"——这是他们给我干的那桩事情取的名称，意思就和"农业"一样。我记得有一次我的母亲把这个词带到一个狗窝里去卖弄时，就是这样解释的，但她没有说"农业"是什么，只说和"壁内热"是同义。格雷太太和赛迪给新来的客人讲这个故事，每天要说十几遍，说我冒着生命危险救了婴儿一命，我们俩都有烧伤为证，于是客人们就把我传来传去，爱抚我，大声说着我的事儿，你可以看出赛迪和她母亲眼里的得意神情；当有人问我是怎么瘸的时，她们神情惭愧，忙转换话题，有时有人对这件事问来问去，纠缠不休时，在我看来，母女俩好像要哭一样。

而这并不是所有的荣誉；不是，男主人的朋友们来了，整整二十个最出色的人把我带进了实验室，讨论我，好像我是一种新发现似的；其中几个人说一只愚蠢的畜生真了不起，这是他们所能想起的最好的本能表现；但是，主人口气激烈地说，"这远超本能；这是理智，许多人凭借拥有理智，可以得到天主拯救，能和你我一起升天，但他们的理智却比不上这只注定无法升天

"冲过来"、"跌跌撞撞"、"大声叫"这几个动作表现小赛迪找到"我"时的欣喜和激动，感人至深。

A Dog's Tale 狗的自述   255

its possession, has less of it that this poor silly **quadruped**[77] that's **foreordained**[78] to perish"; and then he laughed, and said: "Why, look at me—I'm a **sarcasm**[79]! bless you, **with all**[80] my grand intelligence, the only thing I **inferred**[81] was that the dog had gone mad and was destroying the child, whereas but for the beast's intelligence—it's REASON, I tell you!—the child would have perished!"

They disputed and disputed, and I was the very center of subject of it all, and I wished my mother could know that this grand honor had come to me; it would have made her proud.

Then they discussed **optics**[82], as they called it, and whether a certain injury to the brain would produce blindness or not, but they could not agree about it, and said they must test it by experiment by and by; and next they discussed plants, and that interested me, because in the summer Sadie and I had planted seeds—I helped her dig the holes, you know—and after days and days a little shrub or a flower came up there, and it was a wonder how that could happen; but it did, and I wished I could talk— I would have told those people about it and shown then how much I knew, and been all alive with the subject; but I didn't care for the optics; it was dull, and when the came back to it again it bored me, and I went to sleep.

Pretty soon it was spring, and sunny and pleasant and lovely, and the sweet mother and the children patted me and the puppy good-by, and went away on a journey and a visit to their **kin**[83], and the master wasn't any company for us, but we played together and had good times, and the servants were kind and friendly, so we got along quite happily and counted the days and waited for the family.

And one day those men came again, and said, now for the

77. quadruped
    n. 四足动物
78. foreordain
    vt. 注定
79. sarcasm
    n. 讽刺
80. with all
    尽管
81. infer
    vt. 推断
82. optics
    n. 光学
83. kin
    n. 亲戚

的可怜的蠢狗；"说完，他放声大笑，然后又说道：
"啊，看着我——我真可笑啊！我的天哪，尽管我智力超群，但我只推断出的唯一事情就是这只狗疯了，要杀死这个孩子，要不是这个畜生的智力——我告诉你，这是理智！——这个孩子早就死了！"

他们争论不休，而我正是所有争论的中心主题，我真希望母亲能知道我已经得到了这种崇高荣誉；那一定会使她扬眉吐气。

随后，他们又讨论起了他们所谓的光学，讨论大脑受了某种伤是否会导致失明，但他们意见不一，说他们必须马上通过实验来证明；接下来，他们又讨论起了植物，这使我很感兴趣，因为我和赛迪在夏天种过一些种子——你知道，我还帮她挖了一些坑——过了好多天，那里长出了一棵小树或一朵花，真不知道怎么会发生这种事，但它确实发生了，我真希望我能说话——我就要把这件事告诉那些人，让他们看看我知道多少，我对这个问题非常敏感，但我并不关心光学；它枯燥乏味，所以当他们又回到了那个主题时，让我讨厌，我便睡觉去了。

不久，春天来临，阳光明媚，优美宜人，和蔼亲切的母亲和她的孩子们拍拍我和宝宝，跟我们告别，他们要出远门看亲戚去了，男主人没有陪我们，但我们在一起玩，玩得非常开心，仆人们亲切友好，所以我们相处得也十分融洽，我们掐算着日子，等着家人。

有一天，那些人又来了，说现在要实验，于是他们就把宝宝带到了实验室，我也瘸着三只腿走过去，洋

用补叙的手法，借男主人的话，补充交代前面的情节，给人一种恍然大悟之感。使故事有头有尾，前后照应。

他们讨论光学，讨论大脑受了伤是否会导致失明等等，都是为他们用狗仔做实验进行铺垫。

A Dog's Tale 狗的自述   257

test, and they took the puppy to the laboratory, and I limped three-leggedly along, too, feeling proud, for any attention shown to the puppy was a pleasure to me, of course. They discussed and experimented, and then suddenly the puppy shrieked, and they set him on the floor, and he went staggering around, with his head all bloody, and the master clapped his hands and shouted: "There, I've won—confess it! He's a **blind as a bat**[84]!"

And they all said: "It's so—you've proved your theory, and suffering humanity owes you a great debt from **henceforth**[85]," and they crowded around him, and wrung his hand **cordially**[86] and thankfully, and praised him.

But I hardly saw or heard these things, for I ran at once to my little darling, and **snuggled**[87] close to it where it lay, and licked the blood, and it put its head against mine, whimpering softly, and I knew in my heart it was a comfort to it in its pain and trouble to feel its mother's touch, though it could not see me. Then it dropped down, presently, and its little **velvet**[88] nose rested upon the floor, and it was still, and did not move any more.

Soon the master stopped discussing a moment, and rang in the footman, and said, "Bury it in the far corner of the garden," and then went on with the discussion, and I **trotted**[89] after the footman, very happy and grateful, for I knew the puppy was out of its pain now, because it was asleep. We went far down the garden to the farthest end, where the children and the nurse and the puppy and I used to play in the summer in the **shade**[90] of a great elm, and there the footman dug a hole, and I saw he was going to plant the puppy, and I was glad, because it would grow and come up a fine handsome dog, like Robin Adair, and be a beautiful surprise for the family when they came home; so I tried to help him dig, but my lame leg was no good, being stiff,

84. blind as a bat
   有眼无珠
85. henceforth
   adv. 自此以后
86. cordially
   adv. 诚恳地；诚挚地
87. snuggle
   v. 偎依
88. velvet
   adj. 天鹅绒般的；
   柔软的
89. trot
   v. 小跑
90. shade
   n. 荫凉处

洋得意，因为在我看来，对宝宝的任何关心都是一件高兴事。他们讨论一阵之后就实验，后来宝宝突然尖叫了一声，他们把它放在地板上，他摇摇晃晃乱转，满头是血，男主人拍手叫道："好了，我已经赢了——承认吧！他简直瞎得什么也看不见啦！"

他们全都说："是这样——你已经证明你的理论了，从今以后受苦的人应该大大感谢你。"他们把他团团围住，和他亲切握手，表示感谢，还称赞他。

但是，我几乎都没有听见，也没有看见，因为我马上跑到我的小宝贝身边，然后紧紧地依偎到它所在的地方，舔着它的血，它把头靠着我的头，轻声哭泣，我心里明白，尽管它看不见我，但在痛苦和烦恼之中，它能感觉到母亲的触摸，那对它是一种安慰。随后不久，它就倒了下去，天鹅绒般柔软的鼻子贴在地板上，它静静的，再也不动了。

作者以悲悯之心描绘了这感人的一幕。

一会儿，男主人停止了讨论，按铃叫男仆进来，说："把它埋在花园远处那个角落，"说完又继续讨论，我跟在仆人后面一路小跑，非常痛快，充满感激，因为我知道宝宝睡着了，现在不再痛苦了。我们走到花园最远处那端，我跟孩子们、保姆和宝宝夏天经常在大榆树荫下玩耍，仆人在那里挖了一个坑，我看到他要把宝宝栽在地下，非常高兴，因为它会长出来，长成一只像罗宾·阿代尔那样漂亮好看的狗，等女主人和孩子们回家后，会让他们喜出望外；所以，我尽力帮他挖，但我那只瘸腿僵硬，不中用，你知道，你不得不用两条腿，不然就没用。仆人

you know, and you have to have two, or it is no use. When the footman had finished and covered little Robin up, he patted my head, and there were tears in his eyes, and he said: "Poor little doggie, you saved HIS child!"

I have watched two whole weeks, and he doesn't come up! This last week a fright has been stealing upon me. I think there is something terrible about this. I do not know what it is, but the fear makes me sick, and I cannot eat, though the servants bring me the best of food; and they pet me so, and even come in the night, and cry, and say, "Poor doggie—do give it up and come home; don't break our hearts!" and all this terrifies me the more, and makes me sure something has happened. And I am so weak; since yesterday I cannot stand on my feet anymore. And within this hour the servants, looking toward the sun where it was sinking out of sight and the night chill coming on, said things I could not understand, but they carried something cold to my heart.

"Those poor creatures! They do not suspect. They will come home in the morning, and eagerly ask for the little doggie that did the brave deed, and who of us will be strong enough to say the truth to them: 'The humble little friend is gone where go the beasts that perish.'"

挖完坑，埋好小罗宾后，拍拍我的头，眼含泪水，说道："可怜的小狗，你救过他的孩子啊！"

我守了整整两周，他也没有长出来！后面那一周，有一种恐惧已经悄悄向我袭来。我认为这件事有些可怕。我不知道怕的是什么，但这种恐惧让我烦恼，尽管仆人们给我带最好的东西吃，但我都吃不下；他们尽力爱抚我，甚至夜里还过来，哭着说："可怜的小狗——放弃它，回家去吧；不要让我们伤心了！"这些话更使我心惊胆战，让我确信出了什么事儿。我浑身无力；从昨天起，我再也站不起来了。在这个小时里，仆人们望着正在落山的太阳，夜晚的寒气开始袭来，他们说着一些我听不懂的话，但他们的话让我寒彻心扉。

"那些可怜的人！他们不会怀疑。他们明天早上就要回家来，会迫不及待地问起这个做出过英雄壮举的小狗，我们谁会那样坚强，足以对他们说出真相呢：'这个卑微的小朋友去了不能升天的畜生们去的那个地方。'"

阳光明媚，优美宜人，万物复苏，一切都生机勃勃的春天，男主人杀死了"我"的小宝宝。而我却给了主人家的小娃娃以第二次生命。人性与"狗性"的鲜明对照。

"落山的太阳"、"夜晚的寒气"，这些自然环境的描写渲染和衬托出"我"内心无尽的悲凉。

名篇赏析

　　鲜明的人与狗的对比，让人产生这样一种认识：在资本主义社会，人不如狗。"我"的忠勇与人们的残忍、冷酷无情形成了鲜明对比。

　　小说的情节经作者的精心安排，采用层层铺垫、步步设伏的写作手法，使结构紧凑，读后给人浑然一体的感觉。作家娴熟的写作技巧在此也得到了充分体现。当你读罢此篇、掩卷沉思之时，恐怕不只是为一只狗的悲惨遭遇而痛心，更为人性的卑劣而痛心吧！

Oscar Wilde

01 The Giant's Garden

巨人的花园

姓名	奥斯卡·王尔德
出生日期	1854年10月16日
出生地	爱尔兰都柏林
性别	男

成就和特色

　　英国最著名的唯美主义代表作家。他一生中就写过九篇童话，但每一篇都是精品，他的童话作品可以与安徒生童话和格林童话相媲美，童话集有《快乐王子和其他故事》、《石榴屋》，最著名的童话是《巨人的花园》、《快乐王子》、《夜莺与玫瑰》。最体现王尔德才华的不是童话，也不是短篇小说，而是《道连·格雷的画像》等长篇小说，以及《温德米尔夫人的扇子》、《莎乐美》等戏剧作品。

写作背景

　　自私自利的巨人在失去一切之后最终归顺于少年基督，结束了花园里风雪的肆虐。

01

The Giant's Garden

Every afternoon, as they were coming from school, the children used to go and play in the Giant's garden.

It was a large lovely garden, with soft green grass. Here and there over the grass stood beautiful flowers like stars, and there were twelve peach-trees that in the spring-time broke out into **delicate**[1] blossoms of pink and pearl, and in the autumn bore rich fruit. The birds sat on the trees and sang so sweetly that the children used to stop their games in order to listen to them. "How happy we are here!" they cried to each other.

One day the Giant came back. He had been to visit his friend the Cornish **ogre**[2], and had stayed with him for seven years. After the seven years were over he had said all that he had to say, for his conversation was limited, and he determined to return to his own castle. When he arrived he saw the children playing in the garden.

"What are you doing here?" he cried in a very **gruff**[3] voice, and the children ran away.

"My own garden is my own garden," said the Giant; "any one can understand that, and I will allow nobody to play in it but myself." So he built a high wall all round it, and put up a **notice-board**[4].

TRESPASSERS[5] *WILL BE PROSECUTED*[6].

He was a very selfish Giant.

1. delicate
   adj. 精美的；雅致的
2. ogre
   n. 食人妖魔；传说或神说中食人的巨人或妖怪
3. gruff
   adj.（声音）粗哑的；生硬的
4. notice-board
   n. 布告牌
5. trespasser
   n. 入侵者
6. prosecute
   vt. 检举；对某人提起公诉

巨人的花园

　　每天下午放学后，孩子们总是喜欢到去巨人的花园里玩耍。

　　这是一个长有柔软绿草的可爱大花园。草地上到处盛开着像星星一样美丽的鲜花，那里有十二棵桃树，一到春天就绽放出粉红色和珍珠色的精美花朵，秋天则结出累累硕果。鸟儿栖息在树上，唱得非常甜美，孩子们常常停止游戏，侧耳倾听。"我们真开心！"他们相互大声说道。

作者开门见山，设置一个诗情画意般的情景，为后文打下了伏笔。

　　一天，巨人回来了。原来他是去拜访朋友康沃尔郡的食人妖魔了，并和他一起呆了七年。七年结束后，他说完了他要说的话，因为他的交谈是受限制的，所以他决定回到自己的城堡。他到家后，看到孩子们在花园里玩耍。

　　"你们在这里干什么？"他用非常粗哑的嗓音大声问道。于是，孩子们都跑走了。

　　"我自己的花园就是我自己的花园，"巨人说，"任何人都能明白这一点，除了我自己，我不允许任何人在这里玩。"于是，他在花园四周垒起一道高高的围墙，并竖起了一块告示牌。

　　　　　　　擅入者将受到起诉。

这句话如厉声断喝，霹雳般惊扰了天真烂漫的孩子们。

　　他是一个非常自私的巨人。

7. hail
   n. 冰雹
8. rattle
   v. 嘎嘎作响
9. slate
   n. 石板瓦

The poor children had now nowhere to play. They tried to play on the road, but the road was very dusty and full of hard stones, and they did not like it. They used to wander round the high wall when their lessons were over, and talk about the beautiful garden inside. "How happy we were there," they said to each other.

Then the Spring came, and all over the country there were little blossoms and little birds. Only in the garden of the Selfish Giant it was still winter. The birds did not care to sing in it as there were no children, and the trees forgot to blossom. Once a beautiful flower put its head out from the grass, but when it saw the notice-board it was so sorry for the children that it slipped back into the ground again, and went off to sleep. The only people who were pleased were the Snow and the Frost. "Spring has forgotten this garden," they cried, "so we will live here all the year round." The Snow covered up the grass with her great white cloak, and the Frost painted all the trees silver. Then they invited the North Wind to stay with them, and he came. He was wrapped in furs, and he roared all day about the garden, and blew the chimney-pots down. "This is a delightful spot," he said, "we must ask the Hail[7] on a visit." So the Hail came. Every day for three hours he rattled[8] on the roof of the castle till he broke most of the slates[9], and then he ran round and round the garden as fast as he could go. He was dressed in grey, and his breath was like ice.

"I cannot understand why the Spring is so late in coming," said the Selfish Giant, as he sat at the window and looked out at his cold white garden; "I hope there will be a change in the weather."

But the Spring never came, nor the Summer. The Autumn gave golden fruit to every garden, but to the Giant's garden she gave none. "He is too selfish," she said. So it was always Winter

现在，可怜的孩子们没有地方玩耍了。他们不得不设法在大路上玩，但路上尘土飞扬，遍地都是坚硬的石块，他们都不喜欢那里。放学后，他们常常在高大的围墙四周走来走去，谈论着墙内的美丽花园。"我们在那里曾是多么开心啊！"他们彼此说着。

后来，春天到来时，乡村到处都是小花和小鸟。只有这个自私巨人的花园里还是冬天。因为里面没有孩子们，所以小鸟不爱在那里歌唱，树木也忘记了开花。有一次，一朵美丽的花儿从草丛中探出头，但当它看到那块告示牌后，它为那些小孩感到非常难过，便又把头悄悄缩回了地里，睡觉去了。只有雪与霜对此非常开心。"春天已经忘记了这个花园，"它们叫喊道，"这样我们就可以一年到头住在这里。"雪用巨大的白色斗篷盖住了草地，霜也把所有的树木都涂成了银色。接着，它们邀请北风同住，北风也应邀而来。北风裹着毛皮大衣，整天在花园里呼啸，刮掉了烟囱顶管。"这是一个爽快的地方，"它说，"我们必须请冰雹来访。"于是，冰雹就来了。每天他都要在城堡顶乒乒乓乓下三个小时，直到砸烂大多数的石板瓦，随后又尽可能快地围着花园一圈接一圈地飞跑，浑身灰蒙蒙的，呼出的都像冰一样。

作者以比拟的手法来表露心迹。

"我不明白春天为什么来得这么晚呢，"巨人坐在窗前，望着外面雪白寒冷的花园说，"我希望天气会发生变化。"

但是，春天始终没有来，夏天也没有来。秋天把金色的果实送给了每一座花园，但她什么也没有给巨人

there, and the North Wind, and the Hail, and the Frost, and the Snow danced about through the trees.

One morning the Giant was lying awake in bed when he heard some lovely music. It sounded so sweet to his ears that he thought it must be the King's musicians passing by. It was really only a little linnet[10] singing outside his window, but it was so long since he had heard a bird sing in his garden that it seemed to him to be the most beautiful music in the world. Then the Hail stopped dancing over his head, and the North Wind ceased roaring, and a delicious perfume[11] came to him through the open casement[12]. "I believe the Spring has come at last," said the Giant; and he jumped out of bed and looked out.

What did he see?

He saw a most wonderful sight. Through a little hole in the wall the children had crept[13] in, and they were sitting in the branches of the trees. In every tree that he could see there was a little child. And the trees were so glad to have the children back again that they had covered themselves with blossoms, and were waving their arms gently above the children's heads. The birds were flying about and twittering with delight, and the flowers were looking up through the green grass and laughing. It was a lovely scene, only in one corner it was still winter. It was the farthest corner of the garden, and in it was standing a little boy. He was so small that he could not reach up to the branches of the tree, and he was wandering all round it, crying bitterly. The poor tree was still quite covered with frost and snow, and the North Wind was blowing and roaring above it. "Climb up! little boy," said the Tree, and it bent its branches down as low as it could; but the boy was too tiny.

And the Giant's heart melted as he looked out. "How selfish I have been!" he said; "now I know why the Spring would not come here. I will put that poor little boy on the top of the tree,

10. linnet
    n. 红雀
11. perfume
    n. 香气；芳香
12. casement
    n. 窗扉
13. creep
    vi. 蹑手蹑脚地走；爬行

的花园。"他太自私了，"秋天说。于是，那里总是冬天、北风、冰雹，还有霜和雪在树林间跳舞。

一天早晨，巨人睁眼躺在床上，这时他听到一阵美妙的音乐。音乐是那样美妙动听，他想一定是国王的乐师路过。其实，这只是一只小红雀在他的窗外唱歌，但因为巨人好久没有听到鸟儿在花园里歌唱了，所以他似乎感到那是世界上最美妙的音乐。这时，冰雹停止在他的头顶跳舞，北风停止了呼啸，一缕甜蜜的芳香透过敞开的窗扉来到他的身边。"我相信春天终于来了，"巨人说着，从床上跳下来，向窗外望去。

他看到了什么？

他看到了一幕极其美妙的景象。孩子们爬过一个小墙洞悄悄钻了进来，他们正坐在树枝上。他看得到每棵树上都坐着一个孩子。那些树木又迎来了孩子们，感到非常高兴，树上开满了鲜花，并在孩子们的头顶上轻轻晃动着手臂。鸟儿们一边飞翔，一边欢快地鸣叫。草地上，花朵也纷纷仰起脸，露出了欢笑。这是一幅非常可爱的情景。只有一个角落还是冬天。那是花园里最远的一个角落，一个小男孩正站在那里。他个子太小，爬不上树枝，正一边痛哭，一边围着树转来转去。那棵可怜的树仍是完全覆盖着霜和雪，北风在它上面吹刮着、呼啸着。"爬上来，小孩子！"那棵树说着，尽可能低地垂下树枝，但小男孩太小了。

看着窗外的一切，巨人的心融化了。"我曾经是多么自私啊！"他说，"现在我知道为什么春天不愿来这里了。我要把那个可怜的男孩放到树顶上，然后推倒围

这就像一个心里没有春天的人，他怎么可能会有人生的花朵和果实呢？

看到此情此景，巨人会做出什么反应呢？这是本篇的一个重要节点。

The Giant's Garden 巨人的花园   269

and then I will knock down the wall, and my garden shall be the children's playground for ever and ever." He was really very sorry for what he had done.

So he crept downstairs and opened the front door quite softly, and went out into the garden. But when the children saw him they were so frightened that they all ran away, and the garden became winter again. Only the little boy did not run, for his eyes were so full of tears that he did not see the Giant coming. And the Giant **stole up**[14] behind him and took him gently in his hand, and put him up into the tree. And the tree broke at once into blossom, and the birds came and sang on it, and the little boy stretched out his two arms and **flung**[15] them round the Giant's neck, and kissed him. And the other children, when they saw that the Giant was not wicked any longer, came running back, and with them came the Spring. "It is your garden now, little children," said the Giant, and he took a great axe and knocked down the wall. And when the people were going to market at twelve o'clock they found the Giant playing with the children in the most beautiful garden they had ever seen.

All day long they played, and in the evening they came to the Giant to bid him good-bye.

"But where is your little companion?" he said; "the boy I put into the tree." The Giant loved him the best because he had kissed him.

"We don't know," answered the children; "he has gone away."

"You must tell him to be sure and come here to-morrow," said the Giant. But the children said that they did not know where he lived, and had never seen him before; and the Giant felt very sad.

Every afternoon, when school was over, the children came and played with the Giant. But the little boy whom the Giant loved was never seen again. The Giant was very kind to all the

14. steal up
悄悄地靠近；偷偷地接近

15. fling
vt. 急伸；挥动（手臂、腿等）

墙，我的花园将永远成为孩子们的乐园。"他真的为自己过去的所作所为感到非常懊悔。

于是，巨人轻轻走下楼，悄悄打开前门，走出屋门，进入花园。但是，孩子们一看到他，就吓得纷纷跑走了，花园里又变成了冬天。只有那个小男孩没有跑，因为他的眼里充满了泪水，没有看到巨人走过来。巨人悄悄走到他的身后，一只手轻轻托起他，放在那棵树上。那棵树突然绽开了鲜花，鸟儿们也飞来在上面唱起了歌。小男孩伸出双臂搂住巨人的脖子，亲吻他。其他孩子看到巨人不再凶恶，就纷纷跑了回来，春天也跟着来了。"小孩子们，现在这是你们的花园了，"巨人说着，抡起一把大斧，砍倒了围墙。十二点钟，人们去赶集时，发现巨人和孩子们一起在他们从未见过的世界上最美丽的花园里玩耍。

他们玩了整整一天；傍晚时分，孩子们过来，跟巨人告别。

"可是，你们的那个小伙伴在哪里？"他问，"就是我放到树上的那个男孩。"巨人最爱那个男孩，因为男孩吻过他。

"我们不知道，"孩子们答道，"他已经走了。"

"你们一定要告诉他明天务必来这里，"巨人说。但是，孩子们说他们不知道小男孩住在哪里，以前从来没有见过他；巨人感到非常难过。

每天下午放学后，孩子们都来跟巨人一起玩。但是，巨人喜爱的那个小男孩再也没有来过。尽管巨人善待所有的孩子，但他还是渴望见到他的第一个小朋友，

你对世界笑，世界也会对你笑。心态决定一切。换言之，人心换人心。

children, yet he longed for his first little friend, and often spoke of him. "How I would like to see him!" he used to say.

Years went over, and the Giant grew very old and **feeble**[16]. He could not play about any more, so he sat in a huge armchair, and watched the children at their games, and admired his garden. "I have many beautiful flowers," he said; "but the children are the most beautiful flowers of all."

One winter morning he looked out of his window as he was dressing. He did not hate the Winter now, for he knew that it was merely the Spring asleep, and that the flowers were resting.

Suddenly he rubbed his eyes in wonder, and looked and looked. It certainly was a marvellous sight. In the farthest corner of the garden was a tree quite covered with lovely white blossoms. Its branches were all golden, and silver fruit hung down from them, and underneath it stood the little boy he had loved.

Downstairs ran the Giant in great joy, and out into the garden. He hastened across the grass, and came near to the child. And when he came quite close his face grew red with anger, and he said, "Who hath dared to wound thee?" For on the palms of the child's hands were the prints of two nails, and the prints of two nails were on the little feet.

"Who hath dared to wound thee?" cried the Giant; "tell me, that I may take my big sword and slay him."

"Nay!" answered the child; "but these are the wounds of Love."

"Who art thou?" said the Giant, and a strange awe fell on him, and he knelt before the little child.

And the child smiled on the Giant, and said to him, "You let me play once in your garden, to-day you shall come with me to my garden, which is **Paradise**[17]."

And when the children ran in that afternoon, they found the Giant lying dead under the tree, all covered with white blossoms.

16. feeble
   adj. 虚弱的；无力的
17. paradise
   n. 天堂；伊甸园

并且常常提起他。"我是多么想见到他！"他经常说。

好几年过去了，巨人垂垂老矣，身体虚弱。他不能再跟孩子们一起玩耍了，于是他坐在一把巨大的扶手椅上，一边观看孩子们游戏，一边欣赏自己的花园。"我有许多美丽的鲜花，"他说，"但孩子们才是其中最美丽的花朵。"

一个冬天的早晨，他一边穿衣服，一边向窗外望去。他现在已不讨厌冬天了，因为他知道这只是春天在睡觉，花儿在休息。

突然，他惊奇地揉了揉眼，看了又看。的确是奇妙的景象。只见花园最远处的角落有一棵树上开满了可爱的白花，树枝都金灿灿的，枝头上垂挂着银色果实，树下站着他喜爱的那个小男孩。

巨人欣喜万分地奔下楼，跑出门，进了花园。他匆匆穿过草地，跑到孩子面前。而当他完全靠近时，他气得脸色通红，问道："是谁竟敢伤害你？"因为孩子的手掌心上有两个钉痕，一双小脚上也有两个钉痕。

"是谁竟敢伤害你？"巨人叫道，"告诉我，我要拿长剑宰了他。"

"不！"孩子回答说，"这些都是爱的创伤。"

"你是谁？"巨人说，一种奇特的敬畏之情油然而生，于是他跪在小男孩面前。

小男孩露出了微笑，对巨人说道："你让我在你的花园里玩过一次，今天你要跟我到我的花园去，那就是天堂。"

那天下午孩子们跑进花园时，看到巨人躺在那棵树下，已经死了，全身覆盖着白花。

巨人终于悟出了人生的真谛。

是啊，爱的创伤是一种教训，也是一种启发，更是一种对灵魂的拯救。

名篇赏析

　　《巨人的花园》纯净的语言不仅使读者感受到萧瑟冬天的花园、春意盎然的花园、活泼快乐的孩子，更使读者领略了王尔德内心的自我拯救。王尔德写道："我绝不怀疑，一个人至真的时刻，跪在土里，捶打自己的胸膛，倾诉一生里所有的罪恶。"王尔德用自私的巨人内心的情感冲突和死亡告诉读者，他一直追求和探究的纯净灵魂。

William Faulkner

01 *A Rose for Emily*

献给艾米丽的玫瑰

姓名	威廉·福克纳
出生日期	1897年9月25日
出生地	美国密西西比州
性别	男

成就和特色

　　当代美国著名作家，福克纳一生共写了二十部长篇小说和将近一百篇短篇小说。福克纳的小说语言别具一格，深深植根于南方文学传统，善于运用南方方言，生动形象，力透纸背。他的短篇小说大多采用写实手法，情节鲜明，戏剧性强，生活气息浓郁。他认为，短篇小说在艺术高度上仅次于诗歌，因为作家写"长篇小说时可以马虎，但在写短篇小说时则不可以……它要求近乎绝对的精确"。他的小说中许多人物都是现实生活中的人物的改造。他小说中的历史，既包括过去，也包括现在和未来。他的作品最大的外在特点是绵延婉转、结构繁复和词汇精巧。

写作背景

　　这篇小说看似爱情小说，又像侦探小说，还是哥特式小说；它是一首挽歌，缅怀一种失落的文明和随风而逝的精神世界。

01

A Rose for Emily

When Miss Emily Grierson died, our whole town went to her funeral: the men through a sort of respectful affection for a fallen monument, the women mostly out of curiosity to see the inside of her house, which no one save an old man-servant—a combined gardener and cook—had seen in at least ten years.

It was a big, squarish frame house that had once been white, decorated with cupolas[1] and spires and scrolled[2] balconies in the heavily lightsome style of the seventies, set on what had once been our most select street. But garages and cotton gins had encroached[3] and obliterated[4] even the august[5] names of that neighborhood; only Miss Emily's house was left, lifting its stubborn and coquettish[6] decay above the cotton wagons and the gasoline pumps—an eyesore among eyesores. And now Miss Emily had gone to join the representatives of those august names where they lay in the cedar-bemused cemetery among the ranked and anonymous[7] graves of Union and Confederate soldiers who fell at the battle of Jefferson.

Alive, Miss Emily had been a tradition, a duty, and a care; a sort of hereditary[8] obligation upon the town, dating from that day in 1894 when Colonel Sartoris, the mayor—he who fathered the edict[9] that no Negro woman should appear on the streets without an apron—remitted[10] her taxes, the dispensation[11] dating from the death of her father on into perpetuity[12]. Not that Miss Emily would have accepted charity. Colonel Sartoris invented an involved tale to the effect that Miss Emily's father

献给艾米丽的玫瑰

一

艾米丽·格里尔森小姐去世后，我们全镇人都去给她送葬：男人们是出于一种敬慕之情，因为一座丰碑倒下了；女人们大多数则是出于好奇心，想看看她的屋里是什么样子，因为除了一个园丁兼厨师的老男仆，至少已经十年没人进去看过了。

那是一座曾经涂成白色、近似方形的大木屋，坐落在从前最考究的街道上，装饰有十九世纪七十年代具有浓厚的轻快风格的穹顶、尖塔和涡形花纹的阳台。但是，修车厂和轧棉机已经逐步侵占、甚至湮没了那一带威严的名字；只剩下了艾米丽小姐的房子，在棉花车和加油泵上方耸立着固执而妖艳的破败房子——真是有碍观瞻大煞风景。现在艾米丽小姐已经加入了那些威严名字的代表之列，他们躺在雪松环绕的墓地，置身在杰斐逊战役中倒下的南北双方无名士兵墓之间。

艾米丽小姐健在时曾经是一种传统、一种责任和一种关怀；从1894年那天镇长沙多里斯上校——就是他颁布了黑人妇女不系围裙不得上街的法令——免除了她的税款，从她的父亲去世之日起，到她去世为止，这是镇子承担的一种传统债务。倒不是艾米丽小姐乐意接受施舍。是沙多里斯上校杜撰了一个复杂的故事，大意是

艾米丽小姐的去世和全镇男女去给她送葬的不同心态，曾经威严但已破败的房子和十年没有他人踏入的房间，小说一开始就把读者也带到了一种恐怖的氛围里。而艾米丽小姐的去世代表着一座丰碑的倒下，会牵动读者的思绪：这是一座什么样的丰碑呢？

had loaned money to the town, which the town, as a matter of business, preferred this way of repaying. Only a man of Colonel Sartoris' generation and thought could have invented it, and only a woman could have believed it.

When the next generation, with its more modern ideas, became mayors and aldermen[13], this arrangement created some little dissatisfaction. On the first of the year they mailed her a tax notice. February came, and there was no reply. They wrote her a formal letter, asking her to call at the sheriff's office at her convenience. A week later the mayor wrote her himself, offering to call or to send his car for her, and received in reply a note on paper of an archaic[14] shape, in a thin, flowing calligraphy[15] in faded ink, to the effect that she no longer went out at all. The tax notice was also enclosed, without comment.

They called a special meeting of the Board of Aldermen. A deputation[16] waited upon her, knocked at the door through which no visitor had passed since she ceased giving china-painting lessons eight or ten years earlier. They were admitted by the old Negro into a dim hall from which a stairway mounted into still more shadow. It smelled of dust and disuse—a close, dank smell. The Negro led them into the parlor. It was furnished in heavy, leather-covered furniture. When the Negro opened the blinds of one window, they could see that the leather was cracked; and when they sat down, a faint dust rose sluggishly[17] about their thighs, spinning with slow motes[18] in the single sun-ray. On a tarnished[19] gilt easel before the fireplace stood a crayon[20] portrait of Miss Emily's father.

They rose when she entered—a small, fat woman in black, with a thin gold chain descending to her waist and vanishing into her belt, leaning on an ebony[21] cane with a tarnished gold head. Her skeleton was small and spare; perhaps that was why what would have been merely plumpness in another was obesity in her. She looked bloated[22], like a body long submerged[23]

13. alderman
   n. 市参议员

14. archaic
   adj. 陈旧的；古老的

15. calligraphy
   n. 书法；笔迹

16. deputation
   n. 代表团

17. sluggishly
   adv. 慢慢腾腾地；慢吞吞地

18. mote
   n. 微粒；尘埃

19. tarnished
   adj. 失去光泽的；生锈的

20. crayon
   n. 蜡笔；炭笔画

21. ebony
   n. 乌木；黑檀木

22. bloated
   adj. 浮肿的；肿胀的

23. submerged
   adj. 在水中的；水下的

艾米丽小姐的父亲曾经贷款给镇政府，因此作为一种交易，镇政府更喜欢以这种方式偿还。只有沙多里斯上校这一代的人和思想才能杜撰这个故事，也只有女人才会相信。

等思想更现代的下一代人当了镇长和参议员时，这项安排引起了一些小小的不满。那年第一天，他们给她寄去了一张纳税通知单。到了二月，没有回复。他们给她发去一封公函，要求她方便时前往镇治安官办公室。一周后，镇长亲自给她写信，表示愿意登门拜访或派车接她，而得到的回信是一张便条，用褪色墨水写在陈旧的信笺上，书法流利，字迹细小，大意是说她根本不再出门。纳税通知单也附在信中，没有发表意见。

他们召开了一次参议委员会特别会议。一个代表团正式拜访她，敲了敲门，自从八年或十年前她停止讲授瓷器彩绘课以来，没有客人进出过这个房门。那个老黑人把他们让进阴暗的门厅，从那里上楼梯，进入更暗的地方。这里有一股尘封和废弃的气味——是一股沉闷阴湿的气味。黑人领他们走进客厅。客厅里摆设着包有皮套的沉重家具。黑人打开一扇百叶窗后，他们可以看到皮套开裂；等他们坐下来时，一阵淡淡的灰尘从大腿四周缓缓升起，尘粒在那道阳光中慢慢旋转。壁炉前失去金色光泽的画架上立着艾米丽小姐的父亲的炭笔画像。

描写细腻，用笔精准。

她走进来时，他们都站起来。一个肥胖的小女人一身黑衣，一条细细的金表链坠至腰间，消失在了腰带里；她拄着一根乌木拐杖，拐杖头的镶金失去了光泽。她的身架瘦小；也许这就是在别的女人身上仅仅是丰满，在她身上却肥胖的原因。她看上去像长久浸泡在死水里的尸体那样浮肿，具有那种苍白的色调。当客人说明来意后，她那双深陷在满脸隆起肥肉里的眼睛，看上

in motionless water, and of that pallid hue. Her eyes, lost in the fatty ridges of her face, looked like two small pieces of coal pressed into a lump of dough as they moved from one face to another while the visitors stated their errand.

She did not ask them to sit. She just stood in the door and listened quietly until the spokesman came to a stumbling halt. Then they could hear the invisible watch ticking at the end of the gold chain.

Her voice was dry and cold. "I have no taxes in Jefferson. Colonel Sartoris explained it to me. Perhaps one of you can gain access to the city records and satisfy yourselves."

"But we have. We are the city authorities, Miss Emily. Didn't you get a notice from the sheriff, signed by him?"

"I received a paper, yes," Miss Emily said. "Perhaps he considers himself the sheriff...I have no taxes in Jefferson."

"But there is nothing on the books to show that, you see. We must go by the—"

"See Colonel Sartoris. I have no taxes in Jefferson."

"But, Miss Emily—"

"See Colonel Sartoris." (Colonel Sartoris had been dead almost ten years.) "I have no taxes in Jefferson. Tobe!" The Negro appeared. "Show these gentlemen out."

II

So she **vanquished**[24] them, horse and foot, just as she had vanquished their fathers thirty years before about the smell. That was two years after her father's death and a short time after her sweetheart—the one we believed would marry her—had deserted her. After her father's death she went out very little; after her sweetheart went away, people hardly saw her at all. A few of the ladies had the **temerity**[25] to call, but were not received, and the only sign of life about the place was the Negro man—a young man then—going in and out with a market basket.

24. vanquish
vt. 征服；击败

25. temerity
n. 冒失，鲁莽；蛮勇

去就像按在一团生面中的两块小煤球似的，转来转去，时而瞧瞧这张面孔，时而打量那张面孔。

她没有请他们坐。她只是站在门口，默默地听着，直到发言代表结结巴巴把话说完。随后，他们可以听到那块隐藏在金链那端的表在滴答作响。

她的声音单调乏味，冷若冰霜。"我在杰斐逊无税可纳。沙多里斯上校向我解释过。也许你们哪个人可以查一下镇政府档案，就能消除自己的疑虑。"

"但是，我们已经查过了。我们就是镇政府，艾米丽小姐。你没有收到过司法长官亲手签发的通知吗？"

"是的，我收到过一份公文，"艾米丽小姐说。"也许他自以为是司法长官吧……我在杰斐逊没有税可交。"

"可是，纳税册上没有说明这一点，你明白。我们必须按照——"

"去找沙多里斯上校。我在杰斐逊没有税可交。"

"可是，艾米丽小姐——"

"去找沙多里斯上校。"（沙多里斯上校差不多已经死去十年了。）"我在杰斐逊没有税可交。托比！"黑人走了出来。"领这些先生出去。"

二

她就这样把他们打得"人仰马翻"，就像三十年前为那股气味之事击败他们的父辈一样。那是她的父亲去世后两年，也就是在她的亲密爱人——就是我们都相信一定会娶她的那个人——抛弃她后不久。父亲死后，她不大出门；亲密爱人离去后，人们几乎就见不到她了。少数几位女士冒昧拜访，但都吃了闭门羹，而且她的住处周围唯一的生命迹象就是那个黑人男子——当时还是个年轻人——提着一个购物篮进进出出。

A Rose for Emily 献给艾米丽的玫瑰

"Just as if a man—any man—could keep a kitchen properly," the ladies said; so they were not surprised when the smell developed. It was another link between the gross, **teeming**[26] world and the high and mighty Griersons.

A neighbor, a woman, complained to the mayor, Judge Stevens, eighty years old.

"But what will you have me do about it, madam?" he said.

"Why, send her word to stop it," the woman said. "Isn't there a law?"

"I'm sure that won't be necessary," Judge Stevens said. "It's probably just a snake or a rat that nigger of hers killed in the yard. I'll speak to him about it."

The next day he received two more complaints, one from a man who came in diffident **deprecation**[27]. "We really must do something about it, Judge. I'd be the last one in the world to bother Miss Emily, but we've got to do something." That night the Board of Aldermen met—three graybeards and one younger man, a member of the rising generation.

"It's simple enough," he said. "Send her word to have her place cleaned up. Give her a certain time to do it in, and if she don't…"

"Dammit, sir," Judge Stevens said, "will you accuse a lady to her face of smelling bad?"

So the next night, after midnight, four men crossed Miss Emily's lawn and slunk about the house like burglars, sniffing along the base of the brickwork and at the cellar openings while one of them performed a regular sowing motion with his hand out of a sack slung from his shoulder. They broke open the cellar door and sprinkled **lime**[28] there, and in all the outbuildings. As they recrossed the lawn, a window that had been dark was lighted and Miss Emily sat in it, the light behind her, and her upright torso motionless as that of an idol. They crept quietly across the lawn and into the shadow of the locusts that lined the street. After

26. teeming
    adj. 热闹的；群集的；丰富的

27. deprecation
    n. 反对；贬低

28. lime
    n. 石灰

282

"好像只要是男人——任何男人——都能把厨房收拾妥当似的，"女士们说；因此，当那种气味越来越明显时，她们也不感到吃惊，那是芸芸众生的世界和有权有势的格里尔森家之间的另一联系。

邻居一个女人向八十高龄的法官斯蒂文斯镇长抱怨过。

"可是，太太，你让我对此做什么呢？"他说。

"啊，通知她堵住那个气味，"那个女人说。"不是有法律吗？"

"我相信那没必要，"法官斯蒂文斯说。"也许是她的那个黑鬼在院子里打死了一条蛇或一只老鼠。我去对他说说。"

第二天，他又接到了两起投诉，其中一起是来自一个男人，这个男人进来时用的是缺乏自信的反对语气。"法官，我们对这件事真的必须采取行动了。我最不愿打搅艾米丽小姐，但我们不得不采取行动。"那天夜里，参议会——三位老人和一个比较年轻的新一代成员一起开了个会。

"这件事够简单的，"他说。"通知她把房间打扫干净。给她一定时间打扫干净，如果她不……"

"岂有此理，先生，"法官斯蒂文斯说，"你会当着一位女士的面指责她气味难闻吗？"

于是，第二天午夜过后，四个人穿过艾米丽小姐家的草坪，像夜贼一样绕着房子蹑足潜踪，用力嗅着砖砌墙角和地窖口，其中一人一只手从挎在肩上的袋子里拿出什么东西，持续做出播种的动作。他们打开地窖门，在那里和整个外屋都撒上了石灰。他们又穿过草坪时，原来黑暗的一扇窗户亮起了灯，只见艾米丽小姐坐在那里，灯在她身后，她挺直的躯体一动不动，仿佛一尊偶像。他们悄无声息地走过草坪，进入街道两边洋槐树的

a week or two the smell went away.

That was when people had begun to feel really sorry for her. People in our town, remembering how old lady Wyatt, her great-aunt, had gone completely crazy at last, believed that the Griersons held themselves a little too high for what they really were. None of the young men were quite good enough for Miss Emily and such. We had long thought of them as a **tableau**[29], Miss Emily a slender figure in white in the background, her father a **spraddled**[30] silhouette in the foreground, his back to her and clutching a horsewhip, the two of them framed by the back-flung front door. So when she got to be thirty and was still single, we were not pleased exactly, but **vindicated**[31]; even with insanity in the family she wouldn't have turned down all of her chances if they had really materialized.

When her father died, it got about that the house was all that was left to her; and in a way, people were glad. At last they could pity Miss Emily. Being left alone, and a pauper, she had become humanized. Now she too would know the old thrill and the old despair of a penny more or less.

The day after his death all the ladies prepared to call at the house and offer **condolence**[32] and aid, as is our custom Miss Emily met them at the door, dressed as usual and with no trace of grief on her face. She told them that her father was not dead. She did that for three days, with the ministers calling on her, and the doctors, trying to persuade her to let them **dispose of**[33] the body. Just as they were about to **resort to**[34] law and force, she broke down, and they buried her father quickly.

We did not say she was crazy then. We believed she had to do that. We remembered all the young men her father had driven away, and we knew that with nothing left, she would have to cling to that which had robbed her, as people will.

III

She was sick for a long time. When we saw her again, her

29. tableau
    n. 活人画；画面

30. spraddle
    vt. 跨越；叉开腿站立

31. vindicate
    vt. 维护；证明……正确

32. condolence
    n. 哀悼；慰问

33. dispose of
    处理；解决

34. resort to
    诉诸；求助于

阴影之中。一两周后，气味消失了。

　　人们就是这个时候开始真正为她感到难过。我们镇上的人想起了艾米丽小姐的姑奶奶怀亚特老太太最终彻底变疯的事儿，都相信格里尔森一家人对他们实际所处的地位看得有点过高。任何年轻男人都配不上艾米丽小姐和像她一样的女人。长期以来，我们把他们看成是一幅画中的人物：身材苗条、一袭白衣的艾米丽小姐站在背景，她的父亲叉开腿的侧影在前景，背对艾米丽，手握一根马鞭，一扇向后开的前门框住了他们俩的身影。因此，当她快三十岁、依然单身时，我们的确不开心，只是觉得先前的看法得到了证实：即使她家里有精神错乱史，如果真有机会出现，她也不应该统统拒绝。

　　她的父亲去世后，传说留给她的所有财产就是那座房子；在某种程度上，人们感到高兴。他们终于能怜悯艾米丽了。因为无依无靠，贫困交加，所以她变得有人情味了。现在，她也会知道什么是多一便士就激动万分、少一便士就大失所望的那种人皆有之的心情了。

　　她的父亲死后第二天，所有的女士都准备去她家拜访，表示哀悼，愿意援助；按照我们的习俗，艾米丽小姐在家门口迎接她们，穿得和平常一样，脸上没有任何悲痛。她告诉她们说，她的父亲没有死。无论是牧师拜访她，还是医生设法说服她让他们处理尸体，她一连三天都是这样说。正当他们准备诉诸法律和武力时，她垮了下来，于是他们很快埋葬了她的父亲。

　　我们当时还没有说她发疯。我们相信她是不得不这样做。我们记得她的父亲曾经赶走了所有的青年男人，我们也知道什么也没有给她留下，所以她不得不像人们常做的那样紧紧抓住那个剥夺了她一切的人。

这部分读起来会使读者陷入思考：这是一种什么样的气味？艾米丽小姐家里到底发生了什么？

艾米丽小姐年轻时期的生活状况：父亲主宰和控制着她全部的生活，包括爱情。在父亲的保护和专制下，她没有自由，没有思想，这些终会成为她悲剧命运的导火索。

A Rose for Emily 献给艾米丽的玫瑰

hair was cut short, making her look like a girl, with a vague resemblance to those angels in colored church windows—sort of tragic and **serene**[35].

The town had just let the contracts for paving the sidewalks, and in the summer after her father's death they began the work. The construction company came with niggers and mules and machinery, and a foreman named Homer Barron, a Yankee—a big, dark, ready man, with a big voice and eyes lighter than his face. The little boys would follow in groups to hear him **cuss**[36] the niggers, and the niggers singing in time to the rise and fall of picks. Pretty soon he knew everybody in town. Whenever you heard a lot of laughing anywhere about the square, Homer Barron would be in the center of the group. Presently we began to see him and Miss Emily on Sunday afternoons driving in the yellow-wheeled buggy and the matched team of bays from the **livery stable**[37].

At first we were glad that Miss Emily would have an interest, because the ladies all said, "Of course a Grierson would not think seriously of a Northerner, a day laborer." But there were still others, older people, who said that even grief could not cause a real lady to forget **noblesse oblige**[38] without calling it noblesse oblige. They just said, "Poor Emily. Her kinsfolk should come to her." She had some kin in Alabama; but years ago her father had fallen out with them over the estate of old lady Wyatt, the crazy woman, and there was no communication between the two families. They had not even been represented at the funeral.

And as soon as the old people said, "Poor Emily," the whispering began. "Do you suppose it's really so?" they said to one another. "Of course it is. What else could…" This behind their hands; rustling of craned silk and satin behind **jalousies**[39] closed upon the sun of Sunday afternoon as the thin, swift clop-clop-clop of the matched team passed: "Poor Emily."

She carried her head high enough—even when we believed

---

35. serene
   adj. 宁静的，安详的

36. cuss
   vt. 乱骂；咒骂

37. livery stable
   车马出租所；马房

38. noblesse oblige
   n. 贵人应有的品德；地位高则责任重

39. jalousie
   n. 百叶窗

三

　　她病了好长时间。我们再次见到她时，她头发剪短，看上去像一个少女，跟教堂彩色玻璃窗上的那些天使隐约有些相似——有几分悲怆和安详。

　　镇政府刚刚订好了铺设人行道的合同，在她父亲去世的那年夏天开始动工。建筑公司带着黑鬼、骡子和机器来了，工头是个北方佬，名叫霍默·巴伦——个子高大，皮肤黝黑，迅速敏捷，嗓门洪亮，眼睛比脸色淡。小男孩成群结队跟在身后听到他破口大骂那些黑鬼，黑鬼随着铁镐的升降合拍地唱着。没多久，全镇人他都认识了。无论何时你在广场的什么地方听到笑声不断，霍默·巴伦一定是在人群的中心。又过了不久，每到星期天下午，我们就开始看到他和艾米丽小姐乘轻便马车兜起了风。黄轮马车和从马房里挑出的红棕马非常般配。

　　起初，我们都很高兴艾米丽小姐大概是有了一种兴趣，因为女士们都说："格里尔森家的人肯定不会认真考虑一个北方佬，一个打零工的人。"不过，也有其他人，一些年龄较大的人，他们说，即使悲伤也不能让一位真正的女士忘记"贵人举止"，尽管不把它叫作"贵人举止"。他们只是说："可怜的艾米丽。她的亲属应该来到她身边。"她有亲属在阿拉巴马州；但多年前，她的父亲为了那个疯女人怀亚特老太太的财产跟他们闹翻了脸，所以两家之间没有来往。他们连葬礼都没有派人参加。

　　而老人们一说到"可怜的艾米丽"，就开始窃窃私语。"你认为真是那样吗？"他们彼此问道。"当然是。还能是别的什么……"这是他们用手捂住嘴说的；马队轻快的嘚嘚声驶过时，在遮挡星期天午后太阳的百叶窗后面，伸出的绸缎发出了飒飒声："可怜的艾米丽。"

剪短的头发预示着艾米丽小姐与以前生活的决裂，她开始追求自己的幸福，开始与北方佬霍默相恋。

A Rose for Emily　献给艾米丽的玫瑰　**287**

that she was fallen. It was as if she demanded more than ever the recognition of her dignity as the last Grierson; as if it had wanted that touch of earthiness to reaffirm her **imperviousness**[40]. Like when she bought the rat poison, the **arsenic**[41]. That was over a year after they had begun to say "Poor Emily," and while the two female cousins were visiting her.

"I want some poison," she said to the druggist. She was over thirty then, still a slight woman, though thinner than usual, with cold, haughty black eyes in a face the flesh of which was strained across the temples and about the eye sockets as you imagine a lighthouse-keeper's face ought to look. "I want some poison," she said.

"Yes, Miss Emily. What kind? For rats and such? I'd recom—"

"I want the best you have. I don't care what kind."

The druggist named several. "They'll kill anything up to an elephant. But what you want is—"

"Arsenic," Miss Emily said. "Is that a good one?"

"Is…arsenic? Yes, ma'am. But what you want—"

"I want arsenic."

The druggist looked down at her. She looked back at him, erect, her face like a strained flag. "Why, of course," the druggist said. "If that's what you want. But the law requires you to tell what you are going to use it for."

Miss Emily just stared at him, her head tilted back in order to look him eye for eye, until he looked away and went and got the arsenic and wrapped it up. The Negro delivery boy brought her the package; the druggist didn't come back. When she opened the package at home there was written on the box, under the skull and bones: "For rats."

IV

So the next day we all said, "She will kill herself"; and we said it would be the best thing. When she had first begun to be

40. imperviousness
    n. 不受影响；无动于衷

41. arsenic
    n. 砒霜

她把头抬得够高的——即使在我们相信她堕落时也是这样。好像她比以往都更要求人们公认她作为格里尔森家族末代人的尊严；好像她的尊严需要跟世俗接触，以重申她刀枪不入的性格。就像她买老鼠药、砒霜时那样。那是在人们开始说"可怜的艾米丽"后一年多的时候，当时她的两个堂姐妹正在看望她。

"我要买些毒药。"她对药剂师说。她当时三十出头，仍是一个身材纤细的女人，但比往常更瘦，一双黑眼睛冰冷傲慢，脸上的肉在太阳穴和眼窝四周绷得紧紧的，就像你想象中灯塔看守人应有的面部表情。"我要买些毒药，"她说。

"行，艾米丽小姐。要买哪种？是用来毒老鼠之类的吗？我推——"

"我要你们店最有效的毒药，不管哪种都行。"

药剂师说出了好几种。"它们什么都能毒死，连大象都能毒死。可你想要的是——"

"砒霜，"艾米丽小姐说。"砒霜管用吗？"

"是……砒霜？行，小姐。可你想要的是——"

"我想要砒霜。"

药剂师低头看着她。她也看了他一眼，身体挺直，她的脸像一面绷紧的旗帜。"啊，当然可以，"药剂师说。"如果你想要的是这种毒药。不过，法律要求你说明你要用它做什么。"

艾米丽小姐只是盯着他，头向后歪着，以便正视他的眼睛，一直看到他移开目光，去拿来砒霜包好。黑人送货员把那包药给她送过来；药剂师没再出现。她到家打开药包后，只见在盒子上骷髅骨标记下面写着："毒鼠用药"。

小说没有描写恋爱后的艾米丽小姐的幸福生活，却指向了她更加清瘦，更加冰冷孤傲，面无表情，而且亲自购买砒霜，使读者再次感受到了恐怖的气氛。

seen with Homer Barron, we had said, "She will marry him." Then we said, "She will persuade him yet," because Homer himself had remarked—he liked men, and it was known that he drank with the younger men in the Elks' Club—that he was not a marrying man. Later we said, "Poor Emily" behind the jalousies as they passed on Sunday afternoon in the glittering **buggy**[42], Miss Emily with her head high and Homer Barron with his hat cocked and a cigar in his teeth, reins and whip in a yellow glove.

Then some of the ladies began to say that it was a disgrace to the town and a bad example to the young people. The men did not want to interfere, but at last the ladies forced the Baptist minister —Miss Emily's people were **Episcopal**[43]—to call upon her. He would never **divulge**[44] what happened during that interview, but he refused to go back again. The next Sunday they again drove about the streets, and the following day the minister's wife wrote to Miss Emily's relations in Alabama.

So she had blood-kin under her roof again and we sat back to watch developments. At first nothing happened. Then we were sure that they were to be married. We learned that Miss Emily had been to the jeweler's and ordered a man's toilet set in silver, with the letters H. B. on each piece. Two days later we learned that she had bought a complete outfit of men's clothing, including a nightshirt, and we said, "They are married." We were really glad. We were glad because the two female cousins were even more Grierson than Miss Emily had ever been.

So we were not surprised when Homer Barron—the streets had been finished some time since—was gone. We were a little disappointed that there was not a public blowing-off, but we believed that he had gone on to prepare for Miss Emily's coming, or to give her a chance to get rid of the cousins. (By that time it was a **cabal**[45], and we were all Miss Emily's allies to help **circumvent**[46] the cousins.) Sure enough, after another week they departed. And, as we had expected all along, within three

42. buggy
n. 轻型马车

43. Episcopal
adj. 主教制度的；圣公会的

44. divulge
vt. 泄露；暴露

45. cabal
n. 阴谋小集团；帮派

46. circumvent
vt. 规避；巧妙地制止

四

于是，第二天我们都说，"她要自杀"；而且我们说这是再好不过的事儿。我们第一次看到她和霍默·巴伦在一起时，都说："她要嫁给他。"后来，我们又说："她还要说服他。"因为霍默自己说——他喜欢男人们，大家都知道他和年轻人在麋鹿俱乐部一起喝酒，他是一个不想结婚的人。后来，每到星期天下午他们乘着炫丽的轻便马车经过，艾米丽小姐高扬着头，霍默歪戴帽子，嘴叼雪茄，手戴黄手套，握着马缰和马鞭，我们在百叶窗背后说道："可怜的艾米丽。"

后来，有些女士开始说，这对全镇是一种耻辱，也是年轻人的坏榜样。男人们不想干涉，但女人们最后迫使浸礼会牧师——艾米丽小姐一家人都是圣公会成员——去拜访她。那次会谈经过他从未透露，但他再也不愿去了。下个星期天他们又乘马车在街上兜风，第二天牧师的妻子就给艾米丽小姐住在阿拉巴马州的亲戚写去了信。

于是，她家里又有了近亲，我们坐观事态的进展。起先，没有发生什么事儿。随后，我们得到确信，他们即将结婚。我们获悉艾米丽小姐去过首饰店，订了一套银质男人梳妆用具，每件上面都刻有"霍·巴"的字样。两天后，我们得知她买了全套男人服装，包括睡衣，因此我们说："他们已经结婚了。"我们确实高兴。我们之所以高兴，是因为两位堂姐妹甚至比艾米丽小姐更有格里尔森家族的风范。

因此，当霍默·巴伦离开镇子时——街道已经竣工一段时间了，我们一点也不感到惊异。我们对没有当众送行有点儿失望，但我们都相信他离开是为了迎接艾米丽小姐做准备，或者是给她机会打发走两个堂姐妹。

捕风捉影，流言蜚语，往往是毒药。

days Homer Barron was back in town. A neighbor saw the Negro man admit him at the kitchen door at dusk one evening.

And that was the last we saw of Homer Barron. And of Miss Emily for some time. The Negro man went in and out with the market basket, but the front door remained closed. Now and then we would see her at a window for a moment, as the men did that night when they sprinkled the lime, but for almost six months she did not appear on the streets. Then we knew that this was to be expected too; as if that quality of her father which had **thwarted**[47] her woman's life so many times had been too **virulent**[48] and too furious to die.

When we next saw Miss Emily, she had grown fat and her hair was turning gray. During the next few years it grew grayer and grayer until it attained an even pepper-and-salt iron-gray, when it ceased turning. Up to the day of her death at seventy-four it was still that vigorous iron-gray, like the hair of an active man.

From that time on her front door remained closed, save for a period of six or seven years, when she was about forty, during which she gave lessons in china-painting. She fitted up a studio in one of the downstairs rooms, where the daughters and granddaughters of Colonel Sartoris' **contemporaries**[49] were sent to her with the same regularity and in the same spirit that they were sent to church on Sundays with a twenty-five-cent piece for the collection plate. Meanwhile her taxes had been remitted.

Then the newer generation became the backbone and the spirit of the town, and the painting pupils grew up and fell away and did not send their children to her with boxes of color and **tedious**[50] brushes and pictures cut from the ladies' magazines. The front door closed upon the last one and remained closed for good. When the town got free postal delivery, Miss Emily alone refused to let them fasten the metal numbers above her door and attach a mailbox to it. She would not listen to them.

47. thwart
   vt. 挫败；反对

48. virulent
   adj. 恶性的；剧毒的

49. contemporary
   n. 同龄人；同辈人

50. tedious
   adj. 沉闷的；乏味的

（此时已成了一个秘密小集团，我们都是艾米丽小姐的同盟，帮她撵走堂姐妹。）果然，一周后，她们就离开了。而且，就像我们一直盼望的那样，不出三天霍默·巴伦就回到了镇上。一天黄昏时分，一位邻居看到那个黑人让他走进了厨房门。

这是我们最后一次看到霍默·巴伦。艾米丽小姐，我们也有一段时间没有见过了。黑人提着购货篮进进出出，但前门一直关着。偶尔我们会看到她在窗口站一会儿，就像人们撒石灰那天夜里见到的那样，但差不多六个月她没有在街上露面。于是，我们明白这也在意料之中，好像她父亲的品质多次阻碍她作为女人的生活，这种品质非常刻毒、非常狂暴，所以无法消失。

当我们又见到艾米丽小姐时，她已经发福，头发渐渐灰白。在接下来的几年中，头发越变越灰白，直到变得像胡椒盐一样的铁灰色，这时才不再变了。直到她七十四岁去世那天，都还是那种旺盛的铁灰色，就像是一个活跃男人的头发。

铁灰色是一种象征，也是一种意象。

从那时起，除了她大约四十岁那段时期的六七年以外，她的前门一直关闭。那段时期，她讲授瓷器彩绘课。在楼下的一个房间，她布置了一个画室，沙多里斯上校的同时代人都把女儿和孙女送到她那里学画，那样的正规，那样的认真精神，就像星期天送她们上教堂，还给她们二角伍分硬币准备放进捐献盘里的情况一模一样。这时，她的税款已被免除。

后来，新的一代成了镇子的主力军，学画的学生们也长大成人，逐渐离开，她们没有让自己的孩子带着颜料盒、单调乏味的画笔和从女性杂志上剪下的图画到她那里去学画画。最后一个学生离开后，前门就关上了，而且是永远关上了。当镇上实行免费邮递后，只有艾米

Daily, monthly, yearly we watched the Negro grow grayer and more stooped, going in and out with the market basket. Each December we sent her a tax notice, which would be returned by the post office a week later, unclaimed. Now and then we would see her in one of the downstairs windows—she had evidently shut up the top floor of the house—like the carven **torso**[51] of an idol in a niche, looking or not looking at us, we could never tell which. Thus she passed from generation to generation—dear, inescapable, impervious, tranquil, and **perverse**[52].

And so she died. Fell ill in the house filled with dust and shadows, with only a **doddering**[53] Negro man to wait on her. We did not even know she was sick; we had long since given up trying to get any information from the Negro. He talked to no one, probably not even to her, for his voice had grown harsh and rusty, as if from disuse.

She died in one of the downstairs rooms, in a heavy walnut bed with a curtain, her gray head propped on a pillow yellow and moldy with age and lack of sunlight.

V

The Negro met the first of the ladies at the front door and let them in, with their hushed, **sibilant**[54] voices and their quick, curious glances, and then he disappeared. He walked right through the house and out the back and was not seen again.

The two female cousins came at once. They held the funeral on the second day, with the town coming to look at Miss Emily beneath a mass of bought flowers, with the crayon face of her father musing profoundly above the bier and the ladies sibilant and **macabre**[55]; and the very old men—some in their brushed Confederate uniforms—on the porch and the lawn, talking of Miss Emily as if she had been a contemporary of theirs, believing that they had danced with her and courted her perhaps, confusing time with its mathematical progression, as the old do, to whom

51. torso
   n. 人体躯干；躯干雕像
52. perverse
   adj. 违反常情的
53. doddering
   adj. 蹒跚的；老态龙钟的
54. sibilant
   adj. 咝咝作声的；嘶声的
55. macabre
   adj. 恐怖的；令人毛骨悚然的；以死亡为主题的

丽小姐拒绝让人在她的门上方钉金属门牌号，设上邮箱。她不愿理睬他们。

日复一日，月复一月，年复一年，我们看着那个黑人头发渐渐花白，背渐渐佝偻，还是提着购货篮进进出出。每年十二月，我们都寄给她一张纳税通知单，但一周后邮局又退回，无人查收。偶尔，我们会在楼下的一个窗口——她显然已经关闭了房子的顶楼——见到她，就像神龛里的一尊偶像的雕塑躯干，我们从来说不清她是不是在看着我们。就这样，她度过了一代又一代——高贵、宁静，无法逃避，无法接近，有悖常情。

她就这样死了。在一座灰尘满地、影影绰绰的房子里病倒，侍候她的只有一个步履蹒跚的黑人。我们甚至不知道她病了；我们早已不想设法从黑人那里打听任何消息了。他对谁都不说话，说不定对她也不说话，因为他的嗓音好像因废弃不用而变得沙哑生锈了。

她死在楼下的一个房间里，厚重的胡桃木床上挂着床帷，她长满灰发的脑袋靠在枕头上，枕头因天长日久不见阳光而变黄发霉。

五

黑人在前门口迎接第一批女士，让她们进来，她们的声音平静，发出咝咝声，好奇的目光飞快地扫视着，随后黑人不见了。他径直穿过房子，走出后门，再也没有了踪影。

两位堂姐妹马上赶来了。她们第二天就举行了葬礼，全镇人都来看躺在买来的大量鲜花下面的艾米丽小姐，棺材架上方是她父亲深思表情的炭笔画像，女士们发出咝咝声，毛骨悚然；而老年男人——有些人穿着刷过的南方军军装——在走廊上和草坪上谈论着艾米丽小姐，好像她是他们的同时代人，他们相信自己和她跳

从镇上人的议论〝她要嫁给他〞、〝她要说服他〞、〝他们已经结婚了〞到艾米丽小姐数年紧闭的房门，直至她最后的死亡，读者看不清她的爱情和她的生活。这正是作者给我们设的一个迷局。其实，世界本身就是一个让人莫名其妙的迷局。

all the past is not a diminishing road but, instead, a huge meadow which no winter ever quite touches, divided from them now by the narrow bottle-neck of the most recent decade of years.

Already we knew that there was one room in that region above stairs which no one had seen in forty years, and which would have to be forced. They waited until Miss Emily was decently in the ground before they opened it.

The violence of breaking down the door seemed to fill this room with **pervading**[56] dust. A thin, acrid **pall**[57] as of the tomb seemed to lie everywhere upon this room decked and furnished as for a bridal: upon the **valance**[58] curtains of faded rose color, upon the rose-shaded lights, upon the dressing table, upon the delicate array of crystal and the man's toilet things backed with tarnished silver, silver so tarnished that the **monogram**[59] was obscured. Among them lay a collar and tie, as if they had just been removed, which, lifted, left upon the surface a pale crescent in the dust. Upon a chair hung the suit, carefully folded; beneath it the two mute shoes and the **discarded**[60] socks.

The man himself lay in the bed.

For a long while we just stood there, looking down at the profound and fleshless grin. The body had apparently once lain in the attitude of an embrace, but now the long sleep that outlasts love, that conquers even the grimace of love, had **cuckolded**[61] him. What was left of him, rotted beneath what was left of the nightshirt, had become **inextricable**[62] from the bed in which he lay; and upon him and upon the pillow beside him lay that even coating of the patient and biding dust.

Then we noticed that in the second pillow was the **indentation**[63] of a head. One of us lifted something from it, and leaning forward, that faint and invisible dust dry and acrid in the nostrils, we saw a long **strand**[64] of iron-gray hair.

56. pervading
adj. 遍及的；到处弥漫的

57. pall
n. 棺罩

58. valance
n. 帷幔；装饰窗帘

59. monogram
n. 交织文字；由姓名首字母组成的组合图案

60. discarded
adj. 废弃的；丢弃的

61. cuckold
vt. 使戴绿帽子

62. inextricable
adj. 无法解脱的；逃脱不掉的

63. indentation
n. 凹陷；压痕

64. strand
n. 一股；一串；一缕

过舞，说不定还向她求过爱，他们混淆了精确推进的时间，老年人经常这样做，在他们看来，过去的一切不是一条越来越窄的路，而是一大片连冬天也对它无所影响的草地，只是最近十年他们才像窄瓶颈一样同过去隔断了。

我们已经知道楼上那个区域有一个房间，四十年来没有人见过，要进去必须得把门撬开。他们等到艾米丽小姐安葬之后再打开。

猛烈撞开那扇门，似乎让屋里灰尘弥漫。这个布置得像新房一样的房间，好像到处都笼罩着一种淡淡的坟墓一样的酸腐味：褪色的玫瑰色装饰窗帘，玫瑰色的罩灯，梳妆台，一排精致的水晶饰品和失去光泽的白银底男人盥洗用具，白银完全失去了光泽，连刻制的姓名首字母图案都模糊不清了。其中有一个领口和领带，好像是刚取下来一样，拿起它们时，在表面的积尘上留下了淡淡的月牙形痕迹。椅子上挂着一套仔细叠好的衣服；椅子下面有两只寂然无声的鞋和丢弃的短袜。

那个男人就躺在床上。

我们只是久久地站在那里，俯视着那张深沉憔悴、龇牙咧嘴的笑容。显而易见，尸体躺在那里，一度处在拥抱的姿势，但现在那比爱情更持久、甚至战胜扭曲爱情的长眠，已经使他臣服。他剩下的肉体在留下的睡衣下腐烂，已经和他躺着的床粘在一起难以分开；他身上和他身边的枕头上均匀地覆盖着一层日积月累的灰尘。

后来，我们注意到第二只枕头上有人头的压痕。我们中的一个人从上面拿起了一件东西，我们倾身向前，看到一缕铁灰色长发，一股淡淡的干燥发臭的无从觉察的尘埃钻进了鼻孔。

揭开了谜底，让人惊骇，令人震颤，使人久久难以平静。

名篇赏析

　　这篇小说首尾相接，天衣无缝，时序来回颠倒，故事悬念迭出。福克纳没有用意识流的手法向我们展示艾米丽的内心活动，只是通过一系列不按时序排列的事件来表现一个生活在过去时代的女人的悲剧。小说的结尾恐怖得让人窒息，艾米丽小姐毒死了她爱的北方佬，并长期与恋人的尸体共眠。得不到爱情的艾米丽以这种令人毛骨悚然的方式祭奠她此生仅有的一次爱情。读者最终明白了艾米丽小姐家难闻气味、紧锁前门的原因。小说以死亡开始，同时以死亡告终，作者通过对南方贵族艾米丽小姐悲怆荒诞的人生描写，揭示了美国南北融合时期南方淑女在特定历史时期的悲剧命运和旧南方传统文明的失落。